ELEMENTS OF

Literature

LITERATURE OF THE UNITED STATES

FIFTH COURSE

LANGUAGE AND WRITING SKILLS WORKSHEETS

HOLT, RINEHART AND WINSTON

Harcourt Brace & Company

Austin • New York • Orlando • Atlanta • San Francisco • Boston • Dallas • Toronto • London

1997 Reprint by Holt, Rinehart and Winston, Inc.
Copyright © 1995 by Holt, Rinehart and Winston, Inc.

Portions of this work were published in previous editions.

Printed in the United States of America

ISBN 0-03-095732-X

1 2 3 4 5 6 082 99 98 97 96

To the Teacher

The worksheets in this booklet cover a comprehensive range of writing skills instruction and practice. Each chapter of the booklet culminates in a review activity. Worksheets fall into the following categories:

- *Writer's Quick Reference*—These worksheets provide explanations of common usage problems, followed by practice items.
- *Grammar and Usage*—This section is subdivided into chapters on parts of speech; agreement; and verb, pronoun, and modifier usage. The worksheets provide explanation, examples, and activities on key grammar concepts.
- *Phrases, Clauses, Sentences*—The worksheets in this section provide instruction and practice in topics ranging from uses of phrases to effective sentence writing.
- *Mechanics*—These worksheets provide explanations, examples, and practice items on capital letters, punctuation, and spelling and vocabulary.
- *Composition*—The worksheets in this section reinforce students' understanding of the writing process. One chapter focuses on skills related to paragraph and composition structure. Another helps students develop the skills necessary to create a research paper.
- *Resources*—This section of the booklet provides lessons in the use of media resources—including reference materials, newspapers, and dictionaries—and in the conventions of letter writing and manuscript preparation.

To facilitate the integration of language and literature instruction, these *Language and Writing Skills Worksheets* are cross-referenced in the *Annotated Teacher Edition* of *Elements of Literature: Literature of the United States.*

Table of Contents

WRITER'S QUICK REFERENCE

GRAMMAR AND USAGE

CHAPTER 1 PARTS OF SPEECH

CHAPTER 2 AGREEMENT

CHAPTER 3 USING VERBS

CHAPTER 4 USING PRONOUNS

CHAPTER 5 USING MODIFIERS

PHRASES, CLAUSES, SENTENCES

CHAPTER 6 PHRASES

CHAPTER 7 CLAUSES

CHAPTER 8 SENTENCE STRUCTURE

CHAPTER 9 SENTENCE STYLE

CHAPTER 10 SENTENCE COMBINING

MECHANICS

CHAPTER 11 **CAPITALIZATION**

CHAPTER 12 **PUNCTUATION**

CHAPTER 13 **PUNCTUATION**

CHAPTER 14 SPELLING AND VOCABULARY

COMPOSITION

CHAPTER 15 THE WRITING PROCESS

CHAPTER 16 PARAGRAPH AND COMPOSITION STRUCTURE

CHAPTER 17 THE RESEARCH PAPER

RESOURCES

Name _____ Date _____ Class _____

Types of Nouns A

A **noun** is a word used to name a person, a place, a thing, or an idea. A **common noun** is a general name for a person or persons, a place, or a thing. A **proper noun** names a particular person, place, or thing. Common nouns are not capitalized; proper nouns are.

     COMMON NOUN: actor   PROPER NOUN: Emma Thompson

A **concrete noun** names an object that can be perceived by the senses. An **abstract noun** names a quality, a characteristic, or an idea.

     CONCRETE NOUNS: petunia, computer   ABSTRACT NOUNS: enthusiasm, health

Exercise A In the following sentences, underline the common nouns once and the proper nouns twice. On the lines provided, write any proper nouns with the correct capitalization.

              EXAMPLE: 1. The new <u>course</u> will be taught by <u><u>juanita martinez</u></u>.
                    Juanita Martinez

  1. Have you ever read *the crucible* or any other plays by arthur miller? _____

  2. Call miss sacks if you are on her committee. _____

  3. On saturday, june 3, classes in swimming will begin. _____

  4. The louvre, a famous museum in paris, was once a palace. _____

  5. The beach was littered with driftwood that had been blown there by hurricane hugo. _____

Exercise B In the following sentences, classify each underlined noun as concrete or abstract. On the line provided, write *C* if the noun is concrete or *A* if the noun is abstract.

_____ 1. In 1990, August Wilson, who was born in Pittsburgh in 1945, won his second Pulitzer Prize for the <u>play</u> *The Piano Lesson*.

_____ 2. In this play, a brother and sister engage in a conflict over a <u>piano</u>.

_____ 3. The piano becomes a symbol for the <u>ambivalence</u> in the United States toward African American history.

_____ 4. Wilson's <u>discouragement</u> with the treatment of African Americans has spurred him to use theater to raise consciousness.

_____ 5. Wilson has written a series of plays, each set in a different <u>decade</u>.

GRAMMAR/USAGE

Name _____ Date _____ Class _____

Types of Nouns B

A **collective noun** names a group.

    herd (of cows)   squad (of cheerleaders)   fleet (of ships)

A **compound noun** consists of two or more words used together as a single noun. Some compound nouns are written as one word, some as separate words, and others as hyphenated words.

    courthouse   Vietnam Memorial   sister-in-law

Exercise A   In each of the following sentences, decide if the italicized words are collective nouns or compound nouns. On the lines provided, write *collective* or *compound*.

1. This classic film documents the *Fall of Rome*.   _____

2. Is your *sister-in-law* going to be there?   _____

3. In the brush, one stray heifer wandered, lost from the *herd*.   _____

4. *Swarms* of bees surrounded the hives.   _____

5. Haven't you ever been outside *North Dakota*?   _____

6. What is the name of this *group* of stars?   _____

7. The invention was the *brainchild* of a clerk in their offices.   _____

8. Who is the greatest hitter in the history of *baseball*?   _____

9. The *council* will meet again next Tuesday.   _____

10. Everyone in the *band* agreed to meet for practice.   _____

Exercise B   In the following sentences, underline the collective nouns once and the compound nouns twice.

1. The vice-president of the company introduced his family to the committee.

2. Edith, who is my partner on the debate team, uses push buttons to control her wheelchair.

3. A gaggle of Canada geese landed in the back yard of Town Hall.

4. A bill to lower income taxes is being discussed by Congress.

5. Several school organizations, such as the Science Club, need typewriters.

Chapter 1: Parts of Speech

Types of Pronouns A

A **pronoun** is a word used in place of a noun, more than one noun, or another pronoun. The word or words that a pronoun stands for are called the **antecedent** of the pronoun.

> **Kelsey** has a mountain bike that **she** will lend to **me**. [*She* and *me* are pronouns. *Kelsey* is the antecedent of the pronoun *she*.]

A **personal pronoun** refers to the one speaking (first person), the one spoken to (second person), or the one spoken about (third person). A **reflexive pronoun** refers to the subject of a sentence and directs the action of the verb back to the subject. An **intensive pronoun** emphasizes a noun or another pronoun. A **demonstrative pronoun** points out a person, a place, a thing, or an idea.

> PERSONAL PRONOUNS: I asked **him** to return an overdue library book for **me**.
>
> REFLEXIVE PRONOUN: Jared excused **himself** from the meeting.
>
> INTENSIVE PRONOUN: He coolly suggested that I return it **myself**.
>
> DEMONSTRATIVE PRONOUNS: I hate it when he acts like **that**.

Exercise A Underline the pronouns in the following sentences. If the pronoun has an antecedent, underline the antecedent twice. Label each pronoun as *personal*, *reflexive*, *intensive*, or *demonstrative*.

> EXAMPLE: 1. The people of Hong Kong use <u>Chinese</u> and <u>English</u> and have designated <u>them</u> official languages. *personal*

1. On July 1, 1997, the British will relinquish control of Hong Kong, and it will then be governed by China. _____

2. The people of Hong Kong find themselves wondering how they will be affected. _____

3. The Bank of China building in Hong Kong was designed by I. M. Pei, an Asian American himself. _____

4. Shopping in Hong Kong's stores can be fun, and it can be inexpensive too, for the prices of many items—such as cameras and video equipment—are half those of identical items at home. _____

5. In China, when people meet, instead of asking "How are you?" they traditionally ask "Have you eaten yet?" _____

Exercise B In each of the following sentences, underline the type of pronoun indicated in parentheses.

1. I myself have never been to Hong Kong. (intensive)

2. Leona treated herself to dim sum, a meal that she thoroughly enjoyed. (reflexive)

3. This is the postcard I got from Kara when she was in Hong Kong. (demonstrative)

4. She bought that herself in a shop on Man Wa Lane. (personal)

GRAMMAR/USAGE

Name _____ Date _____ Class _____

 **WORKSHEET 4** *Types of Pronouns B*

An **interrogative pronoun** introduces a question. A **relative pronoun** introduces a subordinate clause. An **indefinite pronoun** refers to a person, place, or thing that is not specifically named.

INTERROGATIVE PRONOUN: **Who** took my comb?

RELATIVE PRONOUN: The bike **that** I want has twenty-one speeds.

INDEFINITE PRONOUN: **All** of Hank's finals fall on the same day.

Exercise A Underline the pronouns in the following sentences. Label each pronoun as *interrogative*, *relative*, or *indefinite*.

1. What seems to be Marcia's problem?

2. Each of the cat's newborn kittens seemed incredibly tiny.

3. Inez won one of the leads in the musical that our high school is putting on in the spring.

4. Lomasi told Henry, whom everyone trusted, something in confidence.

5. This is the team that did better than all the rest.

Exercise B In each of the following sentences, underline the type of pronoun indicated in parentheses. There may be more than one of that type of pronoun in the sentence.

1. Everyone who is involved with music in one way or another is preparing for the annual music festival. (indefinite)

2. It's a festival that attracts musicians and fans from all over the state. (relative)

3. Most of the musicians whom I spoke to are excited about the show. (relative)

4. What is each of the bands that are performing going to play? (interrogative)

5. Several of the musicians, whose music many have heard, have won concert competitions. (indefinite)

6. Many other musicians compose their own music, which has yet to be recorded. (relative)

7. All of my friends are going, and my parents, whose taste in music tends toward bluegrass, are going too. (indefinite)

8. However, no one seems to know who is in charge of tickets yet. (indefinite)

9. Whom do I see about advance tickets that are sold at a discount? (interrogative)

10. Somebody must know who it is. (relative)

Name _____ Date _____ Class _____

Adjectives

An **adjective** is a word used to modify a noun or a pronoun. Adjectives modify nouns or pronouns by telling *what kind, which one,* or *how many (how much).* The most frequently used adjectives, *a, an,* and *the,* are called articles.

> **A small, orange** zinnia danced in **the** wind. [The adjectives *small* and *orange* modify *zinnia* and tell what kind; *a* and *the* are articles.]

Some words may be used either as adjectives or as pronouns. Remember that an adjective *modifies* a noun and that a pronoun *takes the place of* a noun.

> ADJECTIVE: I have **another** shoe just like this one somewhere in my room.
>
> PRONOUN: He ate two sandwiches and then asked for **another**.

Sometimes nouns are used as adjectives.

> NOUNS: high school   kitchen   morning
>
> ADJECTIVES: **high school** teacher   **kitchen** sink   **morning** class

NOTE: Don't confuse a noun used as an adjective with a compound noun. If a noun and its modifier are listed together in the dictionary, the word group is a compound noun.

> COMPOUND NOUNS: picket line   horse chestnut

Exercise A   Underline each adjective in the following sentences. Do not include articles.

1. "A funnel cloud has been sighted," the radio announcer said with an urgent voice.

2. Those were the last words Denise Moore heard before the electricity went off and the terrible roar came closer.

3. While Denise took cover in the basement, the wind, wild and powerful, drove a metal pitchfork into the side of a brick building.

4. It sucked the wallpaper from a living room wall but left the wall hangings intact.

5. Afterwards, the local citizens felt that they were lucky because no one had been killed.

Exercise B   Underline each adjective in the following sentences. (Do not include articles.) Then draw an arrow to the word or words that the adjective modifies.

1. Once the Blackfoot people were nomadic, as were other peoples of the Plains.

2. Skilled and resourceful, the Blackfoot hunted buffalo and gathered wild fruits and nuts.

3. When the buffalo vanished, the tribe traveled to another place on the Plains.

4. Many of the legends that come from the Blackfoot reveal their cultural beliefs.

5. Most legends, like the one I just read, are fictional but are based on some facts.

GRAMMAR/USAGE

Chapter 1: Parts of Speech

| WORSHEET 6 | *Action Verbs and Linking Verbs* |

A **verb** is a word used to express an action or a state of being. An **action verb** expresses physical or mental activity.

    PHYSICAL ACTIVITY: sleep, jog, read, speak, dance, type

    MENTAL ACTIVITY: think, wonder, hope, decide, dream, forget

A **transitive verb** is an action verb that takes an object—a word or words that tell who or what receives the action. An **intransitive verb** is an action verb that does not take an object. A verb can be transitive in one sentence and intransitive in another.

    TRANSITIVE VERB: Colleen **washed** her hands.

    INTRANSITIVE VERB: We **washed** before dinner.

A **linking verb** connects the subject with a word that identifies or describes it. The most commonly used linking verbs are forms of the verb *be* and other verbs such as *appear, become, feel, grow, look, remain, seem, smell, sound, stay, taste,* and *turn.* Some linking verbs may be used as action verbs.

    LINKING VERB: Mina **turned** scarlet from embarrassment.

    ACTION VERB: Dwayne **turned** the car around in the driveway.

Exercise A   On the line provided before each sentence, write *AV* if the italicized word is an action verb or *LV* if it is a linking verb.

_____ 1. Hiromi *entered* medical school last fall.

_____ 2. The air often *smells* smoky during autumn.

_____ 3. Simon *feels* more energetic when he exercises in the morning.

_____ 4. In the winter, trees that lose their leaves *look* bare and lifeless.

_____ 5. *Is* it still there?

Exercise B   Underline the verbs in the following sentences. On the line provided, write each verb followed by *TV* for a transitive verb, *IV* for an intransitive verb, or *LV* for a linking verb.

    EXAMPLE: 1. I <u>cradled</u> the puppy, who <u>was</u> asleep in my arms.
            cradled, TV; was, LV

1. While everyone went outside, he remained in the house. _____

2. In ancient Rome, the new year began on March 1, and September was the seventh month of the year. _____

3. In 6000 B.C., the usual transportation for long distances was the camel caravan, which averaged eight miles per hour. _____

4. As we drew near Santorini, I saw its sparkling white houses. _____

5. On those warm, sunny days, the corn grew tall and smelled sweet. _____

Name _____ Date _____ Class _____

The Verb Phrase

A **verb phrase** consists of a main verb and at least one **helping verb** (also called an **auxiliary verb**). Some commonly used helping verbs are forms of the verbs *be, have,* and *do,* as well as other words such as *may, might, must, can, shall, will, could, should,* and *would.*

    We **are studying** Mexican painters in art class.   **Do** you **have** a favorite artist?

    I **could** not **watch** that movie.

NOTE: The word *not,* as well as its contraction (*–n't*), is never part of a verb phrase. Instead, it is an adverb telling *to what extent.*

Exercise A   On the line provided, write the verb phrase from each of the following sentences. Then underline the helping verb(s) in the phrase.

1. Have you ever seen any of Mexican artist Rufino Tamayo's paintings? _____

2. Rufino Tamayo was born in 1899; he died in 1991. _____

3. As a youngster, Tamayo sold fruit in a market in Mexico City, and his eye for color was probably influenced by this experience. _____

4. Some of his work was inspired by the paintings of Spanish artist Pablo Picasso. _____

5. Our art teacher has shown us slides of Rufino Tamayo's paintings. _____

6. Tamayo's paintings are exhibited in major museums throughout the United States and Mexico. _____

7. In 1926, Tamayo went to New York, where he could pursue his goals as an artist. _____

8. Tamayo's painting *Children Playing with Fire* may have been painted in reaction to the Mexican Revolution. _____

9. Tamayo worried that people would destroy themselves and the earth through war. _____

10. Other artists of the 1930s and 1940s did have that same concern. _____

Exercise B   Underline the five verb phrases in the following paragraph. Be sure to include all helping verbs.

    The English language has borrowed many words from other languages. Because a newly borrowed word often sounds unfamiliar, people sometimes do not hear it correctly. They will mispronounce the word and then spell it as if it had come from other, more familiar English words. The wrong spelling hides the true origin of the word and gives the false impression that its source is English. The word *woodchuck,* for example, sounds as if it might have come from two English words, *wood* and *chuck.* Actually, *woodchuck* came from the Cree *otchek.*

GRAMMAR/USAGE

Chapter 1: Parts of Speech

| WORKSHEET 8 | *The Adverb* |

An **adverb** is a word used to modify a verb, an adjective, or another adverb by telling *how, when, where,* or *to what extent (how long* or *how much).*

> The professor arrived **early** for the debate. [*Early* modifies the verb *arrived* and tells *when.*]

> These are **extremely** strenuous exercises. [*Extremely* modifies the adjective *strenuous* and tells *to what extent.*]

> Glinda arrived **quite** late for her appointment. [*Quite* modifies the adverb *late* and tells *to what extent.*]

Exercise A   Underline the adverbs in the following sentences, and draw an arrow to the verb, verb phrase, adjective, or adverb each adverb modifies. A sentence may have more than one adverb.

> EXAMPLE: 1. I danced energetically.

1. Small children need very careful supervision.

2. Hector proudly showed his parents his excellent report card.

3. I never eat in outrageously expensive restaurants.

4. The defendant responded rather sarcastically to the prosecuting attorney.

5. You can eat quite inexpensively in this restaurant.

6. Odessa ran upstairs quickly to get her briefcase.

7. You were driving too fast.

8. The teacher told the students, "Take your essays home for revision, and return them to me tomorrow."

9. Wow! I never knew that skiing could be so exciting!

10. "Do not write on these forms," the officer ordered.

Exercise B   Add adverbs to the two sentences below to make them more interesting and complete. Write your sentences on the lines provided, and underline all the adverbs that you have added.

> EXAMPLE: 1. She called me from Houston with an urgent message.
>
>   *Yesterday, she called me from Houston with an extremely*
>   *urgent message.*

1. Tina was lucky to find her gold ring.

_____

2. The dog waited for its owner's return.

_____

Name _____ Date _____ Class _____

 WORKSHEET 9 | *The Preposition*

A **preposition** is a word used to show the relationship of a noun or pronoun to another word. A preposition introduces a *prepositional phrase*. A prepositional phrase consists of the preposition, a noun or pronoun called the **object of the preposition,** and any modifiers of the object.

> The spider is **in** the web. [*In* is the preposition; *web* is the object of the preposition that ends the prepositional phrase *in the web.*]

A preposition that consists of more than one word is called a **compound preposition.**

> **According to** the weather report, the snow should begin falling soon.

Exercise A   In each of the following sentences, underline each preposition once and the object of the preposition twice. Some sentences have more than one prepositional phrase.

> EXAMPLE: 1. The Incas <u>of</u> <u><u>South America</u></u> offered gifts <u>to</u> their <u><u>gods</u></u>.

1. In spite of the rough terrain, the Incas built an empire along the Andes Mountains.

2. The Incas worshipped the rain god along with the sun god and made many offerings to both.

3. Divers have gathered Incan artifacts from Lake Titicaca, which sits within the Andes Mountains, 12,507 feet above sea level.

4. According to ancient Incan beliefs, mountain ice and water held healing powers.

5. Andean people today maintain a reverent attitude toward the Andes Mountains.

Exercise B   Add prepositional phrases to the following sentences to make them more interesting. Write your sentences on the lines provided and underline the prepositions.

> EXAMPLE: 1. I asked what that contraption was.
>
> <u>Without</u> thinking, I asked what that contraption <u>in</u> the driveway was.

1. Someone sneezed loudly.

_____

2. I will read three books.

_____

3. A hot wind blew angrily.

_____

4. The old car rumbled grumpily.

_____

5. He prepared dinner that night.

_____

GRAMMAR/USAGE

Name _____ Date _____ Class _____

The Conjunction and the Interjection

A **conjunction** is a word used to join words or groups of words. A **coordinating conjunction** connects words or groups of words used in the same way. **Correlative conjunctions** are pairs of conjunctions that connect words or groups of words used in the same way. A **subordinating conjunction** begins a subordinate clause and connects it to an independent clause. A subordinating conjunction may come at the beginning of a sentence.

COORDINATING CONJUNCTION: It began to rain, **so** I didn't go to the game.

CORRELATIVE CONJUNCTIONS: **Either** Alice **or** Yoshiro will drive to the field.

SUBORDINATING CONJUNCTION: **Because** it was raining, we left early.

An **interjection** is a word used to express emotion. It is set off from the rest of the sentence by an exclamation point or a comma.

Gosh! We won!   **Gee**, I'm sorry that I'm late.

Exercise A   Underline the conjunctions in the following sentences. Then, on the line provided, classify each conjunction as *coordinating*, *correlative*, or *subordinating*.

1. Not only did I feel foolish, but I also looked ridiculous.   _____

2. You may not believe me, yet I'm telling the truth!   _____

3. We plan to travel through Europe by train wherever we can.   _____

4. Neither Ken nor Uni had seen the movie.   _____

5. Drain the oil and dispose of it properly.   _____

Exercise B   For each of the following sentences, choose an appropriate subordinating conjunction from the words in parentheses. Write your choice on the line provided.

1. Economists predict economic growth for this quarter, _____ bank officials do not share this optimism. (since, although, because)

2. _____ the aircraft's radio had been damaged, the crew was unable to signal for help. (Until, Since, Although)

3. I didn't call you back _____ I never got your message. (after, even though, because)

4. _____ the survey was made, the architects began their drawings of the new building. (After, Unless, If)

5. Please explain _____ an engine works. (since, as soon as, how)

Exercise C   Underline the interjections in each of the following sentences.

1. Yikes! I can't find my other shoe, and hey, my bus is almost here!

2. Well, it's rather difficult to explain, but I'll try.

Name _____ Date _____ Class _____

Review

Exercise A The following passage contains twenty numbered, italicized words. On the lines provided, identify the part of speech of each italicized word. Base your answer on the way the word is used in the sentence. Use the following abbreviations:

N for noun	**ADV** for adverb
P for pronoun	**PREP** for preposition
ADJ for adjective	**CON** for conjunction
V for verb	**INT** for interjection

EXAMPLE: [1] *Follow* ___V___ the instructions.

In [1] *America* _____ , grammarians are [2] *seldom* _____ heroes to students. The opposite is more likely to be true. Just ask any student [3] *who* _____ is having trouble with high school English. Probably the most important [4] *American* _____ grammarian was Noah Webster, who [5] *died* _____ over a century ago. Today, however, Webster is not widely known for his work as a grammarian. He is famous chiefly for the many dictionaries that have been named [6] *after* _____ him, most of which he had nothing at all to do with.

[7] *One* _____ of the [8] *most* _____ interesting grammarians of the present century was the Harvard scholar George Lyman Kittredge. With a colleague, he [9] *published* _____ in 1913 a book called *Advanced English Grammar.* An [10] *extraordinary* _____ person, Kittredge had no [11] *patience* _____ with [12] *traffic* _____ signs [13] *or* _____ stoplights. He would wave all traffic to a stop with his cane and walk imperiously [14] *across* _____ the street. In his book, Kittredge treated grammar with the same firmness.

[15] *Alas* _____ , Kittredge's book is no longer widely available. This is a pity. What grammarian today would dare to illustrate the nature of the sentence [16] *as* _____ Kittredge did on the first page of his grammar book? One of the first sample sentences on the page [17] *states* _____ categorically, "A man who respects [18] *himself* _____ should never condescend to use [19] *slovenly* _____ language." [20] *Today* _____ grammarians would think twice before preaching to their readers in this manner.

GRAMMAR/USAGE

Exercise B Each of the following sentences contains either one word or two words of the kind specified before the sentence. Find these words and write them on the line provided. Base your answers on the way each word is used in the sentence.

> EXAMPLE: 1. *nouns* We drove past many fields of cotton. *fields, cotton*

1. *pronouns* Cotton cloth is one of the oldest known fabrics in the world.   _____

2. *verbs* Five thousand years ago, the prehistoric inhabitants of India grew and spun cotton.   _____

3. *adverbs* Cotton was also used in ancient Egypt and in ancient China.   _____

4. *prepositions* In Europe, however, cotton was not widely used until the late Middle Ages.   _____

5. *adjectives* Then traders began bringing cotton fabrics into Europe from Mesopotamia and India.   _____

Exercise C Each of the following sentences contains an italicized word that is used twice. This word may function as more than one part of speech. On the lines provided, indicate the part of speech for each use of this word. Use the following abbreviations:

N for noun   ADV for adverb
P for pronoun   PREP for preposition
ADJ for adjective   CON for conjunction
V for verb   INT for interjection

> EXAMPLE: 1. In an obstacle (a) *race* ___N___ , the contestants
> (b) *race* ___V___ over hurdles, climb walls, and scramble through ditches.

1. You can go out (a) *after* _____ your chores are done and (b) *after* _____ dinner.

2. Sure, you can turn the stereo (a) *on* _____ ; the switch is (b) *on* _____ your right.

3. (a) *Well* _____ , it looks like the (b) *well* _____ is finally dry.

4. (a) *Store* _____ the summer stock in the back of the (b) *store* _____ .

5. As you (a) *near* _____ the intersection, look both ways, and pay attention to the cars (b) *near* _____ you.

Exercise D The following passage contains twenty numbered, italicized words. On the lines provided, identify the part of speech of each italicized word. Base your answer on the way the word is used in the sentence. Use these abbreviations: **N, P, ADJ, V, ADV, PREP, CON, INT.**

> EXAMPLE: [1] They saw the *shiny* ___ADJ___ object.

Nearly [1] *every* _____ person knows about the famous gold rushes that

[2] *occurred* _____ in California and in the Klondike during the 1800s. Stories about fortunes

made and lost in the gold fields [3] *near* _____ San Francisco and Dawson have been told and retold. Yet [4] *these* _____ were not the only sites of gold fever on the North American

continent. The discovery and lure of gold had also brought a [5] *swarm* _____ of prospectors

to [6] *northern* _____ Colorado.

[7] *Auraria* _____ is a small town that is now part of Denver. People [8] *flocked* _____

to Auraria in the 1850s [9] *when* _____ they heard tales of [10] *enormous* _____ gold

nuggets in the nearby hills. Formerly an unexplored region [11] *between* _____ two obscure

rivers, Auraria became both a name on the map and a word on people's lips. [12] *It* _____

[13] *soon* _____ had eighteen or twenty stores, twelve [14] *or* _____ fifteen law offices, and

over a thousand people.

In 1859, William Byers established Auraria's first newspaper, [15] *which* _____ he

called the *Rocky Mountain News*. To promote growth, Byers urged Auraria to combine with

Denver City, a [16] *nearby* _____ hamlet. In 1860, the towns did consolidate, [17] *but* _____

the combined city was called Denver. Auraria's name was [18] *largely* _____ forgotten.

[19] *Well* _____ , Byers' dreams to create [20] *growth* _____ certainly came true! By 1890,

Denver was the third largest city west of the Missouri River.

Exercise E Each of the following sentences contains either one word or two words of
the kind specified before the sentence. Find these words and write them on the line
provided. Base your answers on the way each word is used in the sentence.

> EXAMPLE: 1. *verbs* Just a decade ago, the most popular definition of
> *hardware* was "articles that are made of metal."
> *was, are made*

1. *nouns* I am astonished by the incredible operating speed of
modern computers. _____

2. *prepositions* Data fed into a computer can be stored for future use
and retrieved quickly. _____

3. *adjectives* American companies increasingly depend on
electronic equipment. _____

4. *adverbs* Many companies use databanks to obtain up-to-
date information promptly. _____

5. *pronouns* Business executives who once feared electronics are
now ordering personal computers for themselves. _____

GRAMMAR/USAGE

Name _____ Date _____ Class _____

Exercise F Each of the following sentences contains an italicized word that is used twice. This word may function as more than one part of speech. On the lines provided, indicate the part of speech for each use of this word. Use these abbreviations: **N, P, ADJ, V, ADV, PREP, CON, INT**.

EXAMPLE: 1. She (a) *ground* ___V___ the eggshells into the (b) *ground* ___N___ with her shoe.

1. The bright (a) *light* _____ shone through the (b) *light* _____ material.

2. When the tennis ball went (a) *over* _____ the fence, Carmen's partner wanted to start the game (b) *over* _____ .

3. (a) *Color* _____ the letters on the poster with a (b) *color* _____ that is highly visible.

4. Southside's quarterback ran (a) *down* _____ the sidelines on the crucial fourth (b) *down* _____ .

5. (a) *These* _____ socks belong to Diego; (b) *these* _____ are Juanita's; and those are mine.

Name _____ Date _____ Class _____

Agreement of Subject and Verb A

A verb agrees with its subject in **number.** Singular subjects take singular verbs, and plural subjects take plural verbs.

SINGULAR: **Bo Jackson plays** baseball.

PLURAL: The **players,** along with the coach, **fly** to Detroit tomorrow.

Verb phrases must also agree in number with their subjects. The number of a verb phrase is indicated by the form of its first helping (auxiliary) verb.

SINGULAR: **She has** been training for the marathon for months.

PLURAL: The **runners** in the marathon **have** been keeping a steady pace.

Exercise A For each of the following sentences, underline the verb or helping verb in parentheses that agrees in number with the subject. On the line provided, write the subject of each sentence.

1. Lying on the bed (was, were) a blue satin evening dress. _____

2. I (run, runs) ten times around the track every day. _____

3. Under the rotten tree, termites (was, were) burrowing busily. _____

4. (Do, Does) you have another pen? _____

5. The plan I devised (is, are) working perfectly. _____

Exercise B For each of the following sentences, circle the subject of the verb in parentheses. Then underline the verb form that agrees in number with the subject.

EXAMPLE: 1. (Quilting)(has, have) a long and colorful history.

1. During the colonial period, only wealthy women made quilts; however, by the mid-nineteenth century, women throughout the United States (was making, were making) quilts.

2. The abilities that a person would need to make a quilt (include, includes) patience, coordination, and a good sense of color and design.

3. A bag full of colorful bits of cotton and wool fabrics (was put, were put) to good use in a quilt.

4. Fabric from worn-out shirts, as well as from other articles of clothing, (was cut, were cut) into pieces of various shapes and sizes.

5. Several quilters, gathering at one person's home for a quilting bee, often (work, works) on a quilt together.

GRAMMAR/USAGE

Name _____ Date _____ Class _____

Agreement of Subject and Verb B

The following **indefinite pronouns** are always singular: *anybody, anyone, each, either, everybody, everyone, neither, nobody, no one, one, somebody,* and *someone.*

SINGULAR SUBJECT AND VERB: **Everyone** who enjoys sports **likes** this program.

The following indefinite pronouns are always plural: *both, few, many,* and *several.*

PLURAL SUBJECT AND VERB: **Many** who travel to France **visit** Paris.

The following indefinite pronouns may be either singular or plural: *all, any, most, none,* and *some.* These pronouns are singular when they refer to singular words and plural when they refer to plural words.

SINGULAR: **Most** of the book **is** interesting. [*Most* refers to the singular noun *book.*]

PLURAL: **Most** of the students **are** here. [*Most* refers to the plural noun *students.*]

Exercise A For each of the following sentences, underline the subject. Then underline the verb form that agrees in number with the subject.

EXAMPLE: 1. Not <u>one</u> of the pears (look, <u>looks</u>) ripe.

1. Many of the recipes in this cookbook (is, are) adaptable to microwave cooking.

2. Neither of my parents (has, have) any trouble using the metric system.

3. Few of the students (was, were) able to spell *bureaucracy* correctly.

4. None of the written language from the Incan civilization (remain, remains), but scholars have learned about these people through oral communication.

5. Some of the word-processing software for our computer (has, have) arrived late.

Exercise B: Proofreading Most of the following sentences contain verbs that do not agree with their subjects. If the verb does not agree with its subject, write the correct form on the line provided. If the verb agrees with its subject, write C.

EXAMPLE: 1. Each of the issues were resolved. *was*

1. Not all of the members of the class wants to study poetry. _____

2. Everybody in the literature discussion groups have been assigned one poet to study. _____

3. One of the groups want to study some of the works of Marianne Moore. _____

4. Few of the students is familiar with the poetry of Moore. _____

5. After beginning the research, each of the students has realized that analyzing poetry requires technical skills. _____

Name _____ Date _____ Class _____

WORKSHEET 3

Other Problems in Agreement A

A **compound subject** is two or more subjects that have the same verb. A compound subject joined by *and* usually takes a plural verb.

> **Gwendolyn Brooks** and **Judith Viorst are** poets.

However, some compound subjects joined by *and* name only one person or thing. Such compound subjects take singular verbs.

> The **director** and **star** of the movie **is** Barbra Streisand.

Two singular subjects joined by *or* or *nor* take a singular verb.

> Neither **Marco** nor **Raymond has** ever seen an opera.

When a singular subject and a plural subject are joined by *or* or *nor*, the verb agrees with the subject that is nearer to the verb.

> Neither the chorus **members** nor the lead **singer has** come to rehearsal.

Exercise A   For each of the following sentences, circle the subject of the verb in parentheses. Then underline the verb or helping verb that agrees with the subject.

1. Low fares and speed (was, were) incentives for suburbanites to use the new mass transit system.

2. The convenience or the comfort of operating a car, however, (make, makes) many drivers reluctant to use the transit system.

3. Many people do not seem to care that pollution and congestion (results, result) from using the automobile.

4. Neither air pollution nor noise levels in our city (is, are) monitored regularly.

5. The health hazards and psychological effects of smog (have, has) been studied for years.

Exercise B: Proofreading   Most of the following sentences contain verbs that do not agree with their subjects. If the verb does not agree with its subject, write the correct form on the line provided. If the verb agrees with its subject, write *C*.

1. One or both of the Shakespearean plays about Henry IV are likely to be performed this summer.   _____

2. The environmental groups and their opponents has already presented their recommendations to the governor.   _____

3. Neither the affirmative debate team nor the negative one were eager to suggest a solution to the problem.   _____

4. Sandra Cisneros and Maya Angelou is my favorite writers.   _____

5. Rhythm and blues are my favorite kind of music.   _____

GRAMMAR/USAGE

Name _____ Date _____ Class _____

Other Problems in Agreement B

In a question, or in a sentence beginning with *Here, Where,* or *There,* the subject usually follows the verb. Be careful that the subject and the verb agree.

> Here **is** your **ticket**.
>
> Where **are** the **tickets** for Jim and Maria?

A **collective noun** is singular in form but names a group of persons or things. Use a singular verb with a collective noun when the noun refers to the group as a unit. Use a plural verb when the noun refers to the parts or members of the group.

> The team **plays** on Monday. [The team plays together as a unit.]
>
> The team **are** taking turns at bat. [The members of the team take turns at bat.]

An expression of an amount is singular when the amount is thought of as a unit. It is plural when the amount is thought of as many parts.

> Eight dollars **is** the price of a ticket. [The amount is a unit.]
>
> Eight dollars **are** missing from my wallet. [The dollars are separate bills.]

A fraction or percentage is singular when it refers to a singular word and plural when it refers to a plural word.

Expressions of measurement (length, weight, and so on) are usually singular.

> Three quarters of earth **is** covered by water.
>
> Two pints **equals** one quart.

Exercise For each of the following sentences, underline the verb in parentheses that agrees with the subject.

1. Here (is, are) the percentages of last month's sales.

2. Every elementary student learns that three feet (equal, equals) one yard.

3. The hockey team (has, have) all bought new uniforms this year.

4. On our block alone, over two hundred dollars (was, were) collected for the American Cancer Society.

5. A pride of lions (was, were) the subject that commanded the photographer's attention.

6. Three fourths of the proceeds from the sale (go, goes) to charity.

7. Hey, Dad, (there's, there are) no more milk in the refrigerator.

8. (Where's, Where are) her mother and father?

9. The majority of high school juniors (think, thinks) that computer literacy is important.

10. Half of a tank (is, are) not enough gasoline to get to the mountains and back.

Name _____ Date _____ Class _____

WORKSHEET 5

Other Problems in Agreement C

The title of a creative work, the name of an organization, or the name of a country or city takes a singular verb.

    The Third of May **is** one of Francisco Goya's masterpieces.

    United Plastics employs hundreds of people from our area.

Some nouns, such as *civics*, *measles*, and *physics*, are plural in form but singular in meaning.

    The **news comes** on at six o'clock. **Economics is being discussed.**

Nouns that refer to pairs, such as *binoculars* and *scissors*, always take plural verbs.

    Where **are** the **scissors**? Your **trousers need** shortening.

A subject that is a phrase or clause always takes a singular verb.

    What she said about Lydia was hard to believe.

Exercise: Proofreading   Most of the following sentences contain verbs that do not agree with their subjects. If the verb does not agree with its subject, write the correct form on the line provided. If the verb agrees with its subject, write *C*.

1. Microelectronics, the area of electronics dealing with the design and application of microcircuits, have made possible many of the tremendous advances in computers and robotics in recent years. _____

2. Whoever is elected takes office the following month. _____

3. Simple mathematics show that as manufacturing costs rise, profits will decrease unless prices rise. _____

4. Where is my scissors? _____

5. Acme Chemicals are a loyal supporter of the Special Olympics. _____

6. The local news are broadcast on the radio every half hour. _____

7. The best time to call are in the morning. _____

8. The United States produce a large portion of the world's food supply. _____

9. Unfortunately, the statistics does not take into account the vast number of people who refused to answer the questions. _____

10. The Girl Guides, a scouting organization that began in Great Britain, is looking for new members. _____

GRAMMAR/USAGE

Name _____ Date _____ Class _____

WORKSHEET 6

Other Problems in Agreement D

A verb agrees with its subject, not with its predicate nominative.

The leading **crop is** strawberries. **Strawberries are** the leading crop.

Subjects preceded by *every* or *many a(n)* take singular verbs.

Every man and woman **has** spoken. Many an idea **has** been heard.

Use *doesn't* with all singular subjects except the pronouns *I* and *you*. Use *don't* with all plural subjects and with the pronouns *I* and *you*.

He **doesn't** know the answer. I **don't** know it, either.

When a relative pronoun is the subject of an adjective clause, the verb in the clause should agree with the word that the relative pronoun refers to.

Gregory Hines, **who stars** in this movie, is a great dancer.

Exercise A: Proofreading   Most of the following sentences contain verbs that do not agree with their subjects. If the verb does not agree with its subject, write the correct form on the line provided. If the verb agrees with its subject, write *C*.

1. Is the platypus the only one of the mammals that lay eggs?   _____

2. The fact that compact discs does not wear out and does not have
   to be flipped over makes them attractive.   _____

3. Serena was the only one of the students who were chosen to go.   _____

4. Fresh eggs is the major ingredient in meringue.   _____

5. Have every nut and bolt been tightened?   _____

6. These pipes, which was originally installed some fifty years ago,
   are still in good operating condition.   _____

7. The thing I liked best about the city were the subways.   _____

8. Many a hopeful actress return home in a few months.   _____

9. The squadron, which have just taken off, is headed west.   _____

10. Her major achievement was her experiments with plant genetics.   _____

Exercise B   On the line provided, write either *doesn't* or *don't*.

1. Why _____ he even speak to me?

2. They _____ know where her keys are.

3. Cold weather and snow _____ seem to bother the dog at all.

4. _____ Harriet and Gina live in that apartment house?

5. Even though he has a steady job, it _____ pay much.

Name _____ Date _____ Class _____

WORKSHEET 7

Agreement of Pronoun and Antecedent A

A pronoun usually refers to a noun or another pronoun. The word a pronoun refers to is called its **antecedent**. A pronoun agrees with its antecedent in number, gender, and person.

> **Rosalía de Castro,** a Spanish poet, often wrote in **her** native language, Galician.
>
> The **horses** were sleeping in **their** stalls.
>
> **We** got **our** lab partner assignments in biology class today.

Use singular pronouns to refer to indefinite pronouns such as *anybody, each, either, everybody, everyone, neither, no one, nothing, one,* and *something.* Use plural pronouns to refer to the indefinite pronouns *both, few, many,* and *several.* Use singular or plural pronouns to refer to the indefinite pronouns *all, any, most, none,* and *some.*

> SINGULAR: **Some** of your **reasoning** misses **its** mark.
>
> PLURAL: **Some** of your **friends** left **their** things here.

Exercise A: Proofreading   Most of the following sentences contain pronouns that do not agree with their antecedents. If the pronoun does not agree with its antecedent, write the correct form on the line provided. If the pronoun agrees with its antecedent, write *C.*

1. Abdul got the players' autographs and showed it to me.   _____

2. Each of the women provided her own transportation.   _____

3. Some of these people feel that his or her lives are endangered by nuclear power.   _____

4. One of the girls in my class brought their video camera to school.   _____

5. Both of my sisters do her homework on the bus.   _____

Exercise B   Complete each of the following sentences by supplying at least one pronoun that agrees with its antecedent. Use standard formal English.

> EXAMPLE: 1. Each of the girls took *her* turn at bat.

1. All of the workers take _____ breaks at the same time.

2. Miraculously, most of the ancient temple had retained _____ splendor.

3. Everybody in the Brownie troop brought _____ own lunch.

4. Many of the students in our class have turned in _____ reports on the Frida Kahlo exhibit.

5. Looking back, I can see that few of the boys in that class ever gave up _____ goals.

GRAMMAR/USAGE

Chapter 2: Agreement

WORKSHEET 8

Agreement of Pronoun and Antecedent B

Use a plural pronoun to refer to two or more singular antecedents joined by *and*. Use a singular pronoun to refer to two or more singular antecedents joined by *or* or *nor*. When a singular and a plural antecedent are joined by *or* or *nor*, the pronoun usually agrees with the nearer antecedent.

While **Calinda** and **Yvette** were on vacation, I watered **their** plants.

Neither **Mr. Bast** nor the **Rodriguezes** have received **their** recycling bins.

Collective nouns may act as either singular or plural antecedents.

The **team** won all of **its** matches.

The **team** disagree about the color of **their** uniforms.

The title of a creative work or the name of a country, city, or organization takes a singular pronoun.

Hemingway's *For Whom the Bell Tolls* takes **its** title from a poem by John Donne.

Some words, such as *civics*, *measles*, and *physics*, are plural in form but singular in meaning. These words take singular pronouns. Nouns that refer to pairs, such as *shorts* and *pliers*, always take plural pronouns. Nouns preceded by *every* or *many a* take singular pronouns.

Exercise A   Complete each of the following sentences by supplying at least one pronoun that agrees with its antecedent. Use standard formal English.

1. Either Mark or David will take _____ car.

2. Both Ricardo and Paul offered _____ vans to transport the musical equipment.

3. After all these years, neither my studies nor my art has lost _____ appeal for me.

4. After a week, the posse decided _____ should break up.

5. The committee asked Mrs. Marshall and Ms. Lee for _____ opinions.

Exercise B: Proofreading   Most of the following sentences contain pronouns that do not agree with their antecedents. If the pronoun does not agree with its antecedent, write the correct form on the line provided. If the pronoun agrees with its antecedent, write *C*.

1. Taylor Associates, a company new to the area, offers their clients a full range of tax services. _____

2. *Mules and Men* contains tales collected by Zora Neale Hurston. _____

3. Measles may be recognized by their characteristic rash. _____

4. The United Nations will direct their attention to Europe. _____

5. When your eyeglasses are ready, it will be shipped to you. _____

Name _____ Date _____ Class _____

 **Review**

WORKSHEET 9

Exercise A For each of the following sentences, underline the subject of the verb in parentheses. Then underline the verb form that agrees in number with the subject.

EXAMPLE: 1. <u>Both</u> of the brothers (<u>play</u>, plays) in the zydeco band at the Cajun Fest.

1. Neither the Litchfield nor the Torrington exit (is, are) the one you should take.

2. The president, after meeting with several of his advisers, (has, have) promised to veto the proposed tax bill.

3. A medical study of World War II veterans (has, have) concluded that the veterans have the same health prospects as nonveterans.

4. The list of the greatest baseball players of all time (is, are) dominated by outfielders.

5. Babe Ruth, Henry Aaron, Willie Mays, and Joe DiMaggio (is, are) all outfielders on the list.

6. The Mariana Trench, located in the Pacific Ocean near the Mariana Islands, (is, are) the deepest known ocean area in the world.

7. Styles in clothing (seems, seem) to change as often as the weather.

8. (Do, Does) the New York City Triborough Bridge and Tunnel Authority, which oversees the collection of bridge tolls, have a major problem with small Mexican coins?

9. Yes, the Mexican peso, worth a fraction of a cent, (is, are) easily accepted by the present toll machines.

10. These vegetables (doesn't, don't) look fresh.

Exercise B: Proofreading Most of the following sentences contain pronouns that do not agree with their antecedents. If the pronoun does not agree, write the correct form on the line provided. If the pronoun agrees with its antecedent, write C. Use standard formal English.

1. Both Cholanda and Dee Dee gave her ten-minute talks on trees. _____

2. If anyone wants to see an American elm, they should go with Cholanda. _____

3. Neither one of the girls identified their gray birch leaf correctly. _____

4. Everyone who plans to go on a nature hike should be on their guard against poisonous snakes. _____

5. A poisonous snake can usually be identified by either its color or its behavior. _____

6. As for me, my shorts or trousers always have a snakebite kit in its pocket. _____

GRAMMAR/USAGE

7. Most of my friends carry first-aid kits in his or her backpacks. _____

8. The Boy Scouts of America encourages their members to learn first-aid techniques. _____

9. Many a camper has been glad of their knowledge of first aid in an emergency. _____

10. But campers and hikers alike should take care of yourselves while out having fun and learning about nature. _____

Exercise C   Most of the sentences in the following paragraph contain errors in agreement. If the sentence contains an error in agreement, circle the incorrect verb or pronoun, and supply the correct form on the line provided. If the sentence is correct, write C.

EXAMPLE: [1] (Don't) the concept of child prodigies fascinate you? *Doesn't*

[1] Prodigies, people who have immense talent, is born very infrequently. _____

[2] One of the most interesting child prodigies of this century are young Wang Yani of China. _____ [3] Two and a half years were the age at which Wang began painting. _____ [4] Most of her paintings interests me. _____ [5] However, my favorite are the wonderful frolicking monkeys that she painted when she was only five. _____ [6] *Little Monkeys and Mummy* is their title. _____ [7] The people of China has recognized Wang as a prodigy since she was four years old. _____ [8] By the time she was six, she had already painted four thousand pictures. _____ [9] Wet ink and paint is freely mixed in Wang's pictures, producing interesting puddles and fuzzy edges. _____ [10] Honored at home and abroad, Wang Yani is the youngest painter ever to have their works displayed in a one-person show at the Smithsonian Institution. _____

Name _____ Date _____ Class _____

Principal Parts of Regular Verbs

Every verb has four basic forms called the **principal parts**: the *base form*, the *present participle*, the *past*, and the *past participle*. A **regular verb** is one that forms its past and past participle by adding *–d* or *–ed* to the base form.

Base Form	Present Participle	Past	Past Participle
ask	asking	asked	(have) asked
dream	dreaming	dreamed *or* dreamt	(have) dreamed *or* dreamt

Exercise A   On the line provided, write the past or past participle form of the verb in parentheses.

1. Henry Baker _____ at the U.S. Patent Office. (work)

2. He had _____ a list of inventions. (publish)

3. Baker had _____ names of other African American inventors. (collect)

4. In 1900, the Patent Office _____ a survey. (conduct)

5. Baker had _____ numerous letters to many different people. (mail)

6. Newspaper editors had _____ his queries. (receive)

7. Baker's list _____ names of two hundred inventors. (contain)

8. All together, they had _____ four hundred inventions. (create)

9. Thomas L. Jennings _____ a dry-cleaning method. (develop)

10. Baker's second survey _____ up many more inventors. (turn)

Exercise B: Revising   Revise each sentence below, using the past form of the verb instead of the present form. Write your revision on the line provided.

EXAMPLE: 1. Robin pounds the dough into a flat bread.
<u>*Robin pounded the dough into a flat bread.*</u>

1. Dr. Aponte sterilizes her instruments carefully.

_____

2. Just at dusk, a pair of loons call to each other.

_____

3. The ambassadors formalize the treaty with their signatures.

_____

4. The bus stops four times between here and Chicago.

_____

GRAMMAR/USAGE

Name _____ Date _____ Class _____

Principal Parts of Irregular Verbs A

An **irregular verb** forms its past and past participle in some way other than by adding *–d* or *–ed* to the base form. Such verbs form the past or past participle many ways:

CHANGING VOWELS *OR* CONSONANTS: swim, swam, swum; bend, bent, bent

CHANGING VOWELS *AND* CONSONANTS: sleep, slept, slept; do, did, done

MAKING NO CHANGE: let, let, let

Exercise A On the line provided, write the past or past participle form of the verb in parentheses.

EXAMPLE: 1. Godzilla *swung* at the attacking airplanes. (swing)

1. When we got to the video store, you had just _____ . (leave)

2. Unfortunately, I have already _____ most of my weekly allowance. (spend)

3. In an earlier scene, Tarzan had _____ hold of a vine and used it to swing through the trees. (catch)

4. The paintings by Horace Pippin really _____ our interest. (hold)

5. The clown had juggled and had _____ two plates on sticks. (spin)

Exercise B The author of the following silly poem has broken the rules of standard usage just for fun. Each couplet in the poem contains an incorrect past or past participle form of an irregular verb. For each incorrect form shown in italics, provide the correct form. [Note: The poem will no longer rhyme.]

EXAMPLE: 1. Bake, baked; make, *maked*? Hold it—not so fast!
          Verbs that rhyme in the present form may not rhyme
          in the past! _made_

1. Today we fling the same old ball that yesterday we flung;
   Today we bring the same good news that yesterday we *brung*.   _____

2. And we still mind our parents, the folks we've always minded;
   And I may find a dime, just like the dime you *finded*.   _____

3. I smell the crimson rose, the very rose you smelled;
   I'll tell a silly joke today, the same joke you once *telled*.   _____

4. I beep my horn to warn you; I'm sure my horn just beeped;
   I keep all my appointments, the ones I should have *keeped*.   _____

5. I lose my train of thought; my train of thought I've *losed*.
   I use my verbs with care; just see the ones I've used!   _____

Name _____ Date _____ Class _____

Principal Parts of Irregular Verbs B

When forming the past and the past participle of irregular verbs, avoid these common errors:

(1) using the past form with a helping verb

NONSTANDARD: I have never swam in this lake before.

STANDARD: I never **swam** in this lake before.

(2) using the past participle form without a helping verb

NONSTANDARD: She swum to shore to get help.

STANDARD: She **had swum** to shore to get help.

(3) adding –d, –ed, or –t to the base form

NONSTANDARD: We bursted into laughter as soon as we saw the comedian.

STANDARD: We burst into laughter as soon as we saw the comedian.

Exercise A   In each of the following sentences, underline the correct verb form in parentheses.

1. My jeans (shrank, shrunk) in the dryer, and now I can't wear them.

2. Arnie and I (went, gone) to the boat show last week.

3. The troops (drove, drived) the enemy back to the border.

4. I haven't yet (began, begun) writing my report.

5. Until Saturday, Ray had never (gived, given) us cause for alarm.

Exercise B   On the line provided, write the past or past participle form of the verb in parentheses.

1. The tourists had _____ to the desert to see Pueblo dwellings. (come)

2. Jan _____ the cooking, but everyone helped with the cleaning. (do)

3. The silence was _____ by a sudden clap of thunder. (break)

4. West Side High's team easily _____ its opponents. (beat)

5. Miguel _____ up balloons and made decorations for his sister's *quinceañera* party, the celebration of her fifteenth birthday. (blow)

6. As Lou _____ home plate, the fans shrieked with delight. (steal)

7. Had you _____ the time, you'd have done a better job. (take)

8. Ellen had been _____ to attend the regional council. (choose)

9. Joshua had _____ taps on his bugle. (blow)

10. Had they all _____ from the same cup? (drink)

GRAMMAR/USAGE

Name _____ Date _____ Class _____

Principal Parts of Irregular Verbs C

The best way to learn the principal parts of irregular verbs is to memorize them. No single usage rule applies to the different ways that these verbs form their past and past participle forms. Remember that there are some general guidelines you can use. Irregular verbs form the past and past participle by

- changing vowels or consonants
- changing vowels and consonants
- making no change

Exercise: Proofreading Most of the following sentences contain incorrect verb forms. If a verb form is incorrect, write the correct past form on the line provided. If a sentence is correct, write C.

1. When my art class went to an exhibit of African American art, I seen some collages that Romare Bearden had maked. _____

2. Seeing the unusual medium of collage has letted me think about art in a new way. _____

3. Bearden growed up in North Carolina and then spended time studying in New York, Pittsburgh, and Paris. _____

4. Since the 1930s when his art career begun, he has gotten a reputation as a leading abstract artist. _____

5. Instead of specializing in painting or drawing, Bearden finded his niche in the somewhat unusual medium of collage. _____

6. He fashions his artworks out of pieces of colored paper that have been cutted or teared into small shapes. _____

7. Often, he has gave his collages more variety by using pieces from black-and-white or color photographs. _____

8. In his *Blue Interior, Morning,* Bearden has built a composition around a family eating breakfast. _____

9. The materials that he assembled were chose for their textural harmony. _____

10. I could have stand in front of Bearden's collage all day—it was so fascinating! _____

Name _____ Date _____ Class _____

 ## *Troublesome Verbs*
WORKSHEET 5

Certain verbs are troublesome because they are so similar. Study the following verbs:

Lie: The verb *lie (lying, lay, lain)* means "to rest, stay, or recline." *Lie* never takes an object.

Lay: The verb *lay (laying, laid, laid)* means "to put [something] in a place." *Lay* usually takes an object.

Sit: The verb *sit (sitting, sat, sat)* means "to rest in an upright seated position." *Sit* seldom takes an object.

Set: The verb *set (setting, set, set)* usually means "to put [something] in a place." *Set* usually takes an object.

Rise: The verb *rise (rising, rose, risen)* means "to go up" or "to get up." *Rise* never takes an object.

Raise: The verb *raise (raising, raised, raised)* means "to cause [something] to rise" or "to lift up." *Raise* usually takes an object.

Exercise A   For each of the following sentences, underline the correct verb in parentheses.

1. Don't (lie, lay) around all day doing nothing.

2. (Lie, Lay) the petri dish down on the table.

3. The airplane (raised, rose) into the darkening sky.

4. (Sit, Set) down over there with the rest of the class.

5. We (set, sat) around the computer terminal while Mrs. Toro explained the program.

6. Yesterday, we (lay, laid) new tiles on our kitchen floor.

7. The sleeping baby (lay, laid) in the crib.

8. Clothing prices have been (raising, rising) for some time.

9. Your dog has (laid, lain) in the same spot on the porch for hours.

10. The barometer has (raised, risen) steadily for the past twenty-four hours.

Exercise B   Each of the following sayings lacks a verb. Choose the correct verb in parentheses, and write the correct principal part of the verb on the line provided.

1. Let sleeping dogs _____ . (lie, lay)

2. _____ down your burden. (Lie, Lay)

3. Those who would deceive the fox must _____ early in the morning. (rise, raise)

4. I'm _____ on top of the world. (set, sit)

5. If you can't _____ the bridge, lower the river. (rise, raise)

GRAMMAR/USAGE

Chapter 3: Using Verbs

WORKSHEET 6   *Verb Tense*

The **tense** of a verb indicates the time of the action or the state of being expressed by the verb. Every verb has six tenses that are formed from the four principal parts of a verb.

PRESENT: Liz **writes** stories.	PRESENT PERFECT: Jibril **has written** stories.
PAST: Jibril **wrote** a poem.	PAST PERFECT: Before becoming a poet, Liz **had written** stories.
FUTURE: Liz **will (shall) write** poetry.	FUTURE PERFECT: Before next year, Jibril **will (shall) have written** a book of poems.

Exercise A   For each of the following sentences, underline the verb(s). Then, on the line provided, identify the tenses of the verb or verbs in each pair of sentences.

1. a. I took piano lessons for three years.   _____

    b. I have taken piano lessons for three years.   _____

2. a. We do our research on Friday.   _____

    b. We will have done our research on Friday.   _____

3. a. Jane has reported on recent fossil discoveries.   _____

    b. Jane had reported on recent fossil discoveries.   _____

4. a. I made a time line of the Middle Ages on Friday.   _____

    b. I will have made a time line of the Middle Ages on Friday.   _____

5. a. When we got to the airport, the flight left.   _____

    b. When we got to the airport, the flight had left.   _____

Exercise B   On the lines provided, write five original sentences according to the following directions.

1. Using a verb in the *present perfect tense*, write a sentence about a story you have read.

_____

2. Using at least two different verbs, one or more of them in the *past perfect tense*, write two sentences about a movie you have seen.

_____

_____

3. Using at least two different verbs, one or more of them in the *future perfect tense*, write two sentences about a place you would like to visit before a certain time in the future.

_____

_____

Name _____ Date _____ Class _____

Special Problems in the Use of Tenses

Use tense forms carefully to show the correct relationship between verbs in a sentence. When describing events that occur at the same time, use verbs of the same tense. When describing events that occur at different times, use verbs in different tenses to show the order of events.

SAME TIME: Lars **dimmed** the lights and Cassia **opened** the curtain. [past]

DIFFERENT TIMES: Lars **had dimmed** the lights, so Cassia **opened** the curtain. [two different points in the past]

Exercise A Decide if the italicized verbs in each sentence below tell about the same time or different times. On the lines provided, write *S* for same or *D* for different.

_____ 1. We *left* the park as the rain *began*.

_____ 2. By the time the bell *rings*, I *will have finished* my test.

_____ 3. Though the deer *runs* into the thicket, the wolves *follow* it.

_____ 4. They *have loaded* the truck, but the driver *is* not here.

_____ 5. If Jiro *had arrived* ten minutes earlier, he *would have seen* you.

Exercise B Each of the following sentences may contain an error in the use of tenses. Revise the sentences as needed.

EXAMPLE: 1. The holidays will ~~begin~~ *have begun* by the time we arrive in Miami.

1. Francesca promised to bring the Papago basket that she bought in Arizona.

2. Who found that the earth revolved around the sun?

3. In July my parents will be married for twenty-five years.

4. If the books have been cataloged last week, why haven't they been placed on the shelves?

5. We studied *Macbeth* after we learned about the English Renaissance and the Globe Theatre.

6. The graduation valedictory will be delivered by then.

7. Mabel answers the phone and told me of the incident.

8. If you would have waited, I could have given you a ride.

9. I think that digital watches kept the best time.

10. For the past three years, I had no colds.

Name _____ Date _____ Class _____

Progressive and Emphatic Forms

Each verb tense has an additional form called the **progressive form,** which expresses a continuing action or state of being. In each tense, the progressive form consists of the appropriate tense of *be* plus the present participle of the main verb. Some forms also include additional helping verbs.

PRESENT PROGRESSIVE:	is laughing
PAST PROGRESSIVE:	was laughing
FUTURE PROGRESSIVE:	will be laughing
PRESENT PERFECT PROGRESSIVE:	has been laughing
PAST PERFECT PROGRESSIVE:	had been laughing
FUTURE PERFECT PROGRESSIVE:	will have been laughing

The **emphatic form** of a verb is used to express emphasis. This form consists of the present or the past tense of *do* with the base form of the main verb. Only present tense and past tense verbs have emphatic forms.

PRESENT EMPHATIC: A pet certainly **does take** a lot of work.

PAST EMPHATIC: Thanks, your help **did make** a difference.

The emphatic form is also used in questions and in negative statements.

QUESTIONS: **Does** anyone here **have** the computer manual?

NEGATIVE STATEMENTS: No, this tire **doesn't need** air.

Exercise On the line provided, identify the tense and form of the verb in each of the following sentences as either *present, past,* or *future progressive; present perfect, past perfect,* or *future perfect progressive;* or *present* or *past emphatic.*

1. The Warrens will have been living here a month on July 15. _____

2. Don't tell another one of your weird jokes. _____

3. Poor weather conditions had been delaying the shipment. _____

4. Guy is washing the car right now. _____

5. He has been practicing all week for the recital. _____

6. Oh, but I do like your new haircut! _____

7. The pupils were meeting in front of the main building. _____

8. The Michaels will be representing our neighborhood at the citizen's association. _____

9. I'm sorry, but I did not have time for that. _____

10. The Foggy Harbor ferry had been running all night. _____

Name _____ Date _____ Class _____

Active and Passive Voice

Voice is the form a transitive verb takes to indicate whether the subject of the verb performs or receives the action. When the subject of a verb performs the action, the verb is in the **active voice**. When the subject receives the action, the verb is in the **passive voice.**

> ACTIVE: Anita **bought** a bag of oranges. [The subject *(Anita)* performs the action.]
>
> PASSIVE: The bag of oranges **was bought** by Anita. [The subject *(bag)* receives the action.]

In general, the passive voice is less direct, less forceful, and less concise than the active voice. Use the passive voice when you do not know or do not want to reveal the performer of an action or when you want to emphasize the receiver of an action.

> AWKWARD PASSIVE: My bicycle was repainted by Bart.
>
> DELIBERATE PASSIVE: My bicycle was repainted. [The performer is not mentioned and the emphasis is on the bicycle.]

Exercise A   Decide if each italicized verb below is in the active or passive voice. On the line provided, write *A* for active or *P* for passive.

_____ 1. Many beautiful totem poles *were erected* in Alaska.

_____ 2. Maggie *admired* the carvings on one pole.

_____ 3. A fierce eagle's face *was painted* on one.

_____ 4. A sharp, curved beak *had been created.*

_____ 5. One carver *had made* a bear's face.

Exercise B: Revising   On the lines provided, revise the following sentences by changing the passive voice to active voice wherever the change is desirable.

> EXAMPLE: 1. Many cooking methods were invented by early humans.
> *Early humans invented many cooking methods.*

1. At first, roots and berries were gathered and eaten by these people.

_____

2. The discovery that foods taste better if cooked may have been made by them.

_____

3. Slaughtered animals may have been left near the fire by hunters and gatherers.

_____

4. Ovens were formed by early humans from pits lined with stones and hot coals.

_____

GRAMMAR/USAGE

Chapter 3: Using Verbs

WORKSHEET 10   *Mood*

Mood is the form a verb takes to indicate the attitude of the person using the verb. Verbs may be in one of three moods. The **indicative mood** is used to express a fact, an opinion, or a question.

      INDICATIVE MOOD: Tula **translates** articles into Spanish.

The **imperative mood** is used to express a direct command or request.

      IMPERATIVE MOOD: **Show** me how it works.

The **subjunctive mood** has different uses in the past and present tenses. The present subjunctive is used to express a suggestion or a necessity. The past subjunctive is used to express a condition contrary to fact, or to express a wish.

      PRESENT SUBJUNCTIVE: Ms. Hena recommended that I **be** in your class.

      PAST SUBJUNCTIVE: I wish Paula **were** in chemistry class with me.

Exercise A   Identify the mood of the italicized verbs below. On the lines provided, write *IND* for indicative, *IMP* for imperative, or *SUB* for subjunctive.

_____ 1. I wish it *were* Friday instead of Thursday.

_____ 2. If I *were going* sailing, I'd take a sweater.

_____ 3. *Call* me the minute you know the results.

_____ 4. Zoë and my brother *were* good friends in junior high school.

_____ 5. Please *drop* off these clothes for me at the dry cleaner's.

Exercise B: Revising   Most of the following sentences contain errors in the use of verbs. Rewrite those sentences correctly on the lines provided. If a sentence is correct, write *C*.

1. When my dad saw the dented fender, he looked as if he was ready to explode.

_____

2. "I wish that you was not moving so far away," muttered my friend Darwin.

_____

3. Mr. Bao requested that you are the bus monitor on our next class trip.

_____

4. Were you and your two brothers excited about visiting your birthplace in Mexico?

_____

5. Ms. O'Brien asked that Torik is the first to read his report.

_____

Name _____ Date _____ Class _____

 **WORKSHEET 11**   *Using Verbal Tenses Correctly*

The **present participle** or the **past participle** is used to express an action or a state of being that occurs at the same time as that of the main verb. The **present perfect participle** is used to express an action or a state of being that happens before that of the main verb.

> PRESENT PARTICIPLE: **Waking at five,** I heard birds. [The action expressed by *waking* occurs at the same time as the action expressed by *heard*.]
>
> PAST PARTICIPLE: **Wakened at five,** I slowly climbed out of bed. [The action expressed by *wakened* occurs at the same time as the action expressed by *climbed*.]
>
> PRESENT PERFECT PARTICIPLE: **Having wakened at five,** I rose at six. [The action expressed by *having wakened* precedes the action expressed by *rose*.]

The **present infinitive** is used to express an action or a state of being that follows that of the main verb. The **present perfect infinitive** is used to express an action or a state of being that precedes that of the main verb.

> PRESENT INFINITIVE: Tina wanted **to sing**. [The action expressed by *to sing* follows the action expressed by *wanted*.]
>
> PRESENT PERFECT INFINITIVE: Steve claimed **to have heard** her. [The action expressed by *to have heard* precedes the action expressed by *claimed*.]

Exercise: Proofreading   Most of the following sentences contain errors in the use of tenses. Identify each error. Then write the correct form of the verbal on the line provided. If a sentence is correct, write C.

1. Running to the top of the hill, we sat down to rest for a while.

    _____

2. I am glad to have the opportunity to revise my essay, since I have ended up with a higher grade.

    _____

3. The journalists reported the seige to last three weeks.

    _____

4. If a package comes for me, please remember to have put it in a safe place.

    _____

5. Surprised by the rain, I ran for cover.

    _____

GRAMMAR/USAGE

Chapter 3: Using Verbs

 **WORKSHEET 12** *Review*

Exercise A   For each of the following sentences, give the correct form (past or past participle) of the verb in parentheses.

EXAMPLE: 1. The pitcher _struck_ out eleven batters in a row. (strike)

1. Have you ever _____ anything by Gwendolyn Brooks, the lifetime poet laureate of Illinois? (read)

2. We _____ tomato juice with last night's dinner. (drink)

3. How many of you _____ Fernando Valenzuela pitch? (see)

4. I thought my skates had been _____ , but then I finally found them. (steal)

5. He had _____ a play about his experience in Vietnam. (write)

6. Garrett's dad has _____ in a barbershop quartet for years. (sing)

7. We would have bought those Detroit Pistons tickets no matter how much they had _____ . (cost)

8. Female rap groups like Salt 'N Pepa have _____ quite popular lately. (become)

9. Don't you think that the dough for the bread has _____ enough to bake? (rise)

10. LaToya says she has never _____ on a roller coaster. (ride)

11. Have you ever _____ a Japanese dragon kite? (fly)

12. I shivered and _____ after I dented the front fender of Mom's car. (shake)

13. When Mrs. Isayama called my name, I _____ around. (swing)

14. My father has _____ my younger sister to use his power tools without supervision. (forbid)

15. Wanda _____ into the room to greet her friends. (burst)

16. Yesterday, Nguyen and I each _____ about two hundred tennis balls. (hit)

17. Darius had _____ when he went in for the layup. (fall)

18. The government class has _____ to observe the city council in session. (go)

Chapter 3, Worksheet 12, continued

19. I was not aware that the telephone had _____ . (ring)

20. Have you _____ a taste of that delicious tabbouleh yet? (have)

Exercise B: Proofreading   Most of the following sentences contain errors in the use of verbs. Cross out each incorrect verb. Then write the correct verb on the line provided. If a sentence is correct, write C.

EXAMPLE: 1. ~~Lie~~ that knapsack down there.   _Lay_

1. After dinner, we all set around the campfire.   _____

2. The scarf has lain on the floor all morning.   _____

3. Whenever I laid down, the telephone would ring.   _____

4. The cost of oranges has rose sharply this winter.   _____

5. In the morning, I lay the package carefully on the table.   _____

6. We had sat in the stadium for more than five hours.   _____

7. Heavy rains have risen the water level of the creek more than a foot.   _____

8. Lake Mendota lays north of Madison.   _____

9. Please sit the vase of flowers over there by the front window.   _____

10. The huge crane raised the steel girder one hundred feet (about thirty meters).   _____

Exercise C   Some of the following sentences contain errors in the use of verbs or verbals. Circle the incorrect verb, verb phrase, or verbal. Then, on the line provided, give the correct form of the verb.

EXAMPLE: 1. Jan was supposed (to drop) her package off already.
to have dropped

1. Before the program is over, we will hear some great music.   _____

2. Forgetting my lunch, I had no choice but to buy a sandwich at school.   _____

3. He told us that babies saw more than just black and white.   _____

4. The rock group had finished the concert, but the audience called for another set.   _____

5. By the time they had smelled the smoke, the flames had already begun to spread.   _____

6. If Emiliano Zapata would have known the invitation was a trap, he would not have been ambushed at a farm near Cuautla.   _____

7. Jean calls in her advisers and begins to have questioned them about the financial report.   _____

8. How I wish that I was lying on a beach right now!   _____

Chapter 3, Worksheet 12, continued

9. Betty finishes the first draft quickly, but she labored over the
   revision for hours. _____

10. Sarah says she enjoyed working on the kibbutz in Israel last
    summer, but she hardly got a chance to set down the whole time. _____

Exercise D: Proofreading   Most of the sentences in the following paragraph contain errors in the use of verbs. Identify each error. Then supply the correct verb form above the line. If a sentence is correct, write C.

EXAMPLE: [1] After he had lit the candle, Dad ~~begun~~ to recite the first
began
principle of Kwanzaa.

[1] Kwanzaa has been being celebrated by African Americans for more than twenty-five years. [2] This holiday has been created in 1966 by Maulanga Karenga, a professor of Afro-American studies at California State College. [3] Dr. Karenga wished that there was a nonreligious holiday especially for African Americans. [4] If he has not treasured his own background, we would not have this inspiring celebration to enjoy. [5] Professor Karenga has believed that people's heritage should be celebrated by them. [6] Recently, more and more African Americans have began to reserve the seven-day period immediately following Christmas for Kwanzaa. [7] If you would have joined my family for Kwanzaa last year, you would have heard my grandfather's talk about family values and about African Americans who have fought for freedom and honor. [8] We all wore items of traditional African clothing and displayed a red, black, and green flag to symbolize Africa. [9] My parents lay out a wonderful feast each night, and we lit a candle and talked about one of the seven principles of Kwanzaa. [10] I wish I asked you to our house last year for Kwanzaa, and I will definitely invite you this year.

Name _____ Date _____ Class _____

Pronoun Case

Case is the form that a noun or pronoun takes to show how it is used. In English, there are three cases: **nominative, objective,** and **possessive.** Personal pronouns change form in the different cases, as this chart indicates:

		Nominative	Objective	Possessive
SINGULAR	FIRST PERSON:	I	me	my, mine
	SECOND PERSON:	you	you	your, yours
	THIRD PERSON:	he, she, it	him, her, it	his, her, hers, its
PLURAL	FIRST PERSON:	we	us	our, ours
	SECOND PERSON:	you	you	your, yours
	THIRD PERSON:	they	them	their, theirs

Exercise A   Each of the following sentences contains an italicized personal pronoun. On the line before the sentence, write *1* if the pronoun is first person; *2* if it is second person; or *3* if it is third person. Then, write *N* if the pronoun is in the nominative case; *O* if it is in the objective case; or *P* if it is in the possessive case.

EXAMPLE: <u>1—P</u>   1. *Our* favorite writer is Isaac Asimov.

_____ 1. Asimov's father let *him* read science fiction magazines.

_____ 2. *They* inspired Asimov to write his own science fiction stories.

_____ 3. In *my* opinion, one of his best stories is "Nightfall."

_____ 4. Did *you* know that story won a special distinction?

_____ 5. *I* read that the members of the Science Fiction Writers of America named it the best science fiction story of all time.

Exercise B   On the line following each sentence, write the pronoun that completes the sentence correctly. A description of the pronoun appears in parentheses.

1. On Tuesday, we will cast (*first person plural, possessive*) votes. _____

2. Have (*second person singular, nominative*) decided whom to vote for? _____

3. Janeisa hasn't made up (*third person singular, possessive*) mind. _____

4. The candidates have made (*third person plural, possessive*) speeches. _____

5. (*First person plural, nominative*) have qualified candidates. _____

Chapter 4: Using Pronouns

The Nominative Case

The personal pronouns in the **nominative case**—*I, you, he, she, it, we,* and *they*—are used as **subjects** of verbs and as *predicate nominatives.* A **predicate nominative** is a noun or pronoun that follows a linking verb and explains or identifies the subject of the verb. A pronoun that is used as a predicate nominative always follows a form of the verb *be: am, is, are, was, were, be,* or *been.*

SUBJECT: Janet and **I** saw an exhibit of paintings by Seurat.

PREDICATE NOMINATIVE: The captain of the team is **he.**

Exercise   Complete the following sentences by supplying personal pronouns in the nominative case. Then, on the line provided, write *S* if the pronoun is used as a subject or *PN* if the pronoun is used as a predicate nominative. Use a variety of pronouns, but do not use *you* or *it.*

EXAMPLE: __*S*__   1. __*I*__ have been reading about Charles L. Blockson, who became interested in African American heroes as a young student.

_____ 1. When Blockson told his teachers of his interest, it was _____ who said that there had been very few black heroes.

_____ 2. Sure that _____ must be wrong, Blockson started looking for African Americans in the history books.

_____ 3. He began to collect books, and _____ showed him plenty of heroic black Americans.

_____ 4. Blacks had not been inactive in shaping American history, he learned; in fact, _____ had played important roles in most of its key events!

_____ 5. When Blockson's great-grandfather was a teenager, _____ and many other slaves had escaped with the help of the Underground Railroad.

_____ 6. It was _____ who inspired Blockson's lifelong study of the Underground Railroad.

_____ 7. My friend Latisha and _____ read about Blockson's studies in a magazine article and then gave a report in our history class.

_____ 8. Using Blockson's map as a source, _____ and _____ made a simplified map of the main Underground Railroad routes to freedom.

_____ 9. My ancestors escaped from slavery in Kentucky; therefore, _____ must have followed one of the main routes to arrive in Detroit.

_____10. Latisha's great-great-great-grandmother traveled with her younger brother on the Underground Railroad from Virginia to Toronto, and later both _____ and _____ moved here to Detroit to find work.

Name _____ Date _____ Class _____

 **WORKSHEET 3** *The Objective Case A*

Personal pronouns that are used as **objects of verbs**—*me, you, him, her, it, us,* and *them*—are in the **objective case**. A **direct object** follows an action verb and tells *whom* or *what*.

> DIRECT OBJECT: I called Luanne and **them**.

An **indirect object** comes between an action verb and a direct object. It tells *to whom or what* or *for whom or what* the action of the verb is done.

> INDIRECT OBJECT: Zahara sent Janice and **me** a package of gifts.

Exercise A For each of the following sentences, underline the correct form of the pronoun in parentheses.

1. These instructions confuse my brother and (I, me).

2. (He, Him) I like, but don't ask (me, I) about the others.

3. Give the other girls and (she, her) the chemistry assignment.

4. Were they accusing (them, they) or (we, us)?

5. The success of the carwash surprised Mr. Kahn and (him, he).

Exercise B Complete the following sentences by using personal pronouns in the objective case. For each pronoun you add, tell whether it is used as a direct object *(DO)* or as an indirect object *(IO)*. Use a variety of pronouns, but do not use *you* or *it*.

_____ 1. Have you given Nick and _____ the outside reading list?

_____ 2. Did Bob show _____ his autographed copy of Amy Tan's latest book?

_____ 3. With a smile, Mrs. Martin handed Lena, Chris, and _____ their notebooks.

_____ 4. Our teacher has already graded Latoya and _____ on our oral reports to the class.

_____ 5. Ms. Gutiérrez has invited both _____ and _____ to the Diez y Seis Festival.

_____ 6. "Would you tell _____ and her a story?" begged the little boy.

_____ 7. During practice today, the coach taught Patricia and _____ the proper form for the inward dive.

_____ 8. The play gave _____ some ideas for our own skit.

_____ 9. My mother is picking up both you and _____ .

_____ 10. Why don't you write _____ a note and drop it in the mail today?

GRAMMAR/USAGE

Chapter 4: Using Pronouns

The Objective Case B

A **prepositional phrase** consists of a preposition, a noun or pronoun called the **object of the preposition,** and any modifiers of that object. A personal pronoun that is used for the object of a preposition is in the **objective case.**

OBJECT OF THE PREPOSITION: We threw a goodbye party for Sharia and **him.**

A **verbal** is a verb form that is used as another part of speech. **Participles, gerunds,** and **infinitives** are verbals. A personal pronoun in the objective case is used for the object of a verbal.

OBJECT OF A PARTICIPLE: Marco, driving Sandy and **me,** will have room for one more in his car.

OBJECT OF A GERUND: After my grade point average fell, my goal was raising **it.**

OBJECT OF AN INFINITIVE: The city council promised to give **us** a safe park by summer.

Exercise   For each of the following sentences, underline the correct form of the pronoun in parentheses.

1. Would you like to play baseball with Eugenio and (I, me)?

2. These photographs were taken by Dwight and (she, her).

3. We can rely on Theresa and (he, him) for their help.

4. Would you like to sit next to Elaine and (I, me)?

5. There has been much cooperation between the Hispanic Chamber of Commerce and (we, us).

6. Friends like George and (I, me) usually can resolve our differences.

7. When the dog ran out the door, pursuing (he, him) was my only thought.

8. We have been studying the early settlers from England and learning about the help that Native American peoples gave to (they, them).

9. Handing (they, them) the keys, Uncle Jackson cautioned the boys to be careful.

10. Seeing the rocks, the captain tried to steer the ship to avoid (they, them).

Name _____ Date _____ Class _____

The Possessive Case

The personal pronouns in the **possessive case**—*my, mine, your, yours, his, her, hers, its, our, ours, their,* and *theirs*—are used to show ownership or relationship. The possessive pronouns *mine, yours, his, hers, its, ours,* and *theirs* are used in the same ways that the pronouns in the nominative and objective cases are used.

SUBJECT: **Hers** is an enviable situation.

PREDICATE NOMINATIVE: That coat is **mine**.

OBJECT OF VERB: The waiter brought **his** already.

OBJECT OF PREPOSITION: Diego's speech comes after **yours**.

The possessive pronouns *my, your, his, her, its, our,* and *their* are used as adjectives before nouns.

Her story was well written. **Its** ending really surprised me.

A noun or pronoun that precedes a **gerund** must be in the possessive case in order to modify the gerund. Do not confuse a gerund with a **present participle**. Although both end in *–ing,* a gerund acts as a noun, whereas a present participle serves as an adjective. A noun or pronoun that is modified by a present participle should *not* be in the possessive case.

GERUND: **His** swimming is improving. [*Swimming* acts as a noun.]

PARTICIPLE: We saw **him** swimming. [*Swimming* acts as an adjective.]

Exercise A   For each of the following sentences, underline the correct form of the pronoun in parentheses.

1. Fred's speech was slightly better than (my, mine).

2. (Our, Ours) is the last house on the right, just before the appliance store.

3. My graduation is tomorrow, but I don't know the date of (her, hers).

4. You can come in our car if (their, theirs) is full.

5. No, that chair is (his, his's).

Exercise B   Each sentence below contains an italicized word that is either a gerund or a present participle. Before each one, two pronouns appear in parentheses. Underline the pronoun that completes the sentence correctly.

1. I found (him, his) *sleeping* in study hall!

2. I'm tired of (you, your) *borrowing* my clothes.

3. Please don't keep (them, their) *waiting* by the side of the road.

4. (You, Your) *shouting* is really bothering me.

5. He painted (her, hers) *sitting* in the garden.

GRAMMAR/USAGE

Name _____ Date _____ Class _____

Appositives and Elliptical Constructions

An **appositive** is a noun or pronoun placed next to another noun or pronoun to explain or identify it.

    N   APP

    Danny Glover, a **graduate** of San Francisco State, is a talented actor.

PRO   APP

We players need new uniforms.

A **pronoun** used as an appositive is in the same case as the word to which it refers.

    The **contestants,** Charlene and I, received prizes. [The pronoun *I* is in the nominative case because it is in apposition with the subject, *contestants*.]

An **elliptical construction** is a phrase or clause from which words have been omitted. The word *than* or *as* often begins an elliptical construction. A pronoun following *than* or *as* in an elliptical construction is in the same case as it would be if the construction were completed.

    Do you miss Hugo more than **me?** [Do you miss Hugo more than *you miss me*?]

    Do you miss Hugo more than **I?** [Do you miss Hugo more than *I miss Hugo*?]

Exercise A: Proofreading   Cross out any pronouns that are used incorrectly in the following sentences. On the line provided, write the correct form of the pronoun. If a sentence is correct, write *C* on the line.

1. Both actors, Geena Davis and her, deserve to win the award. _____

2. The choir director gave special attention to us altos. _____

3. If us citizens don't work together, our efforts will not succeed. _____

4. Please give we comedians some respect. _____

5. Weren't they your neighbors, Mrs. Wong and him? _____

Exercise B   For each of the following sentences, add words to complete the elliptical clause or phrase. Include the appropriate pronoun form. Then tell whether the pronoun is a *subject* or an *object*. For each sentence, you need to give only one revision.

        EXAMPLE: 1. Jo works longer hours than (I, me). *than I work—subject*

1. No one else in my class is as shy as (I, me). _____

2. The judges gave the prize to Estelle rather than (I, me). _____

3. I have written as many letters as (they, them). _____

4. They sent Lois as many get-well cards as (I, me). _____

5. No one gave more time to good causes than (she, her). _____

Name _____ Date _____ Class _____

WORKSHEET 7

Reflexive and Intensive Pronouns

Reflexive pronouns and **intensive pronouns** (sometimes called **compound personal pronouns**) end in *–self* or *–selves*. Reflexive and intensive pronouns are identical in form, but they are used differently. A **reflexive pronoun** refers to another word that indicates the same individual(s) or thing(s).

Ralph voted for **himself**. [*Himself* refers to *Ralph.*]

An **intensive pronoun** emphasizes another word that indicates the same individual(s) or thing(s).

I made this dress **myself**. [*Myself* emphasizes *I.*]

A pronoun ending in *–self* or *–selves* should not be used in place of a simple personal pronoun.

NONSTANDARD: Luisa bought tickets for herself and myself.

STANDARD: Luisa bought tickets for herself and **me**.

Exercise A For each of the following sentences, label the italicized pronoun as *intensive* or *reflexive* on the line provided. Also, write the word or words that the pronoun refers to or emphasizes. [Note: If the sentence is imperative, the word that the pronoun refers to may be understood.]

EXAMPLE: 1. To get the special beads she wanted for her bead work, Ruthie taught herself how to make them. *reflexive—Ruthie*

1. Before glass and china beads were brought from Europe, Native Americans made different kinds of beads *themselves*. _____

2. Imagine *yourself* hand drilling tiny holes through the center of hundreds of small cylinders of bone, shell, or stone! _____

3. By *itself*, an individual bead doesn't look particularly impressive until you look at it closely. _____

4. I asked Ruthie for some beads so that I can make *myself* a necklace. _____

5. The librarian found the address of a bead distributor for us, but Ruthie and I had to order the materials *ourselves*. _____

Exercise B: Proofreading In each of the following sentences, cross out any pronouns that are used incorrectly. On the line provided, write the correct form of the pronoun.

1. Clarissa and ourselves are holding a party. _____

2. He gave himself and myself a ride on the new scooter. _____

3. Thanks to yourself, the fund drive was a huge success. _____

4. She excused him and myself for being late. _____

Name _____ Date _____ Class _____

Who *and* Whom

Like most personal pronouns, the pronoun *who (whoever)* has three cases. When these pronouns are used to form questions, they are called **interrogative pronouns.** The case of an interrogative pronoun depends on its use in the question.

> NOMINATIVE CASE: **Who** is calling? [*Who* is the subject.]
>
> OBJECTIVE CASE: **Whom** did you call? [*Whom* is the direct object.]
>
> POSSESSIVE CASE: **Whose** hat is this? [*Whose* modifies *hat*.]

When these pronouns are used to introduce a subordinate clause, they are called **relative pronouns.** To choose between *who* and *whom* in a subordinate clause, determine how the pronoun is used in the clause.

> The man **who owns the store** is Mr. Saks. [*Who* is the subject of the clause.]
>
> A man **whom I know** owns a store. [*Whom* is the direct object of the verb *know*.]

Exercise A For each of the following sentences, underline the correct form of the pronoun in parentheses.

1. Eula, (who, whom) hadn't seen me in months, welcomed me.

2. The doctor (who, whom) I consulted listened intently as I spoke.

3. (Who, Whom) did you invite to the prom?

4. To (who, whom) does that jacket belong?

5. Do you know (who, whom) invented the steam engine?

Exercise B For each of the following sentences, underline the correct form of the pronoun in parentheses. Then identify its use in the sentence—as a subject *(S)*, a predicate nominative *(PN)*, a direct object *(DO)*, or an object of the preposition *(OP)*.

> EXAMPLE: __*DO*__ 1. Here are the names of some of the authors (who, whom) we will study this semester.

_____ 1. Betty Smith, the author of *A Tree Grows in Brooklyn*, was an obscure writer (who, whom) became a celebrity overnight.

_____ 2. Her novel is an American classic about a young girl (who, whom) she called Francie Nolan.

_____ 3. Francie, (who, whom) we follow through girlhood to adulthood, had only one tree in her city back yard.

_____ 4. Carson McCullers, (who, whom) critics describe as a major American writer, also wrote a novel about a young girl's coming of age.

_____ 5. (Who, Whom) would not be moved by *The Member of the Wedding*?

Name _____ Date _____ Class _____

Ambiguous and General Reference

A **pronoun** should always refer clearly to its **antecedent**. Avoid an **ambiguous reference,** which occurs when a pronoun refers to either of two antecedents.

> AMBIGUOUS: Dora wrote to Anna while **she** was away. [Who was away?]
>
> CLEAR: While Dora was away, she wrote to Anna.

Similarly, avoid a **general reference,** which occurs when a pronoun such as *it, this, that, which,* or *such* refers to a general idea rather than to a specific noun.

> GENERAL: The storm began at four o'clock. **That** made commuting difficult. [no specific antecedent for *that*]
>
> CLEAR: A storm that began at four o'clock made commuting difficult.

Exercise: Revising The following sentences contain ambiguous or general pronoun references. On the lines provided, revise each faulty sentence. [Note: Although these sentences can be corrected in more than one way, you need to give only one revision.]

> EXAMPLE: 1. Some people still haven't heard about the Civil Rights Memorial, which is unfortunate.
>
> *That some people still haven't heard about the Civil Rights Memorial is unfortunate.*

1. Tonya sent a postcard to Alice after she saw the Civil Rights Memorial at the Southern

   Poverty Law Center in Montgomery, Alabama. _____

   _____

2. Morris S. Dees, cofounder of the Law Center, and other officials wanted to find a top

   architect to create a special memorial. This led them to Maya Lin. _____

   _____

3. My mother remembers reading about Lin at the time she was chosen to design the Vietnam

   Veterans Memorial in Washington, D.C. _____

   _____

4. Before she made up her mind, Lin researched the history of the civil rights movement. That

   convinced her to accept the project. _____

   _____

5. Nowadays, many people come to Montgomery especially to see the Civil Rights Memorial,

   which, of course, benefits the city. _____

   _____

GRAMMAR/USAGE

Name _____ Date _____ Class _____

Weak and Indefinite Reference

A pronoun must always refer clearly to its antecedent. Avoid a **weak reference,** which occurs when a pronoun refers to an antecedent that has not been expressed.

> WEAK: In my Chinese cooking class, I made **one.** [made what?]
>
> CLEAR: In my Chinese cooking class, I made one egg roll.

Similarly, avoid an **indefinite reference,** which occurs when a pronoun such as *it, they,* or *you* refers to no particular person or thing.

> INDEFINITE: In Houston **they** have a chili festival every year. [*They* is unnecessary to the meaning of the sentence.]
>
> CLEAR: Houston has a chili festival every year.

Exercise A: Revising   The following sentences contain weak or indefinite pronoun references. On the lines provided, revise each faulty sentence. [Note: Although sentences can be corrected in more than one way, you need to give only one revision.]

> EXAMPLE: 1. In the newspaper they ran an article about English actor Jeremy Brett as the detective Sherlock Holmes.
>
> *The newspaper ran an article about English actor Jeremy Brett as the detective Sherlock Holmes.*

1. Every time I see Sherlock Holmes on public television's *Mystery!* series, I want to read some more of them. _____

   _____

2. In the article, they talk about Brett's authentic Holmes wardrobe. _____

   _____

3. In some old movies, you see Holmes wearing a deerstalker hat, but he never does in the stories by Sir Arthur Conan Doyle. _____

   _____

4. Holmes is a very theatrical person. One of these is using disguises, such as dressing as a priest in "Final Problem." _____

   _____

5. Throughout Doyle's stories they present Holmes as confident, fair, and dramatic but also as restless, temperamental, and moody. _____

   _____

Chapter 4: Using Pronouns

WORKSHEET 11 *Review*

Exercise A For each sentence in the following paragraph, underline the correct form of the pronoun in parentheses.

Jordan and [1] (I, me) had thought of Impressionism as a French style of painting, and for the most part, we were right. But every artist is influenced by other artists' ideas, whether or not [2] (he or she, him or her) is aware of being influenced. If you have heard of Edgar Degas, you might know that both [3] (he, him) and the American Impressionist Mary Cassatt were very much influenced by exhibitions of Japanese prints that came to Paris. At first glance, Impressionist paintings don't appear very Japanese, but if you look at any one of [4] (they, them) and a Japanese print placed side by side, you can see strong parallels. This morning, Ms. Kent pointed out some of those stylistic similarities to Jordan and [5] (me, myself). Neither of [6] (we, us) two art lovers could possibly mistake the resemblance. "Just between you and [7] (I, me)," said Ms. Kent, "almost all of the Impressionists openly copied ideas from the Japanese." One of my favorite painters is Toulouse-Lautrec, [8] (who, whom) often used the Japanese technique of including a large object in the extreme foreground to lend a feeling of depth to a picture. Both Mary Cassatt and [9] (he, him) learned from the Japanese the principle of cutting figures at the edge of the canvas to achieve a snapshot-like quality. The Japanese technique of juxtaposing different patterned fabrics appealed to Mary Cassatt, and this technique was used by Pierre Bonnard as well as by [10] (she, her).

Exercise B: Proofreading For each of the following sentences that contains an incorrect pronoun form, identify the error, and then write the correct form on the line provided. If a sentence is correct, write C.

EXAMPLE: 1. Neither Karl nor <u>myself</u> could find the book. _____*I*_____

1. Many farm workers voted for Cesar Chavez, who they believed
   would fight for their rights. _____

2. Both her father and herself have artistic talent. _____

3. I can't understand his dropping out of the band during his
   senior year. _____

4. The new exchange students, Michelle and her, already speak
   some English. _____

5. Robert's parents have no objection to him trying to get a job
   after school. _____

Chapter 4, Worksheet 11, continued

6. I thought that Beth and her would make the best officers.   _____

7. They have many more cassette tapes than us.   _____

8. The title of salutatorian goes to whomever has the second
    highest academic average.   _____

9. Who is supposed to sit in this empty seat between Lauren and I?   _____

10. Who do you suppose won the ballroom dance contest?   _____

Exercise C: Revising   Revise each of the following sentences, correcting the pronoun reference. [Note: Although these sentences can be corrected in more than one way, you need to give only one revision.]

1. Everyone is excited about graduation because you have worked so hard for it.

    _____

2. In some parts of Africa, they mine diamonds and sell them to jewelers to be cut.

    _____

3. I received a notice that three of my library books were overdue, which was a
    complete surprise.

    _____

4. Sarah's uncle has a huge vegetable garden, and he keeps them supplied with fresh
    vegetables all summer long.

    _____

5. He spent more than an hour at the clothing store but did not try any on.

    _____

6. Deep-sea fishing isn't very enjoyable to me unless I catch at least one.

    _____

7. When the ship struck the dock, it burst into flames.

    _____

8. The first part of the test will be on chemistry, the second on mathematics, the third
    on physics. This will make it very difficult.

    _____

9. Several of the eyewitnesses described the man as short, others said he was tall, and
    yet others said he was "about average." It confused the police investigators.

    _____

10. Since the show was scheduled for the same night as the intramural play-off game, it
    had to be postponed.

    _____

Name _____ Date _____ Class _____

Adjectives and Adverbs

An **adjective** limits the meaning of a noun or a pronoun. An adjective may also limit the meaning of a gerund—a verbal used as a noun. An **adverb** limits the meaning of a verb or a verbal, an adjective, or another adverb.

> ADJECTIVE: I wore a **cotton** kimono. [*Cotton* limits the word *kimono*.]
>
> ADVERB: Lester hummed **softly**. [*Softly* limits the word *hummed*.]

Linking verbs, especially the forms of the verb *to be* and verbs of sense (*taste, smell, feel,* etc.) are often followed by adjectives that modify the subject of the verb. Action verbs are often followed by adverbs.

> MODIFIES SUBJECT
> OF LINKING VERB: The **hailstones** looked **huge**.
>
> MODIFIES ACTION VERB: I **looked quickly** at my watch.

Exercise For each of the following sentences, underline the correct modifier in parentheses. Then circle the word that it modifies.

1. Rosemary Apple Blossom Lonewolf is an artist whose style is (unique, uniquely) among Native American potters.

2. Lonewolf combines (traditional, traditionally) and modern techniques to create her miniature pottery.

3. In crafting her pots, Lonewolf uses the dark red clay that is (ready, readily) available around the Santa Clara Pueblo in New Mexico, where she lives.

4. These miniatures have a detailed and (delicate, delicately) etched surface called sgraffito.

5. Because of the (extreme, extremely) intricate detail on its surface, a single pot may take many months to finish.

6. The subjects for most of Lonewolf's pots combine ancient Pueblo myths and traditions with (current, currently) ideas or events.

7. One pot, for example, (clear, clearly) depicts a Pueblo corn dancer walking down a city street lined with skyscrapers.

8. Lonewolf uses such images to show that Native Americans can and do adapt (real, really) well to new ways.

9. At first known only in the Southwest, Lonewolf's work is now shown throughout the United States because the appeal of her subjects is quite (broad, broadly).

10. Rosemary Lonewolf's talented family includes her grandfather, father, and son, who are all (high, highly) skilled potters.

GRAMMAR/USAGE

Name _____ Date _____ Class _____

 **WORKSHEET 2** *Comparison*

Comparison refers to the change in the form of an adjective or adverb to show increasing or decreasing degrees in the quality the modifier expresses. The three degrees of comparison are **positive, comparative,** and **superlative.** Most one-syllable modifiers form the comparative and superlative degrees by adding *-er* and *-est.* Some two-syllable modifiers form the comparative and superlative degrees by adding *-er* and *-est.* Other two-syllable modifiers form the comparative and superlative degrees by using *more* and *most.* Modifiers of more than two syllables form the comparative and superlative degrees by using *more* and *most.*

    COMPARATIVE FORMS: bigger, easier, more hopeful, more cautiously

    SUPERLATIVE FORMS: biggest, easiest, most hopeful, most cautiously

To show a decrease in the qualities they express, all modifiers form the comparative and superlative degrees by using *less* and *least.*

    less tired, least tired, less understanding, least understanding

Some modifiers, like those listed below, do not follow the regular methods of forming the comparative and superlative degrees.

    bad, worse, worst   little, less, least   good, better, best   much, more, most

Exercise On the line provided, write the comparative and the superlative forms of each of the following modifiers.

    EXAMPLE: 1. stubborn *more (less) stubborn; most (least) stubborn*

1. readily _____

2. hard _____

3. cheerful _____

4. eager _____

5. quick _____

6. well _____

7. many _____

8. stealthily _____

9. expensive _____

10. enthusiastically _____

Name _____ Date _____ Class _____

Uses of Comparative and Superlative Forms

Use the **comparative degree** when comparing two things. Use the **superlative degree** when comparing more than two.

  COMPARING TWO: Carla is **more** talkative than Kris.

  COMPARING MORE
     THAN TWO: Of all my friends, Vinnie is the **most** talkative.

Exercise A   Complete each of the sentences below by giving the correct form of the modifier on the left. Write the correct form on the line provided.

1. *friendly*   Louise is one of the _____ people in my school.

2. *bad*   That blizzard is the _____ one I've ever seen!

3. *good*   My brother is the _____ player on his team.

4. *dark*   My sister's hair is _____ than mine.

5. *interesting* Of the two books that I read, the first was _____ .

Exercise B   On the line provided, write the correct form of the modifier shown in italics in each sentence below. If a sentence is correct, write *C*.

1. Of the two exercises, the second is the *most difficult*.   _____

2. That would be the *most disastrous* course of action you could possibly consider.   _____

3. My older brother is *less generous* with his possessions than my younger one.   _____

4. He made the *least dangerous* of the two choices.   _____

5. Chris found peeling vegetables the *more boring* of his many household tasks.   _____

6. Corn grew *more abundantly* in the valley than on the hillside.   _____

7. Ben felt that Mr. Renfrew spoke *most candidly* than Mr. Lucas.   _____

8. I know this shade of blue is a closer match than that one, but we still haven't found the *better* match.   _____

9. Although both cars appear to be well constructed, I think that the *most desirable* one is the one that gets better gas mileage.   _____

10. Which of these two hotels is *farthest* from the airport?   _____

GRAMMAR/USAGE

Name _____ Date _____ Class _____

Problems with Comparative and Superlative Forms

A **double comparison** is the use of two comparative forms (usually *-er* and *more*) or two superlative forms (usually *-est* and *most*) to modify the same word. Avoid using double comparisons.

> DOUBLE COMPARISON: This film is more longer than the last one we saw.
>
> STANDARD: This film is longer than the last one we saw.

Include the word *other* or *else* when comparing one member of a group with the rest of the group.

> ILLOGICAL: Arlo is funnier than anyone in his class. [Arlo is a member of the class. Logically, Arlo could not be funnier than himself.]
>
> LOGICAL: Arlo is funnier than anyone **else** in his class.
>
> LOGICAL: Arlo is funnier than any **other** person in his class.

Avoid comparing items that cannot logically be compared.

> ILLOGICAL: Our attendance record is better than Baker High School. [The sentence makes an illogical comparison between an attendance record and a high school.]
>
> LOGICAL: Our attendance record is better than Baker High School's **record.**

Exercise: Revising   On the lines provided, revise the following sentences by correcting the errors in the use of modifiers.

> EXAMPLE: 1. It seems I spend more time doing my biology homework than anyone in my class.
>
> *It seems I spend more time doing my biology homework than anyone else in my class.*

1. This is the most rainiest weather I've ever seen!

   _____

2. Richard felt more stronger than he had the day before.

   _____

3. The newscaster said that the pollen count this morning was higher than any count taken this spring.

   _____

4. Today Jane feels more hopefuller about the outcome of their adventure than she felt last week.

   _____

5. Wendy's paintings are more symbolic than Earl.

   _____

Name _____ Date _____ Class _____

More Problems with Comparative and Superlative Forms

An **incomplete comparison** results when the second part of a comparison can be understood in two ways. State both parts of a comparison completely if there is any possibility of misreading.

ILLOGICAL: She visits me more frequently than Leon. [The elliptical clause *than Leon* may be completed in more than one way.]

LOGICAL: She visits me more frequently than she visits Leon.

LOGICAL: She visits me more frequently than Leon visits me.

A **compound comparison** uses both the positive and comparative degrees of a modifier. Include all the words necessary to complete a compound comparison.

NONSTANDARD: I can ski as well, if not better than, my sister.

STANDARD: I can ski as well as, if not better than, my sister.

Absolute adjectives (such as *complete, equal, perfect, infinite,* and *unique*) express a quality that either exists completely or doesn't exist at all. These adjectives have no comparative or superlative forms because they do not vary in degree. Absolute adjectives may be used in comparisons if the absolute is accompanied by *more nearly* or *most nearly*.

NONSTANDARD: Of all the answers given, Michael's was the most correct.

STANDARD: Of all the answers given, Michael's was the most nearly correct.

STANDARD: Of all the answers given, Michael's was the best.

Exercise: Revising   Each of the following sentences contains an error in the use of a comparison. On the line provided, revise each sentence to correct the error.

EXAMPLE: 1. Which answer is the most complete?

Which answer is the most nearly complete?

1. Did you like the circus better than Keisha?

_____

2. My new wheelchair is as good, or better than, my old one.

_____

3. Nobody I know can draw a more perfect circle than I can.

_____

4. I see my horse as often as, if not more often than, my sister.

_____

5. Of all the teachers, Mrs. Taylor always provides the most complete directions on her tests.

_____

GRAMMAR/USAGE

Name _____ Date _____ Class _____

 **WORKSHEET 6** *Placement of Modifiers*

Place one-word modifiers such as *even, hardly, just, merely, nearly, only,* and *scarcely* immediately before the words they modify. Notice how the meaning of the sentences below change depending on where the modifier is placed.

We **only** answered his questions.

We answered **only** his questions.

A modifying word, phrase, or clause that sounds awkward because it modifies the wrong word or group of words is called a **misplaced modifier**. To correct a misplaced modifier, place the modifier as close as possible to the word or words it modifies.

MISPLACED: High up on the wall, I noticed a spider.

CLEAR: I noticed a spider high up on the wall.

Avoid placing a word, phrase, or clause so that it seems to modify either of two words. Such a misplaced modifier is called a **two-way**, or **squinting, modifier**.

TWO-WAY: Dr. Hena told the man during the operation what to expect.

CLEAR: During the operation, Dr. Hena told the man what to expect.

CLEAR: Dr. Hena told the man what to expect during the operation.

Exercise A   On lines 1.a and 2.a below, write two sentences, using a different one of the following modifiers in each sentence: *even, hardly, just, merely, nearly, only,* or *scarcely*. Then, on lines 1.b and 2.b, rewrite each of the sentences, changing its meaning by moving the modifier.

EXAMPLE: 1. a. *Even Maura was afraid to approach Ms. Sterner.*

b. *Maura was afraid to approach even Ms. Sterner.*

1. a. _____

   b. _____

2. a. _____

   b. _____

Exercise B   The following sentences contain misplaced and two-way modifiers. Correct each sentence by circling the faulty modifier and drawing an arrow to show where it belongs.

EXAMPLE: 1. We saw a lamp in a department store (that cost only ten dollars).

1. We listened eagerly to the stories told by Scheherazade in the *Arabian Nights* munching peanuts and crackers.

2. I showed my friends my new fish, a puffer, brimming with pride.

3. Ralph Ellison said during an interview Richard Wright inspired him to write.

4. Petra walked along the beach, digging for clams without a care in the world.

5. There is a bracelet in the museum that is four thousand years old.

Name _____ Date _____ Class _____

 # Dangling Modifiers

A modifying word, phrase, or clause that does not sensibly modify any word or words in a sentence is called a **dangling modifier**.

DANGLING: To be a good opera singer, clear enunciation is extremely important. [Who is to be a good opera singer?]

CLEAR: To be a good opera singer, a person needs clear enunciation.

CLEAR: A good opera singer needs clear enunciation.

Exercise A Read each sentence below and decide if it is correct or if it contains a dangling modifier. On the line provided, write *C* for correct or *DM* for dangling modifier.

_____ 1. While jogging along Center Street, Elia saw a lost dog.

_____ 2. Looking out the window, a remarkable sight appeared.

_____ 3. Muffled in heavy clothing, the hike up the mountain was tiring.

_____ 4. Standing near the runway, the noise of the jets was deafening.

_____ 5. Worried, dark circles appeared under Nathan's eyes.

Exercise B: Revising The following sentences contain dangling modifiers. On the line provided, revise each sentence so that its meaning is clear and correct.

EXAMPLE: 1. Frightened by our presence, the rabbit's ears perked up and its nose twitched.

Frightened by our presence, the rabbit perked up its ears and twitched its nose.

1. All bundled up in a blanket, the baby's first outing was a brief one.

_____

2. When performing on stage, the microphone should not be placed too near the speaker cones.

_____

3. To help colonial soldiers during the Revolutionary War, Haym Solomon's efforts raised money to buy food and clothing.

_____

4. To work efficiently without sticking, be sure to use the proper solvent and machine oil.

_____

5. When discussing colonial American writers, the contributions of the African American poet Phillis Wheatley should not be forgotten.

_____

GRAMMAR/USAGE

Chapter 5: Using Modifiers

 **WORKSHEET 8**   *Review*

Exercise A: Proofreading   Proofread the following paragraph and correct any errors in the use of modifiers. There may be sentences that need no change.

> EXAMPLE: [1] Of the two forts I've visited, Castillo de San Marcos is the
>   *older*
>   ~~oldest.~~

[1] In fact, Castillo de San Marcos in St. Augustine, Florida, is the most oldest standing fort in the United States. [2] Earlier wood forts had been extremely difficult to defend, but Castillo de San Marcos was built of stone. [3] Before the construction of this fort, Spain had no strong military base that could withstand a real fierce enemy assault. [4] In fact, previous battles with the British had proved that of the two countries, Spain had the least defensible forts. [5] Begun in 1672, the building of Castillo de San Marcos went slow, taking several decades to complete. [6] Replacing the existing nine wood forts in St. Augustine, the new stone fort fared good against attacks. [7] Today, no one is sure which fort was easiest to protect, Spain's Castillo de San Marcos or the British fort in Charleston, South Carolina. [8] However, Castillo de San Marcos, with its 16-foot-thick walls and 40-foot-wide moat, proved to be one of the most strongest forts in the South and was never taken by force. [9] When Florida finally did come under British control, the Spanish felt especially badly about leaving their impressive fort in the hands of their old enemies. [10] Castillo de San Marcos is now a national monument and stands today as a memorial to all those who fought so courageous to guard St. Augustine long ago.

Exercise B: Proofreading   Read each of the following sentences to see if it contains an error in the use of modifiers. Draw a line through each error, and, if necessary, write the correct word or words on the line provided. Use a caret (∧) to show where the added word or words belong in the sentence. If a sentence is already correct, write C on the line.

> EXAMPLES: 1. Marcus plays the guitar ~~beautiful.~~ *beautifully*
>   2. Leila knows more about stars than anyone∧I know.   *else*

1. Nations, like people, can get along well or poor.   _____

2. The situation in the strife-torn country looked bad.   _____

3. The workers handled the explosives very careful.   _____

4. The butter tasted so badly that we were sure it was rancid. _____

5. In order to play the piano well, one has to practice regular. _____

6. According to the newspaper, last week's snowstorm was the worse blizzard of the decade. _____

7. Of the two surgeons, Dr. White Feather is the older and the most experienced. _____

8. The elderly woman in Ward D had more visitors than any patient in the hospital. _____

9. The Yankees lost the game by a single run, but they won the second game easy, 10–2. _____

10. The students thought that Ms. Pong's outfits were the most handsomest clothes they had ever seen. _____

11. The books that we had ordered were slow in arriving. _____

12. The costume fits you perfect and is very becoming. _____

13. I think that Pilar is more happier at summer camp than she thought she would be. _____

14. She usually makes higher grades than anyone in her class. _____

15. The plan sounded good, but it did not work very well. _____

16. The play was more interesting to me than our guest. _____

17. Today, my aunt is feeling as well, if not better than, she did before her surgery. _____

18. On such a beautiful day, who could have a heart more full than mine? _____

19. Of the two solutions, which one is the most nearly correct? _____

20. His handwriting is easier to read than Tim. _____

Exercise C: Revising Most of the following sentences contain errors in the placement of modifiers. On the line provided, revise each faulty sentence so that its meaning is clear. If a sentence is correct, write C.

EXAMPLE: 1. I described my trip to Hawaii to my friends who had never been there when I got back.

When I got back, I described my trip to Hawaii to my friends, who had never been there.

1. Visitors soon learn how important one man can be on vacation in Hawaii.

_____

2. Born in the mid-1700s, the Hawaiian people were united under one government by Kamehameha I.

_____

GRAMMAR/USAGE

3. After capturing Maui, Molokai, and Lanai, Oahu was soon another of Kamehameha's conquests.

_____

4. Kamehameha assured the Hawaiian people when he became the ruler of the entire island they would see peace.

_____

5. By 1810, Kamehameha was certain his conquest would be successful.

_____

6. Having won Kauai and Niihau, Kamehameha's dream of a united country was realized.

_____

7. A hero to his people, Kamehameha's government ruled Hawaii for many years.

_____

8. A statue to honor the great ruler was crafted by Thomas Gould.

_____

9. While being transported across the ocean, the Hawaiian people lost their beloved statue.

_____

10. Though lost at sea, a sculptor made a duplicate.

_____

Name _____ Date _____ Class _____

The Adjective Phrase

A **phrase** is a group of related words that is used as a single part of speech and does not contain both a verb and its subject. A **prepositional phrase** consists of a preposition; a noun, pronoun, or verbal called the **object of the preposition;** and any modifiers of that object.

> **In addition to swimming and running,** Emma likes bicycling. [*Swimming and running* is the compound object of the compound preposition *In addition to.*]

An **adjective phrase** is a prepositional phrase that modifies a noun or a pronoun.

> Judo has been called the gentle art **of self-defense**. [The prepositional phrase modifies the noun *art*.]

An adjective phrase always follows the word it modifies.

> Where is my **magazine about fishing in Texas**? [*About fishing* modifies the subject *magazine. In Texas* modifies *fishing*, which serves as the object of the preposition *about*.]

More than one adjective phrase may modify the same word.

> We just received a letter **from Uncle Jim about Alaska**. [The two phrases *from Uncle Jim* and *about Alaska* modify the noun *letter*.]

Exercise A   In the following sentences, underline each adjective phrase. Then draw an arrow from each phrase to the word that it modifies.

> EXAMPLE: 1. Mr. Ortiz's garden contains flowers of many varieties.

1. The sale on slacks at the department store lasted all day.

2. Eva attended a lecture about etching.

3. The tall tree with the hornet's nest is an oak.

4. I found a book of chemistry notes here yesterday.

5. Stuart and Monica read the poems by W. H. Auden and Marianne Moore.

Exercise B   In the following sentences, underline each adjective phrase once and the word it modifies twice.

1. The instinct for self-preservation is a basic drive in nearly all living things.

2. Yet small Scandinavian animals called lemmings occasionally follow a pattern of self-destruction.

3. Every few years their population exceeds their food supply, and they ford streams and lakes, devouring everything in their path and leaving no trace of vegetation.

4. When they reach the cliffs along the sea, they leap into the water and drown.

5. Explanations of their rush to the sea are only guesses, and the lemming remains a mystery to those who study animal behavior.

SENTENCES

Name _____ Date _____ Class _____

The Adverb Phrase and the Noun Phrase

Like an adjective phrase, an **adverb phrase** is a prepositional phrase. While an adjective phrase modifies a noun or a pronoun, an adverb phrase modifies a verb, an adjective, or an adverb. More than one adverb phrase can modify the same word. Unlike an adjective phrase, an adverb phrase can precede the word it modifies.

> **In the morning,** he rode the new bicycle **for the first time**. [The adverb phrases *in the morning* and *for the first time* both modify the verb *rode*.]

Occasionally, a prepositional phrase may function as a noun.

> **After dusk** is when raccoons become active. [*After dusk* is the subject of the verb *is*.]

Exercise   Circle each prepositional phrase in the following sentences. On the line provided, identify each prepositional phrase as *adjective, adverb,* or *noun*. Be sure to include any prepositional phrase that modifies the object of another preposition.

> EXAMPLE: 1. From out of Africa comes a very interesting instrument.
> *adverb—noun*

1. Varied in size and shape, the family of musical instruments called *mbira* is popular throughout Africa.   _____

2. About the size of a paperback book, *mbiras,* called *kalimbas,* are small boxes made from smooth, warm-colored wood.   _____

3. Because you pluck the steel keys with your thumbs to play melodies, some people call the instrument a thumb box.   _____

4. Below the keys, there is a sound hole like the one on a guitar.   _____

5. When one or more keys are plucked, the notes resonate inside the box.   _____

6. The *kalimba* sounds like a cross between a small xylophone, a music box, and a set of wind chimes.   _____

7. Small in size, it's easily carried in a pocket or backpack, and it is simple to play.   _____

8. Nearly everybody enjoys the soft, light sound, even if the player hits a wrong note with both thumbs!   _____

9. During the sixteenth century, Portuguese explorers from along the East African coast noted instruments similar to the *kalimba*.   _____

10. In 1586, Father Dos Santos, a Portuguese traveler, wrote that native *mbira* players pluck the keys lightly, "as a good player strikes those of a harpsichord," producing "a sweet and gentle harmony of accordant sounds."   _____

Name _____ Date _____ Class _____

Participles and Participial Phrases

A **verbal** is a form of a verb used as a noun, an adjective, or an adverb. One kind of verbal is called a **participle**, a verb form that is used as an adjective. There are two kinds of participles—**present participles** and **past participles**. Present participles end in *-ing*, while most past participles end in *-d* or *-ed*.

> A **growing** teenager needs a **balanced** diet. [The present participle *growing* modifies the noun *teenager*. The past participle *balanced* modifies the noun *diet*.]

A **participial phrase** consists of a participle and all of the words related to the participle. Do not confuse a participle used as an adjective with a participle that is part of a verb phrase.

> PARTICIPIAL PHRASE: **Twirling his pencil,** Mitch considered the last question on the test. [*Twirling his pencil* modifies the noun *Mitch*.]

> VERB PHRASE: Mitch **was twirling** his pencil. [The participle appears with a helping verb and is part of a verb phrase.]

An **absolute phrase** consists of a participle and the noun or pronoun it modifies. The entire phrase is used to modify an independent clause.

> **Winter having come early,** we were unprepared for the blizzard. [*Having come early* modifies the noun *Winter*. The absolute phrase modifies the independent clause by telling *why* we were unprepared.]

Exercise A   Each sentence below contains an italicized participial phrase. Underline the noun or pronoun that each phrase modifies.

1. The baby, *crying from hunger,* awakened everyone in the house.

2. *Cooked too long,* the roast was dry and tasteless.

3. *Spinning on our skates,* we attracted the attention of all the other skaters.

4. The money *collected by the students* went toward their class trip.

5. Mika saw a rabbit *hiding under the bush.*

Exercise B   Each of the following sentences contains at least one participial phrase. Underline each participial phrase. On the line provided, identify the word or words the phrase modifies. If the participle is part of an absolute phrase, write *absolute*.

1. Our champion, smiling broadly, entered the hall.

   _____

2. Forty adders coiled together is an alarming sight, but close contact is the way these snakes stay warm.

   _____

3. The salmon, deriving the pink color of its flesh from its diet, feeds on shrimplike crustaceans.

   _____

4. The car loaded, our vacation was ready to begin.

   _____

5. Trained on an overhead trellis, a white rosebush growing in Arizona covers eight thousand square feet of aerial space.

   _____

SENTENCES

Name _____ Date _____ Class _____

Gerunds and Gerund Phrases

A **gerund** is a verb form that ends in *-ing* and is used as a noun.

SUBJECT: **Studying** always makes Trevor hungry.

PREDICATE NOMINATIVE: My favorite pastime is **sailing**.

DIRECT OBJECT: Boris likes **hiking**.

INDIRECT OBJECT: Ada gave **reading** a high priority.

OBJECT OF PREPOSITION: The girls earn money by **baby-sitting**.

A **gerund phrase** consists of a gerund and all of the words related to the gerund.

Tony's parents saw **his waiting on tables** as a good way to earn money for college. [The gerund phrase is the object of the verb *saw*. The possessive pronoun *his* and the adverb phrase *on tables* modify the gerund *waiting*.]

Exercise A   Underline the gerunds in the following sentences. On the line provided, identify each gerund as a *subject*, a *direct object*, an *indirect object*, a *predicate nominative*, or an *object of a preposition*.

EXAMPLE: 1. By reading the newspaper daily, you will become an informed citizen. *reading—object of a preposition*

1. Do you enjoy skiing? _____

2. I sometimes dream about diving. _____

3. My Navajo grandmother thinks that weaving would be a good hobby for me. _____

4. I have been giving camping a fair try, but I still do not like it. _____

5. Exercising is part of my daily routine. _____

Exercise B   Underline the verbal phrase in each of the following sentences. On the line provided, identify each phrase as a *participial phrase* or a *gerund phrase*.

1. Dr. Mae Jemison became an astronaut by placing among the best fifteen candidates out of two thousand applicants. _____

2. Appointed principal of the Mason City Iowa High School in 1881, Carrie Chapman Catt became the city's first female superintendent. _____

3. The Nineteenth Amendment to the Constitution, adopted in 1920, was largely the result of Catt's efforts. _____

4. Working for *Life* throughout her long career, Margaret Bourke-White was the first female war photographer. _____

5. Phyllis McGinley, a famous writer of light verse, began her professional writing while she was still in college. _____

Name _____ Date _____ Class _____

Infinitives and Infinitive Phrases

An **infinitive** is a verb form that can be used as a noun, an adjective, or an adverb. An infinitive usually begins with *to*.

> NOUN: Alani offered **to help**. [*To help* is used as a direct object.]
>
> ADJECTIVE: This is the coat **to buy**. [*To buy* modifies *coat*.]
>
> ADVERB: Arthur was unable **to sleep**. [*To sleep* modifies *unable*.]

An **infinitive phrase** consists of an infinitive and all of the words related to the infinitive. The entire infinitive phrase can be used as a noun, an adjective, or an adverb.

> INFINITIVE PHRASE: Motega was asked **to sing louder**. [The infinitive phrase *to sing louder* is used as a noun that is the object of the verb *asked*. The infinitive *to sing* is modified by the adverb *louder*.]

Exercise A   Underline the infinitive in each of the following sentences. On the line provided, tell whether it is used as a noun *(N)*, an adjective *(ADJ)*, or an adverb *(ADV)*. If the infinitive is used as a noun, indicate whether it is a subject *(S)*, a direct object *(DO)*, or a predicate nominative *(PN)*. If the infinitive is used as a modifier, underline the word it modifies twice.

> EXAMPLE: _ADJ_   1. That day, your father was a <u>sight</u> to see.

_____ 1. I'd do almost anything to avoid cleaning my room.

_____ 2. David Robinson slam-dunked the ball with one second to go!

_____ 3. Oops! I forgot to buy milk on my way home.

_____ 4. In our judicial system, to prosecute the defendant in criminal cases is the job of the state.

_____ 5. Anita's task was to interview all qualified applicants.

Exercise B   Complete each of the following phrases or sentences by adding an infinitive or infinitive phrase that serves as the part of speech indicated in parentheses.

> EXAMPLE: 1. Enrique has a bicycle *(adjective)*
>
> *Enrique has a bicycle to sell.*

1. I have a responsibility *(adjective)*

_____

2. The student council's objective was *(noun)*

_____

3. My little sister is not allowed *(adverb)*

_____

4. I am working at a restaurant this summer *(adverb)*

_____

SENTENCES

Name _____ Date _____ Class _____

Appositives and Appositive Phrases

Types of Phrases:

PREPOSITIONAL PHRASE: Tracy went **to the library** and got a book **on civics.**

PARTICIPIAL PHRASE: **Looking over my shoulder,** I noticed the cat.

GERUND PHRASE: **Going to movies** is Paolo's favorite pastime.

INFINITIVE PHRASE: I need **to know your date of birth.**

Another kind of phrase is the *appositive phrase.* An **appositive** is a noun or a pronoun placed beside another noun or pronoun to identify or explain it. An **appositive phrase** consists of an appositive and its modifiers.

APPOSITIVE: Your friend **Ramla** called after you left.

APPOSITIVE PHRASE: Jesse Sheng, **the vice president of the bank,** sent me a card.

Exercise A   Underline the appositive phrase in each sentence below.

1. Denise Chapman, the first woman to be elected sheriff in our county, was cited for bravery.

2. Our local technician can fix any electronic device: computers, VCRs, anything.

3. Rio de Janeiro, one of the most exciting cities in the world, is filled with tourists.

4. Once a tangle of weeds and brambles, our yard was transformed by my father.

5. Jan Matzeliger, the inventor, was pictured on a recent stamp.

Exercise B   On the line provided, identify each italicized phrase in the following paragraph as a prepositional phrase *(PREP)*, a participial phrase *(PART)*, a gerund phrase *(GER)*, an infinitive phrase *(INF)*, or an appositive phrase *(APP)*. Do not separately identify a prepositional phrase that is part of a larger phrase.

Each year, thousands of Americans travel [1] *to hundreds of vacation spots in the United States and other countries* _____. [2] *Anticipating all kinds of weather and activities* _____ , many eager travelers pack far too much clothing and equipment. The most effective way to pack is [3] *to set out clothes for the trip* _____ and then to put half of them back [4] *in the closet* _____ . Of course, travelers should give particularly careful thought to walking shoes, [5] *the most important item of apparel on any sightseeing trip* _____ . Experienced travelers pack only two or three changes of casual clothing, even if they plan [6] *to be away for some time* _____ . [7] *Taking out the smallest piece of luggage they own* _____ , they study its capacity. It is possible to pack enough clothes for three weeks in small luggage, [8] *perhaps a duffel bag or shoulder bag* _____ . Passengers can carry such bags onto an airliner and avoid [9] *waiting at the baggage claim area* _____ . For most people, [10] *doing a bit of hand laundry every few days* _____ is preferable to spending their vacation burdened with heavy suitcases.

Chapter 6: Phrases

WORKSHEET 7 | *Review*

Exercise A   Each of the following sentences contains a prepositional phrase. First, underline the phrase. Then on the line provided, tell how the phrase is used. Write *ADJ* for an adjective phrase or *ADV* for an adverb phrase.

EXAMPLE: _ADV_   1. In colonial days many Americans could not read.

_____ 1. Free public education did not exist at that time.

_____ 2. The fees for elementary schooling were usually not large; nonetheless, many families could not afford them.

_____ 3. While most of the towns and cities had schools, many rural districts did not.

_____ 4. Wealthy rural families hired tutors or sent their sons to boarding schools.

_____ 5. However, a member of the family was the only teacher a daughter had.

Exercise B . On the line provided, identify each italicized phrase in the following sentences. Write *PREP* for a prepositional phrase or *PART* for a participial phrase. Then give the word or words each phrase modifies. Do not separately identify a prepositional phrase that is part of a participial phrase.

EXAMPLE: 1. *Delighted by the play*, the critic applauded *with great enthusiasm.* PART—critic: PREP—applauded

1. Mahalia Jackson, *called the greatest gospel singer in history*, would sing only religious songs. _____

2. Her version of "Silent Night" was one *of the all-time best-selling records* in Denmark. _____

3. *Setting out in a thirty-one-foot ketch*, Sharon Sites Adams, a woman *from California*, sailed *across the Pacific* alone. _____

4. *Having been rejected by six publishers*, the story *of Peter Rabbit* was finally published privately *by Beatrix Potter*. _____

5. *Known for his imaginative style*, architect Minoru Yamasaki designed the World Trade Center, *located in New York City*. _____

6. *In 1932*, Amelia Earhart, *trying for a new record*, began her solo flight *over the Atlantic*. _____

7. Maria Tallchief was a ballerina *in the New York Ballet Company*. _____

8. *Dancing to wide acclaim in both the United States and Europe*, she was known *for her interpretation* of Stravinsky's Firebird. _____

9. *Continuing her research on radium* after her husband's death, Marie Curie received the Nobel Prize *in chemistry*. _____

10. *First elected to the House of Representatives in 1968*, Shirley Chisholm was the first black female member *of Congress*. _____

SENTENCES

Chapter 6 Worksheet 7, continued

Exercise C On the line provided, identify each italicized phrase in the following sentences. Write *PREP* for a prepositional phrase, *PART* for a participial phrase, *GER* for a gerund phrase, or *INF* for an infinitive phrase. Do not separately identify a prepositional phrase that is part of a larger phrase.

EXAMPLE: 1. *Celebrating the strength of the human spirit*, Christy Brown's book My Left Foot tells the story *of his life*. PART, PREP

1. Christy Brown, *born with cerebral palsy*, was unable to *speak a single word*. _____

2. Everyone, *including his family*, assumed he had very little intelligence, because he could not express himself *to them*. _____

3. Christy's left foot was the only limb he could control, and one day he succeeded in *grabbing a piece of chalk with it* and began *to write the word "mother" on the wooden floor*. _____

4. Christy's family, *amazed at this remarkable achievement*, suddenly realized that *his leading a full, rewarding life* was not an impossible dream. _____

5. *Typing the entire manuscript with his left foot*, Christy Brown was eventually able *to tell his story in this inspiring book about his life*. _____

Exercise D Each of the following sentences contains an italicized phrase. On the line provided, identify each phrase. Write the correct abbreviation from the following list:

PREP = prepositional phrase   **INF** = infinitive phrase
PART = participial phrase   **APP** = appositive phrase
GER = gerund phrase

EXAMPLES: _PREP_ 1. The curtains *in the study* were dark.

GER 2. *Running in place* is part of the exercise routine.

_____ 1. The angry driver jumped *from the damaged car*.

_____ 2. *Shocked greatly*, they stood silent and still.

_____ 3. An excellent form of exercise is *walking vigorously for an hour each day*.

_____ 4. We followed the deer's trail for several miles; then, *discouraged by our fruitless tracking*, we gave up.

_____ 5. *To rest awhile* seemed advisable.

_____ 6. The park's prize attraction, *an obsolete tank*, was my small brother's favorite "mountain."

_____ 7. *Finishing a theme* is sometimes hard.

_____ 8. Dorothea Lange's task was *photographing migrant workers*.

_____ 9. After the heavy rain began, I no longer wanted *to go to the movies*.

_____10. A frog that did not jump would be a strange kind *of frog*.

Name _____ Date _____ Class _____

Independent Clauses and Subordinate Clauses

A **clause** is a group of words that contains a verb and its subject and that is used as part of a sentence. An **independent** (or **main**) **clause** expresses a complete thought and can stand by itself as a sentence.

                                       S   V

INDEPENDENT CLAUSE: Korea celebrates its Memorial Day in June.

                                  S V   S   V

INDEPENDENT CLAUSES: I play the guitar, and George sings.

A **subordinate** (or **dependent**) **clause** does not express a complete thought and cannot stand alone as a sentence.

       SUBORDINATE CLAUSE: The day is named for Micajah Autry, **who is considered a hero**.

       SUBORDINATE CLAUSE: **Where you go,** I go.

Exercise A   Decide if each item below is an independent clause or a subordinate clause. Then, in the space provided, write *I* for independent or *S* for subordinate.

_____ 1. Cuba is the largest island in the Greater Antilles.

_____ 2. Where more than eight thousand different species of plants grow.

_____ 3. That more than seven thousand insect species live there.

_____ 4. The royal palm is the national tree.

_____ 5. Since Cuba is home to some thirty species of bats.

Exercise B   On the line provided, identify each italicized word group in the following paragraph as an independent clause or a subordinate clause. Write *I* for independent or *S* for subordinate.

            EXAMPLE: [1] ____*I*____ *How are eggs processed in a large processing plant?*

[1] _____ Large plants are *where most eggs are processed today.* [2] _____ After an egg is laid, *it gently rolls along the slanted floor of the hens' cage to a narrow conveyor belt.* [3] _____ Several narrow conveyor belts converge into one wide belt *that runs directly into the processing plant.* [4] _____ *As soon as the eggs reach the processing plant,* they are automatically sprayed with detergent and water. [5] _____ The eggs then pass through a specially lit inspection area, *where defective eggs can be identified and removed.* [6] _____ After the eggs are weighed, *they are separated by weight into groups.* [7] _____ Each group of eggs goes onto a separate conveyor belt, *which leads to a forklike lifting device.* [8] _____ This device lifts six eggs at a time, *while the empty egg cartons wait two feet below it.* [9] _____ *The eggs are gently lowered into the cartons,* which are then shipped to grocery stores and supermarkets. [10] _____ *What is truly amazing* is that no human hands ever touch the eggs during the entire process.

SENTENCES

Name _____ Date _____ Class _____

 **WORKSHEET 2** *The Adjective Clause*

An **adjective clause** is a subordinate clause that modifies a noun or a pronoun. Usually, an adjective clause begins with a *relative pronoun*, such as *who, whom, whose, which,* or *that.* This pronoun relates the clause to the word or words that the clause modifies.

> ADJECTIVE CLAUSE: Celia Cruz, **who has been called the Queen of Salsa,** began singing in the 1940s. [The relative pronoun *who* relates the adjective clause to the noun *Celia Cruz.* It also serves as the subject of the verb *has been called.*]

An adjective clause may begin with a *relative adverb*, such as *when* or *where.*

> ADJECTIVE CLAUSE: I live near First Avenue, **where I catch the bus.** [The clause *where I catch the bus* modifies the noun *First Avenue.*]

Exercise A   Underline the adjective clause in each of the following sentences. Then draw an arrow to the word that the clause modifies.

> EXAMPLE: Robbie entered the library where they had first met.

1. Sara went to the Bureau of Vital Statistics, where she hoped to find the answer.

2. Red is a color that often signals danger.

3. The passengers suffered delays that they thought were intolerable.

4. The lake which we visit every summer is called Clear Lake.

5. Kaulana is the only one of you who is always punctual.

Exercise B   Underline the adjective clause in each of the following sentences. On the line provided, tell whether the relative pronoun is used as the *subject, direct object,* or *object of a preposition* in the adjective clause.

> EXAMPLE: 1. Theo, who is the editor of the school newspaper, wrote an article about the inhumane treatment of laboratory animals. *subject*

1. The book which he needs was ordered yesterday.   _____

2. In March many countries have festivals that can be traced back to ancient celebrations of spring.   _____

3. The nominee was a politician whom everyone admired.   _____

4. It's not easy to understand someone who mumbles.   _____

5. The horse that I rode had a white blaze on her face.   _____

Name _____ Date _____ Class _____

 **WORKSHEET 3** *The Noun Clause*

A **noun clause** is a subordinate clause used as a noun. A noun clause may be used as a subject, a predicate nominative, a direct object, an indirect object, the object of a preposition, or an object of a verbal.

SUBJECT: **Whoever wants to come with us** is welcome.

PREDICATE NOMINATIVE: The results were not **what we had expected**.

DIRECT OBJECT: I understand **how that works**.

INDIRECT OBJECT: Ying Par will give **whoever asks** some help.

OBJECT OF A PREPOSITION: Sam told his story to **whomever he could get to listen**.

OBJECT OF A VERBAL: We resolved to send **whatever we could** to the flood survivors.

Noun clauses are usually introduced by *that, what, when, where, whether, who, whoever, whom, whomever, whose, why,* and *how*. The word that introduces a noun clause may or may not have another function in the clause.

Exercise A Underline the noun clause in each of the following sentences.

1. Garrett Morgan recognized that a mask was needed to keep people safe from poisonous gas.

2. Whoever wore the mask would be safe.

3. What Morgan did invent was the earliest traffic signals.

4. I saw a demonstration of how they worked.

5. No one can deny that traffic signals prevent accidents.

Exercise B Underline the noun clause in each sentence. Then identify how the clause is used. On the line provided, write *S* for subject, *DO* for direct object, *IO* for indirect object, *OP* for object of a preposition, or *PN* for predicate nominative.

EXAMPLES: _*OP*_ 1. Please address your letter to <u>whoever manages the store</u>.

_*DO*_ 2. Do you know <u>where the new municipal center is</u>?

_____ 1. Would you please tell me what the past tense of the verb *swing* is?

_____ 2. Give whoever calls me my office number.

_____ 3. Whatever you decide will be fine with me.

_____ 4. Was that color what you wanted?

_____ 5. The stranded crew survived with whatever had been aboard their raft.

SENTENCES

Chapter 7: Clauses

 **WORKSHEET 4** ## *The Adverb Clause*

An **adverb clause** is a subordinate clause that modifies a verb, an adjective, an adverb, or a verbal. An adverb clause tells *how, when, where, why, to what extent,* or *under what condition.* Adverb clauses are introduced by **subordinating conjunctions,** such as *after, although, before, if, since, so, than, unless, wherever,* or *while.*

> MODIFYING MAIN VERB: **Wherever you travel,** people will usually help you. [The adverb clause modifies the verb phrase *will help.* The subordinating conjunction is *wherever.*]

> MODIFYING ADJECTIVE: This speaker sounds much better **than the one we heard first.** [The adverb clause modifies the adjective *better.* The subordinating conjunction is *than.*]

Part of a clause may be left out when the meaning can be understood from the context of the sentence. Such a clause is called an **elliptical clause.**

> ELLIPTICAL CLAUSE: **Although** [she was] **tired,** the soldier remained at her post.

Exercise A   Underline the adverb clause in each of the following sentences.

1. When we visited Kyoto, we stayed in a ryokan.

2. We removed our shoes before we entered our room.

3. While we were at dinner, someone made our beds.

4. We brought very little luggage, since the ryokan provided robes.

5. The water in the bath was much hotter than I had expected!

Exercise B   Underline the adverb clause in each of the following sentences. On the line provided, give the word or words that the clause modifies. Then state whether the clause tells *how, when, where, why, to what extent,* or *under what condition.* [Note: If a clause is elliptical, be prepared to supply the omitted word or words.]

> EXAMPLE: 1. <u>If we stop by the mall,</u> we might be late for the movie.
> *might be; under what condition*

1. Your trip to New York will not be complete unless you see the Alvin Ailey American Dance Theater.   _____

2. Because he was late so often, he bought a watch.   _____

3. As soon as you're ready, we will leave.   _____

4. The company entered the international scene, selling where no competition existed.   _____

5. This test is easier than Mr. Lincoln's.   _____

Name _____ Date _____ Class _____

WORKSHEET 5 *Review*

Exercise A Each of the following sentences contains an italicized clause. On the line provided, identify the italicized clause as *IND* for independent or *SUB* for subordinate clause.

_____ 1. *Although Spanish is the chief language of South America*, dozens of other languages are spoken there.

_____ 2. The official language of Brazil, *which is by far the largest of the South American countries*, is Portuguese.

_____ 3. *The Inca language is still spoken by several million people* who live in Ecuador, Peru, and Bolivia.

_____ 4. If you go to Guyana, *you will find many Hindus and Moslems* whose ancestors came from Asia and who still speak Hindi and other Indian languages.

_____ 5. Dutch, of course, is the official language of Suriname (Dutch Guiana), and *French is spoken throughout French Guiana.*

Exercise B Each of the following sentences contains a subordinate clause. First, find this clause and underline it. Then, on the line provided, identify the kind of subordinate clause it is. Write *ADJ* for adjective clause, *ADV* for adverb clause, or *N* for noun clause.

_____ 1. The educational systems of most South American countries are different from the system that we are accustomed to in the United States.

_____ 2. The Spanish and Portuguese settlers who colonized South America brought with them the educational traditions of their native countries.

_____ 3. Although the colonists established many schools and universities, they did not try to provide education for everyone.

_____ 4. They assumed that schooling was necessary only for people of the professional classes.

_____ 5. Today nearly all South American countries have laws that call for compulsory elementary education for all children.

_____ 6. Often the laws cannot be put into effect, however, since money for teachers, schools, and textbooks is lacking.

_____ 7. In Bolivia, which has the lowest literacy rate in South America, about one third of the population cannot read and write.

_____ 8. One reason for this low rate is that many Bolivians are mountain dwellers.

_____ 9. It is hard to provide schooling for these people because they live in isolated mountain villages and speak a number of different dialects.

_____10. Many South American children who do go to school quit at the end of three or four years.

Exercise C Each of the following sentences contains a subordinate clause. First, find this clause and underline it. Then, on the line provided, identify the kind of subordinate clause it is. Write *ADJ* for adjective clause, *ADV* for adverb clause, or *N* for noun clause.

_____ 1. While almost all South American countries have state-supported secondary schools and universities, relatively few students expect to go on to these schools.

_____ 2. Following the European tradition, the secondary schools usually offer an academic program that emphasizes classical studies and foreign languages.

_____ 3. The teaching in a secondary school may consist largely of scholarly lectures on which the students are expected to take complete notes.

_____ 4. Whoever graduates from a secondary school has finished his or her general education.

_____ 5. Students may not go to universities unless they want to prepare for specialized professions like law and medicine.

Exercise D Underline the subordinate clause in each of the following sentences. On the line provided, tell whether the subordinate clause is used as an *adjective* or a *noun*. Then give the word that each adjective clause modifies, and state whether each noun clause is used as a *subject*, a *direct object*, an *object of a preposition*, or a *predicate nominative*.

> EXAMPLE: 1. Until recently, most scientists believed that the giant
> sequoias of California were the oldest living trees on earth.
> *noun; direct object*

1. Now, however, that honor is given to the bristlecone pine, a small, gnarled tree that few people have ever heard of. _____

2. Botanists estimate that some bristlecone pines are more than six thousand years old. _____

3. The oldest sequoias are only 2,500 years old, according to those who study the trees. _____

4. Whoever respects hardiness has to respect the bristlecone. _____

5. The high altitude of the Rocky Mountains, the bristlecone's natural habitat, is what makes the tree grow so slowly. _____

6. Some people think that the bristlecone pine looks frightening. _____

7. The trademark by which they are known is their gnarled, stunted look. _____

8. The bristlecone's needles, which stay on the branches for twelve to fifteen years, are extraordinarily long-lived. _____

9. Botanists tell us that the bristlecone is a member of the foxtail family. _____

10. Like all members of this family, the bristlecone has needle clusters that resemble a fox's tail. _____

Name _____ Date _____ Class _____

The Sentence

A **sentence** is a group of words that expresses a complete thought. A sentence begins with a capital letter and ends with a period, a question mark, or an exclamation point. Do not be misled by a group of words that looks like a sentence but that does not make sense by itself. Such a word group is called a **sentence fragment**.

SENTENCE FRAGMENT: The window in the kitchen.

SENTENCE: The window in the kitchen refused to open.

Exercise A   Decide if the following groups of words are sentence fragments or complete sentences. On the line provided, write *F* if an item is a fragment or *S* if an item is a sentence.

_____ 1. Hercules defeated Hydra.

_____ 2. A plant thought by some to have great healing powers.

_____ 3. How many pages of the article in the magazine?

_____ 4. Kiyo, wearing her soccer uniform, posed for her team picture.

_____ 5. As my grandmother observes about the weather.

_____ 6. In Greek mythology, Demeter was an earth goddess.

_____ 7. After she retired, Mrs. Renfrew decided to live in the country.

_____ 8. A solitary turtle crossing the road.

_____ 9. What a marvelous idea for a story that is!

_____10. Rebecca had flung open the door and raced down the stairs.

Exercise B: Revising   Decide whether the following items are sentences or fragments. If an item contains only complete sentences, write *C* on the line provided. If the item contains fragments, rewrite the item as one or two complete sentences.

1. Hisao Watanabe, the orchestra's guest conductor. Walked onto the stage.

   _____

2. The young conductor, who was born in Tokyo, Japan. Having studied piano and trumpet at the Chicago Musical College of Roosevelt University.

   _____

3. Augusta Read Thomas wrote the piece that we heard. Commissioned by the New York Youth Orchestra's musical director, Samuel Wong.

   _____

4. Ms. Thomas dedicated *Ritual, An Overture Concertante* to Samuel Wong. She wanted to thank him for giving her the chance to compose the work.

   _____

SENTENCES

Name _____ Date _____ Class _____

 **WORKSHEET 2** *Subject and Predicate*

A sentence consists of two parts: a **subject** and a **predicate**. The **subject** tells *whom* or *what* the sentence is about. The **predicate** tells something about the subject.

          SUBJECT   PREDICATE
  The beautiful Rocky Mountains | attract many visitors.

    PREDICATE   SUBJECT   PREDICATE
  Where has | Marlene | been going on the weekends?

In these examples, all the words labeled *subject* make up the **complete subject,** and all the words labeled *predicate* make up the **complete predicate**.

A **simple subject** is the main word or group of words that tells *whom* or *what* the sentence is about. A **simple predicate** is a verb or verb phrase that tells something about the subject.

         SIMPLE SUBJECT: My mother's **hometown** is Kalamazoo, Michigan.

        SIMPLE PREDICATE: **Could** the calculator **have** possibly **been** incorrect?

Exercise   For each of the following sentences, underline the simple subject once and the simple predicate twice. Be sure to include all words in a verb phrase.

          EXAMPLE: 1. In feudal Japan, the samurai, members of the military
                    class, ruled society with an iron hand.

1. The people of the peasant class lived in terror of these landlord-warriors.

2. A samurai's powerful position gave him the right to kill any disobedient or disrespectful peasant.

3. Did anyone in Japan refuse to serve the samurai?

4. There was a dedicated group of rebels called ninja, which means "stealers in."

5. Off to the barren mountain regions of Iga and Koga fled the ninja people with their families.

6. There, they could train their children in the martial arts of *ninjutsu*.

7. Lessons in camouflage, escape, and evasion were taught to children as young as one or two years of age.

8. Childhood games also provided practice in both armed and unarmed combat.

9. The ninja struck at the samurai in any way possible.

10. In time, the ninja warriors gained a reputation all over Japan.

Chapter 8: Sentence Structure

Compound Subjects and Verbs

A **compound subject** consists of two or more subjects that are joined by a conjunction and that have the same verb. A **compound verb** consists of two or more verbs that are joined by a conjunction and that have the same subject.

COMPOUND SUBJECT: **Eggs, milk,** and **butter** are ingredients for making muffins.

COMPOUND VERB: Ian **collected** his thoughts and **began** to write.

Exercise A   Underline the compound parts in each of the following sentences. Then, on the line provided, write *CS* for compound subject or *CV* for compound verb.

_____ 1. News, weather, and sports are reported each night at 6:00 P.M.

_____ 2. Either Mark or his cousin Sara will pick you up at the bus stop.

_____ 3. The driver turned off the road, parked on a side street, and waited.

_____ 4. Increased wages and additional benefits were products of the negotiations.

_____ 5. The poet Valéry rose before dawn each morning and wrote for hours.

Exercise B: Revising   Combine each set of sentences to create one sentence with a compound subject or a compound verb. Write each new sentence on the line provided.

EXAMPLE: 1. Kelley put on her helmet and knee pads. Then she pulled on her in-line skates.

Kelley put on her helmet and knee pads and then pulled on her in-line skates.

1. Swimming is a popular summer sport. Boating is a popular summer sport, too.

_____

2. Juan dropped his duffel bag on the sand. Juan then spread his beach towel. After that, he stretched lazily.

_____

3. My cat always recognizes the sound of my father's car. The cat meets my father at the door.

_____

4. Oats and soybeans are important grain crops. Corn and wheat and alfalfa are important grain crops, also.

_____

SENTENCES

Name _____ Date _____ Class _____

 **WORSHEET 4** *Finding the Subject*

To find the subject of a sentence, ask *Who?* or *What?* before the verb.

Elmore wrote to his grandmother. [*Who wrote? Elmore wrote.*]

(1) The subject of a sentence expressing a command or request is always understood to be *you*, although *you* may not appear in the sentence. The subject of a command or a request is *you* even when the sentence contains a **noun of direct address**—a word naming the one or ones spoken to.

        REQUEST: [*You*] Please bring me that book of poems.

        COMMAND: Mariana, [*you*] turn out your light and go to sleep.

(2) The subject of the sentence is never in a prepositional phrase.

Some of these poems are difficult to understand. [*Poems is the object of the preposition of. Some is the subject of the sentence.*]

(3) The subject of a sentence expressing a question usually follows the verb or part of the verb phrase. Turning the question into a statement will often help you find the subject.

Whose poem do **you** like the best? [*You (do) like whose poem the best.*]

(4) The words *there* and *here* are never the subject of a sentence.

There are several **books** of poetry on the shelf. [*What are? Books are.*]

Exercise A   Underline the subject once and the verb twice in the following sentences. If the subject is understood to be *you*, write *you* on the line provided.

_____ 1. Here is a poem by Alice Walker, African American poet and Pulitzer Prize winner.

_____ 2. Wasn't Alice Walker dismissed from college once because of her participation in a civil rights demonstration?

_____ 3. Didn't she later win a scholarship to Sarah Lawrence College?

_____ 4. There are several copies of *The Color Purple* by Alice Walker in our school library.

_____ 5. Claudia, please pick up a copy of *The Color Purple* at the library.

Exercise B   Decide if the underlined word in each of the following sentences is the subject. If it is, write *C* on the line provided. If it is not, find the subject and circle it.

_____ 1. Was Langston Hughes <u>one</u> of the most influential African American poets of his day?

_____ 2. <u>Gregory</u>, listen to the rhythm in the poem "Harlem" by Langston Hughes.

_____ 3. <u>There</u> is a line in that poem about "a raisin in the sun."

_____ 4. <u>Lorraine Hansberry</u>, the playwright, took the title of *A Raisin in the Sun* from that poem.

Name _____ Date _____ Class _____

WORKSHEET 5

Direct and Indirect Objects

A **complement** is a word or a group of words that completes the meaning of a verb. *Direct objects* and *indirect objects* are two types of complements. A **direct object** is a word or word group that receives the action of a verb or that shows the result of the action. A direct object tells *whom* or *what* after a transitive verb. An **indirect object** is a word or word group that comes between a transitive verb and a direct object and that tells *to whom* or *to what* or *for whom* or *for what* the action of the verb is done.

               IO   DO

Liana read her **sister** a **story**.

                    IO   DO

The librarian handed **me** the **pile** of books.

A verbal may have complements.

    The last thing he remembered was **giving Liana** his **keys**. [*Keys* is the direct object of the gerund *giving*, and *Liana* is the indirect object.]

Exercise A Decide whether the underlined words in the following sentences are direct objects or indirect objects. On the line provided, write *DO* for a direct object or *IO* for an indirect object.

_____ 1. Amy Tan writes <u>stories</u> based on her family history.

_____ 2. In her books, Amy Tan gives <u>readers</u> a glimpse into her Chinese heritage.

_____ 3. The stories that she heard growing up gave her <u>material</u> for her books.

_____ 4. Tan explores the <u>relationship</u> between Chinese American mothers and their daughters in her book *The Joy Luck Club*.

_____ 5. Tan offered her <u>editor</u>, her <u>agent</u>, and her <u>family</u> thanks for their help and encouragement while she wrote her first novel.

Exercise B In the following sentences, underline the indirect objects once and the direct objects twice.

1. N. Scott Momaday's Native American parents gave him the Kiowa name *Tsoai-talee*.

2. My teacher told us the name and its meaning, which is "Rock-Tree Boy."

3. A childhood visit to his grandmother's house offered Momaday lasting impressions that he would later describe in his book *The Names*.

4. The Pulitzer Prize Committee awarded the writer the 1969 fiction prize for his book *House Made of Dawn*.

5. Do you still have the copy of Momaday's *The Way to Rainy Mountain* that I lent you?

SENTENCES

Name _____ Date _____ Class _____

WORKSHEET 6 *Objective Complements*

A **direct object** receives or shows the result of the action of a verb. A direct object tells *whom* or *what* after a transitive verb. An **indirect object** comes between a transitive verb and a direct object and tells *to whom* or *to what* or *for whom* or *for what* the action of the verb is done.

        IO   DO
Luis showed **Terry** the **solution** to the math problem.

Another type of complement is an *objective complement*. An **objective complement** is a word or word group that helps complete the meaning of a transitive verb by identifying or modifying the direct object. Only a few verbs take objective complements: *consider, make,* and verbs that can be replaced by *consider* or *make,* such as *appoint, call, choose, dye, elect, keep, name, cut, paint,* and *sweep.* An objective complement may be a noun, an adjective, or a participle.

The judges called Jeremy the most promising **pianist** at the recital. [The noun *pianist* identifies the direct object *Jeremy*.]

Helen's friends consider her **mature** and **giving.** [The adjective *mature* and the participle *giving* modify the direct object *her*.]

A verbal can take an objective complement.

The committee voted **to name her** the new committee **chair.** [*Her* is the direct object of the infinitive *to name,* and the objective complement *chair* identifies *her*.]

Exercise A Identify the objective complements in the following sentences. Write the complements on the lines provided.

1. My grandfather declared Julia's lasagna delicious.   _____

2. He called eating both a necessity and a pleasure.   _____

3. His friends dubbed him "The Connoisseur."   _____

4. Granddad appointed my sister Julia taster of his new recipes.   _____

5. She considers the job fulfilling and exciting.   _____

Exercise B Underline each complement in the following sentences. Then, in the space above each sentence, identify each complement as a direct object *(DO)*, an indirect object *(IO)*, or an objective complement *(OC)*.

                                DO
EXAMPLE: 1. Candles have great <u>appeal</u> as decorative objects.

1. Every year, the United States consumes many tons of paraffin for candle making.

2. Nowadays, candle making offers hobbyists a relaxing and rewarding pastime.

3. Candlemakers can make candles by dipping a wick into melted wax.

4. Incense mixed into the melted wax will give your candles a pleasant scent.

5. Candlemakers also dye candle wax various colors.

Name _____ Date _____ Class _____

WORKSHEET 7 — *Subject Complements*

A **subject complement** is a word or word group that completes the meaning of a linking verb and that identifies or modifies the subject. There are two kinds of subject complements: the **predicate nominative** and the **predicate adjective**. A **predicate nominative** is a word or group of words that follows a linking verb and that refers to the same person or thing as the subject of the verb. A **predicate adjective** is an adjective that follows a linking verb and that modifies the subject of the verb.

    PREDICATE NOMINATIVES: The alternates are **Lisa, Tanya,** and **I.**

    PREDICATE ADJECTIVES: These oranges are **sweet** and **juicy.**

NOTE: Do not confuse a verbal used as a predicate nominative with a participle used as the main verb in a verb phrase.

    PREDICATE NOMINATIVE: My favorite pastime is **swimming** in Barton Springs.

    VERB: He **is swimming** in Barton Springs.

Exercise A   Underline the linking verb twice and the subject complement(s) once in each of the following sentences. On the line provided, indicate whether the complement is a *predicate nominative* or a *predicate adjective.*

    EXAMPLE: 1. Slowly, the sky <u>became</u> <u>dark</u>. *predicate adjective*

1. The most common deer in India is a species of axis deer. _____

2. Wilhelm Roentgen was the discoverer of the X-ray. _____

3. The violin solo sounded beautiful. _____

4. The animals near the burning forest were growing restless. _____

5. Harriet Tubman was active in the Underground Railroad. _____

6. Is Raymond Dawson the author of *The Chinese Experience*? _____

7. How contented my uncle seemed in his remote cottage on the Outer Banks of North Carolina. _____

8. Should Bill be the leader of the expedition? _____

9. Rebel groups were the targets of the regime's search. _____

10. The food at the banquet was boring and colorless. _____

Exercise B   On the line provided, add a subject complement to each group of words below to make a complete sentence.

1. Sara, at the age of eighty-four, was _____

2. After his retirement, Detective Forbes became _____

3. When he completed his driving test, Sergio felt _____

4. All of the gardens in the tiny Japanese village were _____

SENTENCES

Name _____ Date _____ Class _____

WORKSHEET 8

Classifying Sentences by Structure

According to their structure, sentences are classified as *simple, compound, complex,* or *compound-complex*. A **simple sentence** has one independent clause and no subordinate clauses. However, it may have a compound subject or a compound verb. A **compound sentence** has two or more independent clauses but no subordinate clauses.

> SIMPLE: You and Doyle may each bring a guest.
>
> COMPOUND: You and Doyle leave now; your guests will follow.

A **complex sentence** has one independent clause and at least one subordinate clause. A **compound-complex sentence** has two or more independent clauses and at least one subordinate clause.

> COMPLEX: As I practiced my speech, I grew calmer.
>
> COMPOUND-COMPLEX: Before class started, I grew nervous, so I practiced my speech again.

Exercise   On the line provided, classify each of the following sentences as simple *(S)*, compound *(CD)*, complex *(CX)*, or compound-complex *(CC)*.

> EXAMPLE: ___*S*___ 1. Using the pith of the papyrus plant, ancient Egyptians made the first paper.

_____ 1. Charles Drew did research on blood plasma and helped develop blood banks.

_____ 2. Supposedly, if the month of March comes in like a lion, it goes out like a lamb.

_____ 3. The Malays believe that sickness will follow the eating of stolen foods.

_____ 4. When World War I ended in 1918, many people thought that there would be no more wars; but twenty-one years later, World War II began.

_____ 5. In his letter to Mrs. Bixby, Abraham Lincoln consoled her for the loss of several sons and hoped that time would ease her sorrow.

_____ 6. After the announcement of the final score, all of us fans cheered the team and clapped enthusiastically.

_____ 7. In England and Wales, salmon was once king, yet few salmon rivers remain.

_____ 8. The English philosopher Thomas Hobbes once aspired to be a mathematician, but he never fulfilled this ambition.

_____ 9. As an older woman, Queen Elizabeth I always wore a dark-red wig, so no one knew whether her own hair had grayed or not.

_____10. Professional tennis star Zina Garrison-Jackson devotes time to training and encouraging young inner-city tennis players.

Name _____ Date _____ Class _____

WORSHEET 9

Classifying Sentences by Purpose

Sentences may be classified according to purpose. A **declarative sentence** makes a statement. It is followed by a period. An **interrogative sentence** asks a question. It is followed by a question mark. An **imperative sentence** makes a request or gives a command. It is usually followed by a period. A very strong command, however, is followed by an exclamation point. An **exclamatory sentence** expresses strong feeling or shows excitement. It is followed by an exclamation point.

> DECLARATIVE: Fruit juice is good for you**.**
>
> INTERROGATIVE: Will you support this recommendation**?**
>
> IMPERATIVE: Please pass the prune juice**.**
> Watch out for the bus**!**
>
> EXCLAMATORY: That tastes terrible**!**

Exercise   On the line provided, identify each of the following sentences. Write *D* for declarative, *INT* for interrogative, *IMP* for imperative, or *E* for exclamatory. Then supply the appropriate end mark after the last word in each sentence.

_____ 1. Anyone with a little free time and a generous heart can help make the world of books available to people with visual impairments

_____ 2. For example, have you ever wondered how Braille schoolbooks for sight-impaired students are created

_____ 3. Imagine dozens and dozens of volunteers, all with their fingers flying across the keys of machines that look much like miniature typewriters

_____ 4. Different combinations of six keys on the machines make the raised-dot patterns that represent letters and numbers in Braille

_____ 5. First, Braille typists take a course to learn how to use the machines

_____ 6. Once you learn how, typing in Braille isn't difficult at all

_____ 7. If I participate, can I work at home in my spare time

_____ 8. What rewarding volunteer work this is

_____ 9. When I considered how much time I wasted every week, I decided to use that time constructively by volunteering to help create Braille textbooks

_____ 10. If you know someone who might be interested in participating, help him or her find out how to get in touch with the Braille Association in your community

SENTENCES

Chapter 8: Sentence Structure

WORKSHEET 10 *Review*

Exercise A   On the line after each sentence, write the simple subject and the verb. Be sure to include all parts of a verb phrase and all parts of a compound subject or verb.

EXAMPLE: 1. There are many varieties of spoken English.
Subject: varieties   Verb: are

1. All of us recognize the differences in English pronunciations—for instance, the difference between American and British pronunciations.

   _____

2. We are also familiar with many of the varieties of American speech.

   _____

3. We know Texans by their drawl and recognize Bostonians by their pronunciations of *a*'s and *r*'s.

   _____

4. Usually, however, an educated Texan and an educated Bostonian write a nearly identical kind of English.

   _____

5. In fact, the Texan and the Bostonian share this written brand of English with most other writers of English in all parts of the world.

   _____

6. Almost any book or article in English is completely understandable to English-speaking people worldwide.

   _____

7. Some people dislike this uniformity and prefer variety in written language.

   _____

8. But can you imagine a spelling book with different directions for each different local dialect?

   _____

9. A word such as *idea* would be spelled *idea, idear, idee,* or even *uhdeeuh,* according to the different speech habits of different writers.

   _____

10. Would the use of many different spellings for the same word be a help or a hindrance in world communication?

   _____

Exercise B On the line provided, identify the sentence part or parts indicated in parentheses. Be sure to include all parts of a compound subject or verb. Write the first word and the last word of a complete subject or predicate. Separate these words with a dash.

EXAMPLE: 1. *(predicate adjective, complete subject)* The people of New Orleans are famous for their creativity with food as well as with music.
famous, The—Orleans

1. *(complete subject)* Both Creole cooking and Cajun cooking flourish in the kitchens of the city's French Quarter. _____

2. *(complete predicate)* Some visitors to New Orleans have trouble telling the difference between these two similar styles of food preparation. _____

3. *(indirect object, direct object)* My aunt, a restaurant critic, showed me the differences between Creole cooking and Cajun cooking. _____

4. *(verb, direct object)* The French founders of New Orleans developed the savory Creole style of cooking. _____

5. *(predicate nominative)* The beignet (a square doughnut) and *boudin* (a spicy, savory sausage) are tasty local favorites from French cuisine. _____

6. *(complete predicate)* In Creole dishes, there are also tangy traces of Spanish, African, and Caribbean cooking. _____

7. *(predicate nominative)* Cajun cooking is Creole's peppery country cousin and was born in the rural bayou areas surrounding New Orleans. _____

8. *(predicate adjectives)* My aunt's favorite Cajun treat, alligator gumbo, is wonderfully thick and spicy. _____

9. *(complete subject, direct object)* A little red shellfish used in many Cajun dishes resembles a tiny lobster. _____

10. *(objective complement)* They're New Orleans crawfish, and I declare them the tastiest morsels I've ever eaten! _____

Exercise C Write the proper punctuation at the end of each sentence. Then, on the line provided, write *D* for declarative, *INT* for interrogative, *IMP* for imperative, or *E* for exclamatory. There may be more than one correct answer for some sentences.

EXAMPLE: ___E___ 1. That certainly was an extraordinary meeting*!*

_____ 1. Dr. Elizabeth Blackwell opened a hospital in 1853

_____ 2. Would you mind staying after class to help clean up in here

_____ 3. What a day I've had

_____ 4. Don't move from that spot

_____ 5. Think before you speak

Chapter 8, Worksheet 11, continued

Exercise D On the line provided before each of the following sentences, identify the type of sentence it is. Write *S* for simple, *CD* for compound, *CX* for complex, or *CC* for compound-complex.

_____ 1. Explorers who probe the world beneath the sea have made many important scientific discoveries.

_____ 2. Undersea exploration requires sophisticated equipment to enable divers to breathe and to protect them from water pressure.

_____ 3. For centuries, divers went thirty to forty feet (nine to twelve meters) beneath the surface without equipment; others used diving bells in shallow water.

_____ 4. Divers have greater freedom and more mobility when they use the aqualung that Jacques-Yves Cousteau helped invent in 1943.

_____ 5. Cousteau's inventions have brought about many changes in undersea exploration; his observation vehicle, which he calls a "diving saucer," enables divers to stay underwater for long periods of time.

Name _____ Date _____ Class _____

Coordinating Ideas

Ideas of equal weight in a sentence are called **coordinate ideas**. To give equal emphasis to two or more **independent clauses**—clauses that express complete thoughts—link them with a connecting word, appropriate punctuation, or both. The result is a **compound sentence**.

Winter was hard**, but** spring came early.

Ice had broken great branches off of many trees**; nevertheless,** new growth was everywhere.

The meadows came alive; tiny shoots of grass sprouted up everywhere.

Different connectives show different kinds of relationships between independent clauses.

ADDITION	CONTRAST	CHOICE	RESULT
also	but	either . . . or	accordingly
and	however	neither . . . nor	consequently
as well as	nevertheless	nor	hence
both . . . and	still	or	therefore
likewise	yet	otherwise	thus

You can also use connecting words to coordinate words or phrases in a sentence. The result is a compound element in your sentence.

Daffodils and tulips bloomed. [compound subject]

Songbirds **returned and built their happy nests.** [compound predicate]

Exercise On the line provided, use an appropriate connecting word and punctuation to join each of the following items.

1. At one time, Irish Americans were the big names in boxing _____ African Americans now dominate this field.

2. Many Irish American boxers grew up in rough neighborhoods of large cities

   _____ it is not surprising that boxing appealed to them.

3. You might have heard the name John L. Sullivan _____ "Gentleman Jim" Corbett.

4. Eugene O'Neill won several Pulitzer Prizes for literature _____ he also won the Nobel Prize for literature.

5. You may not have heard of the Irish American Philip Barry

   _____ he was the author of *The Philadelphia Story.*

SENTENCES

Chapter 9: Sentence Style

WORKSHEET 2

Subordinating Ideas in Adverb Clauses

You can express ideas so that one is grammatically subordinate to another. A **subordinate clause** is a group of words that has a subject and a verb and depends on the sentence's main clause for its full meaning. An **adverb clause** is a subordinate clause that modifies a verb, an adjective, or an adverb in a sentence. A subordinating conjunction introduces an adverb clause. The list below shows subordinating conjunctions you can use to express the following relationships between the main clause and the adverb clause: *time or place, cause or reason, purpose or result,* or *condition.*

TIME OR PLACE: after, as, before, since, until, when, whenever, where, wherever, while

CAUSE OR REASON: as, because, even though, if, since, that, unless, whereas, while

PURPOSE OR RESULT: so that, in order that

CONDITION: although, even though, if, provided that, unless, while

Exercise For each of the following sentences, write an appropriate subordinating conjunction in the blank. The hint in parentheses tells you what kind of relationship the conjunction should express. Do not use the same conjunction twice.

1. _____ it is called a lake, Moraine is really a three-acre pond located beneath a high majestic ridge on Grapetree Mountain. (*condition*)

2. _____ we visited Lake Moraine, we heard wild geese and saw beavers building dams. (*time*)

3. _____ we were sitting by the tent one summer evening, a snowshoe hare crept from behind the pine trees to eat lettuce from our hands. (*time*)

4. Lake Moraine is now threatened _____ acid rains are destroying the brook trout that live there. (*cause or reason*)

5. _____ acid pollutants from factory fumes enter the atmosphere, they fall to the earth in rain and snow. (*time*)

6. High-altitude ponds get heavy doses of acid rains _____ the mountains trap moisture-bearing air masses. (*cause or reason*)

7. _____ the acid pollutants end up in the mountain ponds, fish (especially trout) suffer and die in great numbers. (*time*)

8. Many remote trout ponds are encased in granite _____ little soil or organic matter exists to trap or buffer the acid rain. (*purpose or result*)

9. _____ it is possible to develop acid-tolerant strains of trout, a program of selective breeding will take many years. (*condition*)

10. Ponds like Lake Moraine will become trout graveyards _____ we don't combat the effects of acid rain. (*condition*)

Name _____ Date _____ Class _____

WORKSHEET 3

Subordinating Ideas in Adjective Clauses

You can subordinate an idea in a sentence by putting the idea in an adjective clause. An **adjective clause** modifies a noun or pronoun in a sentence. An adjective clause usually begins with *who, whom, whose, which, that,* or *where*.

Before you use an adjective clause in a sentence, decide which idea you want to emphasize. Then put the idea you want to emphasize in the independent clause and the other information in an adjective clause.

> Gabriel García Márquez, **who is one of my favorite authors**, wrote *Love in the Time of Cholera*. [This sentence emphasizes that Márquez wrote *Love in the Time of Cholera*.]

> Gabriel García Márquez, **who wrote *Love in the Time of Cholera***, is one of my favorite authors. [This sentence emphasizes that Márquez is a favorite author.]

Exercise: Revising Change the emphasis in each of the following sentences. Emphasize the idea that is now in the adjective clause, and subordinate the idea that is now in the independent clause. You may have to delete some words, change the word order, or use a different word to begin the new subordinate clause.

1. N. Scott Momaday, who writes eloquently about Native American culture, won a Pulitzer

   Prize for the novel *House Made of Dawn*. _____

   _____

2. *House Made of Dawn*, which was published in 1968, focuses on a Native American man's struggle to reconcile traditional tribal values with modern-day American life.

   _____

   _____

3. Momaday spent his boyhood on several different reservations, where he acquired extensive knowledge of Native American history and culture.

   _____

   _____

4. Momaday's book *The Way to Rainy Mountain*, which gives a perceptive account of Native American life, focuses on the history and culture of the Kiowa tribe.

   _____

   _____

5. Momaday, who has also published two collections of poems, considers himself primarily a

   poet. _____

   _____

SENTENCES

Chapter 9: Sentence Style

WORKSHEET 4 | *Weak Coordination*

In writing, it's important to show the relative importance of ideas and their logical connections. If you overuse coordination, you end up with **weak coordination**. One symptom of weak coordination is *weak focus*, or poor definition of the main point or details. Another is *weak connections*, or fuzzy bridges between ideas.

WEAK: Our guide was inexperienced, and we enjoyed the tour, and the museum was new. [What is the main idea of the sentence? Are all three clauses equally important?]

BETTER: Although our guide was inexperienced, we enjoyed the tour of the new museum.

Avoid weak coordination. Check each compound sentence to be sure that every clause is equally important and therefore best linked by the coordinating conjunctions *and, but, for, nor, or, so,* or *yet.* If not, subordinate an idea by placing it in a subordinate clause or phrase.

Exercise: Revising   Each of the following sentences contains weak coordination. On the lines provided, correct the sentences. You may move, add, or delete words as needed.

EXAMPLE: 1. Most people know George Washington was the first President of the United States, and many people don't know much about his early career.

Although most people know George Washington was the first President of the United States, many people don't know much about his early career.

1. George Washington served in a Virginia regiment, and he served in the last French and Indian War. _____

   _____

2. He was appointed commander of the Virginia forces in 1755, but he was only twenty-three years old. _____

   _____

3. In 1758, he resigned his commission, and the war in Virginia was over at this time.

   _____

   _____

4. During the next fifteen years, Washington led the life of a typical Virginia planter, so he devoted his time to his plantation and to politics. _____

   _____

5. In 1775, Washington was appointed commander in chief of the Continental Army, and the Continental Congress had unanimously voted this appointment. _____

   _____

Name _____ Date _____ Class _____

Parallel Structure

Use the same grammatical form to express equal, or parallel, ideas. Applying the same grammatical form to equal ideas creates **parallel structure**. Use parallel structure when you link coordinate ideas.

> NOT PARALLEL: I work to save my money and for helping my family. [infinitive paired with a gerund]

> PARALLEL: I work to save my money and to help my family. [infinitive paired with an infinitive]

Use parallel structure when you compare or contrast ideas.

> NOT PARALLEL: She liked astronomy more than to study the literature of ancient peoples. [noun contrasted with an infinitive]

> PARALLEL: She liked astronomy more than the literature of ancient peoples. [noun contrasted with a noun]

Use parallel structure when you link ideas with correlative conjunctions (*both . . . and, either . . . or, neither . . . nor, not only . . . but also*).

> NOT PARALLEL: Henry Cisneros has served as both the mayor of San Antonio and in the President's Cabinet.

> PARALLEL: Henry Cisneros has served as both the mayor of San Antonio and a member of the President's Cabinet. [Note that the correlative conjunctions are placed directly before the parallel terms.]

Exercise: Revising Make the following sentences parallel by putting the ideas in parallel form. You may delete, add, or move some words.

1. Decide which foods to eat by evaluating their caloric content, their nutritional value, and how they might affect your complexion. _____

    _____

2. An enchilada requires less effort to make than to bake a cake from scratch. _____

    _____

3. To try exotic foods and seeing historical sights are reasons some Americans plan

    international vacations. _____

    _____

4. Either Jamal will be in the school orchestra or on the track team.

    _____

5. Two habits we acquired in Costa Rica were to eat a large meal at noon and taking a siesta

    afterward. _____

    _____

SENTENCES

Chapter 9: Sentence Style

WORKSHEET 6

Sentence Fragments

A sentence expresses a complete thought. If you punctuate a part of a sentence as if it were a complete sentence, you create a **sentence fragment**. In general, avoid sentence fragments.

A phrase is a group of related words that doesn't contain a subject and a verb. Because a phrase doesn't express a complete thought, it can't stand on its own as a sentence.

FRAGMENT: Had run to the top of the hill in two minutes flat.

SENTENCE: Nico **had run to the top of the hill in two minutes flat.**

FRAGMENT: To provide a secure environment for the children. Parents monitor all school activities.

SENTENCE: **To provide a secure environment for the children,** parents monitor all school activities.

A **subordinate clause** contains a subject and a predicate but doesn't express a complete thought and can't stand alone as a sentence.

FRAGMENT: We are planning to have a big family picnic in the park this Saturday. If it doesn't rain.

SENTENCE: We are planning to have a big family picnic in the park this Saturday **if it doesn't rain.**

Exercise: Revising The following items contain fragments. Revise each item to include the fragment in a complete sentence.

1. Nat Love, who was born a slave in Tennessee, became a cowboy. When he was just fifteen years old. _____

   _____

2. An expert horseback rider, Love traveled throughout the West. Driving cattle on the open range. _____

   _____

3. After taking first prize in a riding, roping, and shooting contest in Deadwood, South Dakota, became known as Deadwood Dick. _____

   _____

4. In 1907, published his autobiography, *The Life and Adventures of Nat Love, Better Known in Cattle Country as "Deadwood Dick."* _____

   _____

5. The book both true stories and tall tales about Love. And other famous characters of the Old West. _____

   _____

 **WORKSHEET 7** ## *Run-on Sentences*

Two or more sentences that run together as if they were a single thought create a **run-on sentence**. There are two kinds of run-on sentences: the *fused sentence* and the *comma splice*. A **fused sentence** has no punctuation at all between the two complete thoughts. A **comma splice** has just a comma between them. There are many ways to correct a run-on sentence.

1. You can make two sentences.
2. You can use a comma and a coordinating conjunction.
3. You can change one independent clause to a subordinate clause.
4. You can use a semicolon, with or without a conjunctive adverb.

Exercise: Revising   The following sentences are confusing because they're run-on sentences. On the lines provided, revise each run-on sentence by using the method given in parentheses. Whether you coordinate ideas or subordinate an idea, make sure your revised version shows the appropriate relationship between the ideas.

EXAMPLE: 1. England's Victorian era is named for the reign of Queen Victoria it lasted from 1837 to 1901. (*subordinate clause*)

England's Victorian era, which lasted from 1837 to 1901, is named for the reign of Queen Victoria.

1. The Victorian Era was a time of extreme delicacy and tact in language direct references to the body were considered offensive in polite society. (*two sentences*)

_____

_____

2. The word *limb* had to be used instead of *leg* or *arm,* even a reference to the "leg" of a chair was considered impolite. (*semicolon*) _____

_____

3. In reference to poultry, the thigh was called the second joint the leg was called the first joint or the drumstick. (*comma and coordinating conjunction*) _____

_____

4. Delicate language was carried to an even greater extreme by some people, they referred to a bull as a "gentleman cow." (*subordinate clause*) _____

_____

5. This kind of delicate language seems funny to us now, even today we use indirect language to replace words and phrases that might be considered offensive. (*semicolon and conjunctive adverb*) _____

_____

_____

SENTENCES

Chapter 9: Sentence Style

 **WORSHEET 8** *Unnecessary Shifts*

Avoid making unnecessary shifts in sentences. Sometimes, a shift in subject is necessary to express the meaning you intend.

Take these forms to the front office where the secretary will process them.

Often, though, a shift in subject, tense, or voice in mid-sentence can create an awkward or confusing sentence.

AWKWARD: Writers should avoid an unnecessary shift in subject or else you will create an awkward sentence. [unnecessary shift in subject]

REVISED: You should avoid an unnecessary shift in subject, or else you will create an awkward sentence.

AWKWARD: The family is the center of Arab society, and Arabs tended to be identified by the family to which they belong. [unnecessary shift in tense]

REVISED: The family is the center of Arab society, and Arabs tend to be identified by the family to which they belong.

AWKWARD: The pony bucked, and its rider was thrown off. [unnecessary shift from active voice to passive voice]

REVISED: The pony bucked and threw off its rider.

Exercise: Revising On the line provided, revise each of the following sentences to correct any unnecessary shift in tense, voice, or subject. If the sentence contains a shift that is necessary to express its meaning, write C.

1. The wind was strong that day, but the kite never got off the ground.

   _____

2. Fans are urged to make reservations so that you will be assured seats.

   _____

3. David booted the computer; then, he types in the command for the program.

   _____

4. After Tawanda read the recipe carefully, the vegetables were cut by her.

   _____

5. Although a dozen divers searched the submerged vessel, no trace of the treasure was located.

   _____

Name _____ Date _____ Class _____

WORKSHEET 9

Varying Sentence Beginnings

Varied sentence beginnings hold a reader's attention.

USE A SINGLE-WORD MODIFIER: Carefully, Roscoe aimed. [adverb]

USE A PHRASE MODIFIER: With precise timing, Roscoe shot. [prepositional phrase]

Shooting quickly, Roscoe hit the bull's eye. [participial phrase]

To win the match, Roscoe had to outshoot Kareem. [infinitive phrase]

USE A CLAUSE MODIFIER: Because he stayed calm, Roscoe won the tournament. [adverb clause]

Exercise: Revising   On the lines provided, revise each of the following sentences by varying their beginnings. The hint in parentheses will tell you which type of beginning to use. You may add or delete words or change word forms as needed.

1. People have used signs and gestures to communicate their thoughts since prehistoric times. *(phrase)*

   _____

   _____

2. A system of commonly understood gestures often helped different Native American nations communicate with each other. *(single-word modifier)*

   _____

   _____

3. Nations in the Plains area spoke many different languages, so a well-developed sign language was essential for trading. *(clause)*

   _____

   _____

4. The scope of the sign language grew as more groups settled on the Plains. *(clause)*

   _____

   _____

5. Gestures, such as the one meaning "peace," could be used by strangers and were known by many nations. *(phrase)*

   _____

   _____

SENTENCES

Chapter 9: Sentence Style

WORSHEET 10 *Varying Sentence Structure*

You can improve your style by varying the structure of your sentences. Use a mix of simple, compound, complex, and compound-complex sentences in your writing.

In Greater Boston, about 12 percent of the cats have extra toes on each forepaw [*simple*]. These cats are called *polydactyl*, which comes from a Greek word meaning "many digits" [*complex*]. The ancestors of these cats probably came from Europe in the colonial era, but nobody is absolutely sure [*compound*]. The cats were popular passengers on merchant ships because they controlled the shipboard rat population, and they were popular in Boston households as well [*compound-complex*].

Exercise: Revising   On the lines provided, revise the following paragraphs to create variety in sentence structure. Continue your revision on an additional sheet of paper if necessary.

Both *Fahrenheit* and *centigrade* refer to temperature scales. The two terms differ in origin as well as in meaning. Fahrenheit takes its name from the eighteenth-century German physicist Gabriel Daniel Fahrenheit. He devised the scale. On the Fahrenheit scale, the freezing point of water is 32 degrees. Its boiling point is 212 degrees.

The term *centigrade* is derived from the Latin words *centum* and *gradus*. *Centum* means "hundred." *Gradus* means "step" or "degree." On the centigrade scale, the freezing point of water is 0 degrees. Its boiling point is 100 degrees. Another word for *centigrade* is *Celsius*. Anders Celsius was an eighteenth-century Swedish astronomer. He established the centigrade scale.

_____

_____

_____

_____

_____

_____

_____

_____

_____

_____

_____

_____

_____

_____

Name _____ Date _____ Class _____

WORSHEET 11

Revising to Reduce Wordiness

Skilled writers make every word count. Avoid using unnecessary words in your writing.
To avoid wordiness, keep these three points in mind.

1. Use only as many words as you need to make your point.
2. Choose simple, clear words and expressions over complicated ones.
3. Don't repeat words or ideas unless absolutely necessary.

When editing, you might take out unnecessary words, simplify your language, change a
clause to a phrase, or reduce a phrase or a clause to a word or two.

Exercise   On the lines provided, revise the following sentences to reduce wordiness.

1. George Herman "Babe" Ruth was one of the most talented, skilled, and gifted baseball
   players of all time. _____
   _____

2. Altogether, Ruth won nearly 70 percent of all the games he pitched. _____
   _____

3. Ruth had a staggering lifetime total of 714 home runs; that number of home runs is an
   extraordinary record. _____
   _____

4. He pitched twenty-nine consecutive scoreless innings in a row. _____
   _____

5. Ruth, who is now in the Baseball Hall of Fame, is immortal and famous forever.
   _____

6. When Yankee stadium opened in 1923, it was given the nickname "The House That Ruth
   Built." _____
   _____

7. Ruth was also a remarkable pitcher who could strike out many players.
   _____

8. In the field, without a doubt he was unquestionably one of the best fielders in baseball.
   _____

9. Jaime views clips of the legendary Babe Ruth poised momentously at the bat.
   _____

10. Jaime admires and regards highly Babe Ruth's style. _____
    _____

SENTENCES

Chapter 9: Sentence Style

WORSHEET 12 *Review*

Exercise A Each of the following sentences contains a blank where a subordinating conjunction has been omitted. From the lettered list of subordinating conjunctions that follows the sentence, choose the one that will best fill the blank. Write the letter of your choice in the blank provided at the left.

_____ 1. _____ most students know the answer to it, an enduring trivia question is "What are the five Great Lakes?"
(a) When   (b) Before   (c) Although   (d) If

_____ 2. It is important to take good notes _____ you start to write the paper.
(a) after   (b) because   (c) unless   (d) before

_____ 3. _____ so many people wanted to see the exhibit, the art gallery extended its hours.
(a) Because   (b) So that   (c) Even though   (d) Until

_____ 4. Do not volunteer for this assignment _____ you are willing to work at least four extra hours a week.
(a) if   (b) while   (c) unless   (d) after

_____ 5. He tried to allot his time _____ he could finish his chemistry project in time for the science fair.
(a) whereas   (b) so that   (c) if   (d) although

Exercise B: Revising Weak coordination and faulty parallelism make the following paragraphs confusing. On the lines provided, revise each faulty sentence to make it clear and smooth. You may need to add, delete, or rearrange some words in the sentences. Remember to check the placement of correlative conjunctions.

For most writers, the road to fame is long and a difficult path. But Amy Tan published *The Joy Luck Club* in 1989, and she became an instant celebrity. *The Joy Luck Club* topped the bestseller list soon after its publication, and it was Tan's first novel.

Tan is a Chinese American writer, and she writes skillfully about the lives of second-generation Chinese Americans. In *The Joy Luck Club* and her second novel, *The Kitchen God's Wife*, she portrays family relationships both with humor and insightfully.

_____

_____

_____

_____

_____

Chapter 9, Worksheet 12, continued

_____

_____

_____

_____

_____

_____

_____

_____

_____

_____

Exercise C: Revising On the lines provided, revise the following word groups to eliminate fragments, run-ons, and unnecessary shifts.

1. Many great Americans had little or no formal education, among these are political leaders, writers, artists, scientists, and business executives.

   _____

   _____

2. Eleanor Roosevelt had little formal education. Susan B. Anthony the equivalent of a high school education.

   _____

   _____

3. When Abraham Lincoln was a young man, he was working in a general store. At the same time studied books on law.

   _____

   _____

4. Although Carl Sandburg left school when he was thirteen years old. He later went on to Lombard College after serving in the army during the Spanish-American War.

   _____

   _____

5. Booker T. Washington walked five hundred miles to enroll himself for classes at Hampton Institute, later, he founded Tuskegee Institute.

   _____

   _____

SENTENCES

Chapter 9, Worksheet 12, continued

Exercise D: Revising   On the lines provided, revise the following paragraph to vary the sentence beginnings and sentence structure.

The temperature-humidity index is important. It is abbreviated as *THI*. It indicates comfort or discomfort. It has a scale. The scale is based on the inter-action between relative humidity and temperature. THI readings vary. You can have a reading of ten. At ten, few people will feel uncomfortable. You can have a reading of seventy-five. At seventy-five, most people will feel uncomfortable.

_____

_____

_____

_____

_____

_____

_____

_____

Exercise E: Revising   On the lines provided, revise the following sentences to eliminate wordiness.

1. During Saturday morning cartoons, children are exposed to too much televised violence on television. _____

    _____

    _____

2. By the age of sixteen, the average television watcher will have already seen and witnessed about eighteen thousand televised murders. _____

    _____

    _____

3. On the screen are acts of violence; machine guns, bombs, and other weapons that shoot and kill are common and often seen on television. _____

    _____

    _____

4. This issue is one that has been a growing concern to many people who think about this important issue. _____

    _____

    _____

Name _____ Date _____ Class _____

Combining by Inserting Single-Word Modifiers and Prepositional Phrases

Combine related sentences by taking a key word or phrase from one sentence and inserting it into another sentence.

> ORIGINAL: The young man answered the reporter. The young man's answer was confident.
>
> COMBINED: **Confidently,** the young man answered the reporter.

Sometimes you can take a word from one sentence and insert it directly into another sentence as a modifier. Other times you will need to change the word into an adjective or adverb before you can insert it.

> ORIGINAL: A dusty road stretched before us. The road was endless.
>
> COMBINED: A dusty road stretched **endlessly** before us.
>
> *or*
>
> An **endless,** dusty road stretched before us.

Exercise   On the lines provided, combine each group of short, related sentences by inserting adjectives, adverbs, or prepositional phrases into the first sentence. You may change the forms of some words before you insert them. Add commas if necessary.

> EXAMPLE: 1. The Iroquois moved to the Northeast. They moved in the thirteenth century. They left the Mississippi region.
>
> *In the thirteenth century, the Iroquois moved from the Mississippi region to the Northeast.*

1. The Iroquois formed a confederation. The confederation was powerful. The Iroquois formed the confederation in the Northeast. _____

   _____

2. A central council of the confederation made decisions. The council made decisions unanimously. _____

   _____

3. Women nominated delegates. These women were from the confederation. They nominated delegates to the central council. _____

   _____

4. The Iroquois developed trade routes. The trade routes were extensive. The trade routes were along waterways and trails. _____

   _____

5. Hunting was an important element. It was an element in Iroquois society. It was always an important element. _____

   _____

SENTENCES

Name _____ Date _____ Class _____

Combining by Inserting Participial Phrases

A **participial phrase** contains a participle and words related to it. It acts as an adjective.

> EXAMPLE: **Thrusting a burning torch into the cave,** the archaeologists gasped in unison, **surprised at their find.**

Sometimes you can take a participial phrase from one sentence and insert it directly into another sentence. Other times you will need to change a verb into a participle before you can insert the idea into another sentence.

> ORIGINAL: Karen sat at her desk. She was writing a letter.
>
> COMBINED: Karen sat **writing a letter** at her desk.
>
> ORIGINAL: The lake froze solid during the bitter blizzard. The lake became impossible to navigate by canoe.
>
> COMBINED: **Frozen solid during the bitter blizzard,** the lake became impossible to navigate by canoe.

Be sure to place a participial phrase close to the noun or pronoun you want to modify. Otherwise, your sentence may express a meaning you did not intend.

> MISPLACED: Holding an umbrella, the small dog barked at the woman.
>
> IMPROVED: The small dog barked at the woman **holding an umbrella.**

Exercise   On the lines provided, combine each sentence pair below. First, reduce the second sentence to a participial phrase. Then, insert the phrase into the first sentence.

> EXAMPLE: 1. Recycling helps reduce pollution. Recycling transforms useless trash into new materials.
>
> *Transforming useless trash into new materials, recycling helps reduce pollution.*

1. Waste paper becomes wet, soft pulp. A container called a pulper processes it into pulp.

   _____

2. Next, a spinning cylinder helps clean the pulp. The cylinder removes paper clips, staples, and other trash. _____

   _____

3. A water removal machine further processes the pulp. It squeezes out chemicals, ink, and other liquids. _____

   _____

4. The pulp forms a thick substance. It becomes thick as it is mixed with clean water.

   _____

5. When dry, the material forms clean, white sheets of paper. It dries as it is rolled in layers.

   _____

Name _____ Date _____ Class _____

Combining by Inserting Appositive Phrases

An **appositive phrase** consists of an appositive and its modifiers. An appositive phrase identifies or explains a noun or pronoun in a sentence.

    A greyhound, **a sleek dog with an intelligent appearance,** met us at the door.

Sometimes you can combine two sentences by placing one of the ideas in an appositive phrase.

TWO SENTENCES: This chemical is an ingredient in the solution used for developing film. The chemical can irritate the breathing passages.

ONE SENTENCE: This chemical, **an ingredient in the solution used for developing film,** can irritate the breathing passages.

or

A possible irritant to the breathing passages, this chemical is an ingredient in the solution used for developing film.

NOTE: An appositive phrase should be placed directly before or after the noun or pronoun it modifies. An appositive phrase should be set off by a comma or commas.

Exercise   On the lines provided, combine each pair of sentences by turning one of the sentences into an appositive phrase.

EXAMPLE: 1. Calligraphy is an elegant form of handwriting. It requires a special pen or brush.
Calligraphy, an elegant form of handwriting, requires a special pen or brush.

1. Calligraphy has been used for over two thousand years to decorate books and paintings. It is an ancient art form. _____

   _____

2. Chinese calligraphy is done with a paint brush. Chinese calligraphy is the oldest form of calligraphy. _____

   _____

3. In the seventh century A.D., Japanese artists learned calligraphy from the Chinese. The Chinese were the first masters of the art. _____

   _____

4. Islamic artists developed Kufic writing. Kufic writing is one of the most graceful styles of calligraphy. _____

   _____

5. In Islamic countries, you can see sentences from the Koran inscribed in beautiful calligraphy on buildings. The Koran is the Islamic holy book. _____

   _____

SENTENCES

Name _____ Date _____ Class _____

Combining by Coordinating Ideas

You can combine sentences that contain equally important words, phrases, or clauses by using coordinating conjunctions (*and, but, for, or, nor, so, yet*) or correlative conjunctions (such as *both . . . and, either . . . or, neither . . . nor*).

ORIGINAL: Suddenly, the jet veered sharply to the right. Then it disappeared into the clouds.

COMBINED: Suddenly, the jet veered sharply to the right **and** then disappeared into the clouds.

ORIGINAL: The defense attorney had known nothing of the startling new evidence. Neither did the prosecutor.

COMBINED: **Neither** the defense attorney **nor** the prosecutor had known about the startling new evidence.

You can also form a compound sentence by linking independent clauses with a semicolon and a conjunctive adverb (such as *however, likewise, subsequently*) or with just a semicolon.

The jury is still out; **consequently,** no verdict is expected today.

Follow all safety procedures; your life depends on it.

Exercise   Combine each of the following pairs of sentences according to the directions given in parentheses.

1. Bernard Malamud has written many short stories. He has also written several novels.

   (Form a compound direct object.) _____

   _____

2. One of author and journalist Norman Mailer's most famous books is *The Naked and the Dead.* Another of his famous books is *The Executioner's Song. (Form a compound predicate nominative.)*

   _____

   _____

3. Allen Ginsberg's poetry celebrates modern life. Allen Ginsberg's poetry criticizes modern life. *(Form a compound verb.)* _____

   _____

4. Alfred Stieglitz was part of the modern art movement. In fact, he helped usher it in. *(Form a compound sentence with a semicolon.)* _____

   _____

5. In his gallery, Stieglitz displayed the work of a young artist named Georgia O'Keeffe. Later, the two were married. *(Form a compound sentence with a conjunctive adverb.)*

   _____

   _____

Name _____ Date _____ Class _____

Combining by Subordinating Ideas

You can combine related sentences by placing one idea in a subordinate clause (an **adjective clause,** an **adverb clause,** or a **noun clause**). An **adjective clause** modifies a noun or pronoun. You can change a sentence into an adjective clause by replacing its subject with *who, whom, whose, which,* or *that.*

> ORIGINAL: The Chickasaw once lived in the Southeast. They traditionally speak Muskogean.
>
> REVISED: The Chickasaw, **who traditionally speak Muskogean,** once lived in the Southeast.

An **adverb clause** modifies a verb, an adjective, or another adverb in the main clause. To make a sentence into an adverb clause, add a subordinating conjunction such as *although, after, because, if, when, where,* or *while.*

> ORIGINAL: They lived in the Southeast. They were forced to leave.
>
> REVISED: They lived in the Southeast **until they were forced to leave.**

A **noun clause** is a subordinate clause used as a noun. A noun clause often begins with a word such as *that, how, what, whatever, who,* or *whoever.* You may also have to delete or move some words.

> ORIGINAL: In 1837, the U.S. government moved the Chickasaw to a new land. That land is now Oklahoma.
>
> REVISED: In 1837, the U.S. government moved the Chickasaw to **what is now Oklahoma.**

Exercise For each of the following items, turn one sentence into the type of subordinate clause indicated in parentheses. Then insert the subordinate clause into the other sentence.

1. The Chickasaw caught fish in an interesting way. It involved poison. *(adjective clause)*

   _____

2. They threw a mild poison into a lake or pond. The poison was made out of walnut bark. *(adjective clause)*

   _____

   _____

3. The poison took effect. The Chickasaw would spear the fish. *(adverb clause)*

   _____

4. The Chickasaw built pole-frame structures out of materials from the forest. My grandfather showed me how they did this. *(noun clause)* _____

   _____

SENTENCES

Chapter 10: Sentence Combining

WORKSHEET 6   *Combining Sentences*

You can combine the words and ideas in separate sentences in several ways: by inserting single-word modifiers; by inserting prepositional, participial, or appositive phrases; by coordinating ideas; and by subordinating ideas.

Exercise   Using all the sentence-combining skills you have learned, revise the following paragraph for style. Use your judgment about which sentences to combine and how to combine them. Don't change the meaning of the original paragraph.

     Mildred ("Babe") Didrikson Zaharias was born in Beaumont, Texas, around 1911. She was considered one of the finest track-and-field performers of all time. Babe gained national attention in 1930. She competed in a track-and-field meet in Dallas. She won two events. She broke the world record in a third event. The event was the long jump. Babe competed in the Olympic games in 1932. She entered the high jump, the long jump, and the hurdles. She set records in all of these events. They were world records. Only two of these records were made official. Babe's high-jump performance was disqualified. It was disqualified over a technicality. Babe was a champion in women's track and field for more than a decade. She was a world champion in track and field. Babe later became a world champion golfer.

_____

_____

_____

_____

_____

_____

_____

_____

_____

_____

_____

_____

_____

_____

_____

_____

_____

Name _____ Date _____ Class _____

WORKSHEET 7   *Review*

Exercise A   Each of the following items consists of two short, choppy sentences. Combine the sentences as directed.

EXAMPLE: 1. Baltimore is a city rich in history. With the development of such facilities as the National Aquarium and Harborplace, Baltimore has become a dynamic, modern metropolis. (Combine into one sentence, using an *appositive*.)

With the development of such facilities as the National Aquarium and Harborplace, Baltimore, a city rich in history, has become a dynamic, modern metropolis.

1. Fort McHenry lies just across the harbor. Fort McHenry is where Francis Scott Key saw "the star-spangled banner" waving. (Combine into one sentence, using the word *where*.)

   _____

2. The Smithsonian Institution now houses the original fifteen-star flag. This flag was made in Baltimore by Mary Young Pickersgill. (Combine into one sentence, using the word *which*.)

   _____

3. The Baltimore and Ohio Railroad was completed in 1827. Baltimore grew rapidly.

   (Combine into one sentence, beginning with *After*.) _____

   _____

4. The city today is a financial, industrial, and shipping center. The city expanded steadily.

   (Combine into one sentence, beginning with a *participial phrase*.) _____

   _____

5. Visitors should also recognize another fact. Baltimore has a literary tradition. (Combine

   into one sentence, using the word *that*.) _____

   _____

Exercise B   Combine each of the following items. You may have to add, delete, or change some words in the sentences. Add punctuation where necessary. Cross out any unnecessary words, and write your changes above the line.

EXAMPLE: 1. The Peale Museum ^which^ opened in 1814. ~~It~~ is one of the nation's oldest museum buildings.

1. Work on Baltimore's Washington Monument began in 1815. It ranks as the first

   major memorial to George Washington.

2. In the harbor are three historic ships. Baltimoreans point to them with pride.

3. The U.S.S. *Constellation* is anchored next to a working replica of a Baltimore clipper. The *Constellation* is the world's oldest ship still afloat.

4. Monument Street is the site of the first "urban homesteading." This homesteading resulted in the restoration of many fine homes.

5. The journalist H. L. Mencken believed that Baltimore was an especially civilized city. He praised it glowingly.

Exercise C   Revise the following paragraph for style. Using subordinate clauses, appositives, and any other means you wish, combine the ideas in the passage into smooth sentences. Write your improved version on the lines provided or on a separate sheet of paper.

    The Sahara is a formidable desert. It is a barren expanse of sand. It is dotted here and there with sunbaked oases. One of the early oases was Taghaza. It was called "the salt city." Its houses and mosques were built of blocks of salt. The salt-block buildings were roofed with camel skins. Taghaza was an unattractive village. Its mines provided traders in the Mali kingdom with salt. Salt was a commodity that was worth its weight in gold.

_____

_____

_____

_____

_____

_____

_____

_____

_____

_____

_____

_____

_____

_____

_____

_____

_____

Chapter 11: Capitalization

First Words

Capitalize the first word in every sentence.

> **G**leefully, the boy tore into his birthday presents.

Capitalize the first word of a sentence following a colon.

> The press release closed with the following plea: **W**e urge anyone with information to contact the local police.

Capitalize the first word of a direct quotation. When quoting from a writer's work, capitalize the first word of the quotation only if the writer has capitalized it.

> Before the pilot started his engines, he shouted, "**S**tand clear."
>
> What are the "slings and arrows of outrageous fortune" to which Hamlet refers?

Traditionally, the first word of a line of poetry is capitalized.

> **M**yself when young did eagerly frequent
> **D**octor and Saint, and heard great argument . . . .
>   Omar Khayyám, *Rubáiyát*

Capitalize the first word of a statement or a question inserted in a sentence without quotation marks.

> What I meant to say was, **P**lease accept my apology.

Capitalize the first word of a resolution following the word *Resolved*.

> Resolved: **T**hat the school term be extended to twelve months.

Exercise   For the following sentences, strike through each letter that is not capitalized correctly and write the correct form above it.

> EXAMPLE: 1. H̶asn't anyone found the cat's kittens yet?

1. He closed his speech with the following words: come and join us in the trash cleanup.

2. I'm having trouble with the first line of my poem, "on a short, stout bump of a hill."

3. Resolved: that meetings will be held on the first Tuesday of each month.

4. Their reply began, "thank you for your most gracious invitation."

5. what everyone wanted to know was, who would speak out against the injustice?

6. There was no explanation: nobody could understand why he was absent.

7. Do you know the Elizabeth Barrett Browning poem that begins "how do I love thee. . . ."?

8. he said he was "Sorry" for the intrusion.

9. Dolores's expression said, why is this happening?

10. My mother asked, "who used the bathroom last?"

MECHANICS

Chapter 11: Capitalization

WORSHEET 2 *Conventional Situations, the Pronoun I, and the Interjection O*

Capitalize the first word in the salutation and the closing of a letter.

Dear Mr. Paul,   **Dear Jemma,**   **Yours truly,**   **Sincerely,**

Capitalize the Roman numerals and letters in an outline as well as the first word in each heading and subheading.

> **I. Computer acquisition**
> **A. Hardware**
> **1. Central processing unit**
> **2. Peripherals**
> **B. Software**

Capitalize the interjection *O* and the pronoun *I*. The interjection *O* is usually used only for invocations and is followed by the name of the person or thing being addressed. Don't confuse it with the common interjection *oh*, which is capitalized only when it appears at the beginning of a sentence and which is always followed by punctuation.

Exercise A   In each of the following sentences, strike through each letter that is not capitalized correctly and write the correct form above it.

> EXAMPLE: 1. My classmate Emilio and *I* spent the entire afternoon doing research for our report.

1. The idea of a pencil with an eraser attached was conceived by Hyman I. Lipman in 1935, and Oh, what a good idea that was.

2. Well, i think i'll need, Oh, about thirty chairs for the party.

3. Marco read the last line of the poem aloud: "Blow mighty wind, o breath of the sky!"

4. My dear, of course the bank where i have my checking account is federally insured.

5. Change the heading to read "II. deciduous trees."

Exercise B: Proofreading   The following letter has five errors in capitalization. Correct each error.

dear Tom,

thank you for sending me a copy of your outline. Let me direct your attention to "B. Gas energy" under "IV. alternatives." This section seems incomplete; therefore, i am sending you an update of our policies. The package should arrive in, Oh, about a week. I look forward to reading your finished article.

Sincerely,

Juan Ramirez

Name _____ Date _____ Class _____

Proper Nouns and Adjectives: People, Places, Things

Capitalize proper nouns and proper adjectives. A **common noun** is a general name for a person, a place, a thing, or an idea. Common nouns are capitalized only if they begin a sentence, a direct quotation, or in most cases, a line of poetry. Common nouns are also capitalized if they are part of a title. A **proper noun** names a particular person, place, thing, or idea. **Proper adjectives** are formed from proper nouns.

COMMON NOUN:	mountain	country	writer
PROPER NOUN:	Andes	Peru	Franz Kafka
PROPER ADJECTIVE:	Andean	Peruvian	Kafkaesque

In proper nouns made up of two or more words, do not capitalize articles, prepositions of fewer than five letters, the word *to* in an infinitive, or coordinating conjunctions.

the Maharani of Indore   His Grace the Duke of Devonshire

Capitalize the given names of persons and animals. Some names contain more than one capital letter. Usage varies in the capitalization of *van, von, du, de la,* and other parts of many multiword names. Always verify the spelling of a name.

Jessye Norman   Rin Tin Tin   Vincent van Gogh   Diane Di Prima

Abbreviations such as *Ms., Mr., Dr.,* and *Gen.* should always be capitalized. Capitalize the abbreviations *Jr.* and *Sr.* following a name, and set them off with commas. Also capitalize Roman numerals (*I, III,* etc.) but do *not* set them off with commas. Capitalize descriptive names and nicknames.

Brig. Gen. Sue Turner   Sammy Davis, Jr.   Douglas Wylie III

Exercise   The following words and phrases are not capitalized correctly. Write the words and phrases correctly on the lines provided.

1. dr. kanawha _____

2. Mr. and mrs. Chin _____

3. benin civilization _____

4. eudora welty _____

5. african sculpture _____

6. Elizabeth i _____

7. Martin Luther King, jr. _____

8. Felix The Cat _____

9. Andrew "old hickory" Jackson _____

10. Catherine the great _____

Name _____ Date _____ Class _____

Proper Nouns and Adjectives: Geographical Names

Capitalize geographical names. However, words such as *north, western,* and *southeast* are not capitalized when they indicate direction.

West Indies   west of the Pecos   Southern California   southern Haig County

The abbreviations of names of states are always capitalized. In addresses, abbreviations such as *St., Ave., Dr.,* and *Blvd.* are capitalized. Words such as *city, street,* and *park* are capitalized only when they are part of a name. In general, words such as *city, state,* and *county* are not capitalized. The second word in a hyphenated number begins with a small letter.

Forty-second St., New York City, N.Y.   the first street north of the park

Exercise   Most of the following words and phrases are not capitalized correctly. Circle each capital letter that should be lowercase (small), and circle each lowercase letter that should be capitalized. If the item is correct, make no revision.

EXAMPLE: 1. the Ⓝorthern tip of Ⓜaine

1. mojave desert
2. high in the andes mountains
3. south africa
4. the Nazca desert
5. 502 west hunter street
6. the city north of Bucyrus, Ohio
7. a tropical Island
8. cape Horn
9. hawaii volcanoes national park
10. a north american actor

11. Chesapeake bay
12. skiing on the lake
13. new york's tourists
14. hendry county
15. Mississippi river
16. Pikes peak
17. gulf of tonkin
18. south of Twenty-Second street
19. Interstate 4
20. San Diego

Name _____ Date _____ Class _____

Proper Nouns and Adjectives: Organizations, Buildings, etc.

MECHANICS

Capitalize the names of organizations, teams, business firms, institutions, buildings and other architectural structures, and government bodies.

    Boys Choir of Harlem   Jackson and Sons Bicycle Shop   Department of Justice

Do not capitalize words such as *democratic, republican,* and *socialist* when they refer to principles or forms of government. Capitalize such words only when they refer to a specific political party. The word *party* in the name of a political party may or may not be capitalized. Do not capitalize words such as *building, hospital, theater, high school, university,* and *post office* unless they are part of a proper noun.

    Republican candidate   Golden Gate Bridge   Vernon High School
    democratic ideals   a covered bridge   my high school

Capitalize the names of historical events and periods, special events, holidays and other calendar items, and time zones. Do not capitalize the name of a season unless the season is being personified or unless it is part of a proper noun.

    Reconstruction   the Winter Festival   Bronze Age   Father's Day

Exercise Most of the following words and phrases are not capitalized correctly. Circle each capital letter that should be lowercase (small), and circle each lowercase letter that should be capitalized. If the item is correct, make no revision.

    EXAMPLE: 1. the (w)ar of 1812

1. the bureau of american ethnology
2. the Chess Club
3. Pittsburgh steelers
4. veterans day
5. mission san juan capistrano
6. fourth of july
7. spring cleaning
8. Democratic Convention
9. Spelman college
10. tuesday, march 13
11. Luella's auto paint & body
12. great wall of China
13. special olympics
14. a socialist system of government
15. the communist party
16. cuban revolution
17. the red cross
18. the Heidelberg string quartet
19. the museum of the american indian
20. Eastside hospital

Chapter 11: Capitalization

Proper Nouns and Adjectives: Nationalities, etc.

Capitalize the names of nationalities, races, and peoples.

    South African   Arab   Native American   Irish

Capitalize the brand names of commercial products. A noun that follows a brand name is not capitalized. Capitalize the names of ships, trains, aircraft, spacecraft, monuments, awards, planets, and any other particular places, things, or events. Do not capitalize the words *sun* and *moon*. Do not capitalize the word *earth* unless it is used along with the names of other heavenly bodies that are capitalized.

Apple computer	U.S.S. *Saratoga*	Washington Monument
Pluto	National Merit Scholarship	Yellow Brick Road

Do not capitalize the names of school subjects, except for languages and course names followed by a number. Do not capitalize class names such as *senior, junior,* and *sophomore* unless they are part of a proper noun. As a rule, nouns identified by a number or letter are capitalized.

physics	a sophomore at Reed High School	Box 1A
History II	Senior Fun Week	Room 13

Exercise   Most of the following words and phrases are not capitalized correctly. Circle each capital letter that should be lowercase (small), and circle each lowercase letter that should be capitalized. If the item is correct, make no revision.

        EXAMPLE: 1. Ⓢpanish 2

1. the world cup
2. spaceflight to mars
3. the louisiana world exposition
4. german class
5. the Vietnam Veterans memorial
6. The distance between Earth and Mars
7. el galindo tortillas
8. What on Earth!
9. asian culture
10. a cadillac convertible
11. medal of honor
12. a bantu tradition
13. chemistry
14. algebra II
15. *glamorous glennis* (aircraft)
16. the senior prom
17. orange blossom special
18. your junior year
19. chinese cuisine
20. the Moon's shadow

Name _____ Date _____ Class _____

Titles of People

Capitalize a title belonging to a particular person when it comes before the person's name. In general, do not capitalize a title used alone or following a name. Some titles, however, are by tradition capitalized. If you are unsure of whether or not to capitalize a title, check in a dictionary.

Mayor Taylor	General Eisenhower	Doctor Patricia Valdez
London's **mayor**	a **general** in the U.S. Army	the new **doctor**

A title is usually capitalized when it is used alone in direct address. Capitalize words showing family relationships when used with a person's name but *not* when preceded by a possessive. A word showing a family relationship is also capitalized when used in place of a person's name, unless it is preceded by a possessive.

Did **Mom** get to meet your **brother**, **Major**?

My **uncle** Marty warmly greeted **Aunt** Mae.

Exercise For each of the following sentences, strike through each letter that is not capitalized correctly and write the correct form above it.

EXAMPLE: 1. Trish's grandfather plays tennis with ~~u~~ncle ~~w~~ill every
Saturday.

1. Last year, aunt joan showed the three retrievers at several dog shows.

2. Your Mom is one of the best reporters for the city paper, according to the paper's editor.

3. Every evening grandma walks two miles with capt. Warnick.

4. My great-grandfather received a card from president Clinton.

5. Speakers will include former secretary of transportation Elizabeth Dole.

6. Do you think the snow caused the accident, lieutenant?

7. Both dad and uncle Gary are looking forward to the canoe race.

8. My cousin Barbara is studying opera with professor Caroline Estes.

9. Charles Curtis, a relative of my Mom's, was vice president under Herbert Hoover.

10. Did you really meet former prime minister Margaret Thatcher?

Chapter 11: Capitalization

Titles of Works

Capitalize the first and last words and all important words in titles of works, including those shown in the list below.

books	musical compositions	TV and radio programs
cartoons	periodicals	speeches
essays	plays	stories
historical documents	poems	works of art

Unimportant words include articles (*a, an, the*), prepositions with fewer than five letters (*of, in, to, for, from, with*), and coordinating conjunctions (*and, but, for, nor, or, so, yet*). The first word of a subtitle is always capitalized. The article *the* is often written before a title but is not capitalized unless it is part of the official title.

Organic Gardening	State of the Union Address
The Weary Blues: A Book of Verse	the *Daily Comet*
WBUR's "Car Talk"	Michelangelo's *David*

Always capitalize the first element in a hyphenated compound used as a title. Capitalize other elements only if they are nouns or proper adjectives or if they have equal force with the first element. Do not capitalize the second element if it is a participle that modifies the first element or if the two elements make up a single word.

"The Cause-and-Effect Essay"   French-American Alliance   Arabic-speaking

Capitalize the names of religions and their followers, holy days and celebrations, holy writings, and specific deities and venerated beings. The words *god* and *goddess* are not capitalized when they refer to the deities of ancient mythology. Pronouns that refer to a deity may or may not be capitalized.

Exercise   On the line provided, rewrite each item, correcting any errors in capitalization.

1. great earth mother, a Native American deity _____

2. a copy of the magna carta _____

3. Willa Cather's novel *o pioneers!* _____

4. *up from slavery* by Booker T. Washington _____

5. Henry Ossawa Tanner's painting *the banjo lesson* _____

6. a shinto shrine _____

7. *American Usage and Style: the Consensus* _____

8. Dia de los Reyes, or the feast of the epiphany _____

9. a statue of the goddess kali _____

10. Channel 61's *the world of bonsai* _____

Name _____ Date _____ Class _____

Review

Exercise A   Most of the items below are not capitalized correctly. Circle each capital letter that should be lowercase (small), and circle each lowercase letter that should be capitalized. If the item is correct, make no correction.

EXAMPLE: 1. "O Captain, my Captain"

1. East of Albuquerque

2. a teacher of History

3. Rideau canal

4. written in latin

5. a navajo song

6. President Ford

7. the treaty of Ghent

8. an Island in Lake Erie

9. Route 10

10. Hansberry's *A Raisin In The Sun*

11. the Polish Ambassador

12. my Cousin Ana

13. Mayfair motor Inn

14. Sepulveda boulevard

15. a Computer company

16. the mountains of Colorado

17. on Columbus day

18. Thirty-Fourth Street

19. Charles Adams, jr.

20. a Siamese Cat

Exercise B: Proofreading   Read each of the following sentences to see if it contains any errors in capitalization. If the sentence does contain errors, correctly write the word or words that are in error on the line provided. Supply capital letters where they are needed.

1. Chicago, located on Lake Michigan, is home to the world's busiest Airport, the Museum of Science and Industry, and the Art Institute of Chicago.

   _____

2. His Grandfather told us what he remembered about the Second World War, including incidents from the battle of the Bulge.

   _____

3. Last Saturday my father and I went to Carbondale to visit southern Illinois University, where my brother is a Sophomore majoring in chemical engineering.

   _____

4. Tom O'Grady, the Treasurer of Flynn & Weber, inc., once worked for the U.S. Department of Commerce as an accountant.

   _____

5. February 15 is Susan B. Anthony day, commemorating the Birthday of the well-known crusader for women's rights.

   _____

Chapter 11, Worksheet 9, continued

Exercise C: Proofreading   In the following paragraphs, strike through each letter that is not correctly capitalized, and change lowercase letters to capitals or capital letters to lowercase as necessary.

EXAMPLE: [1] Among the many unusual scenes that Captain Christopher Columbus witnessed on his arrival in America was that of native Hispaniolans playing games with balls made of latex.

[1] Latex is the white liquid that oozes from plants like the rubber tree, guayule, Milkweed, and dandelion. [2] Latex balls were also used by the mayans. Unlike the ballgames that you may have played with your Brother or Sister, Mayan games were sacred rituals. [3] According to the *Book Of counsel*, an ancient Mayan document, the games reenacted the story of twins who became immortal. [4] Ballgames were so important to the Mayan culture that, along with stately masks of their Gods, Mayan artists rendered statues of ballplayers. Mayan builders erected large stone stadiums for playing. [5] Although columbus did not note his encounters with latex, other explorers did. One explorer recorded the Mayans' fascinating practice of coating their feet with a protective layer of the milky liquid.

[6] Latex does not hold up well in extreme temperatures. It was used in europe only for rubbing out pencil marks (hence the term *rubber*), until Charles Goodyear became fascinated with the substance and declared that the "elastic gum" glorified god. [7] Goodyear's discovery of vulcanization enabled the successful commercial production of rubber and earned him the public admiration of emperor Napoleon III. [8] In the next decades, Brazil increased its rubber production thousands of times over, as Eric R. Wolf points out in *Europe And The People Without History*. [9] Indeed, rubber became such an essential part of our lives that the U.S. army once asked a young Major named Eisenhower to study the matter. [10] Wisely, major Eisenhower advised the military to maintain its own source of this valuable commodity.

Name _____ Date _____ Class _____

Using End Marks in Sentences

A **statement** (or **declarative sentence**) is followed by a period.

Thomas Edison invented the electric light bulb.

A **question** (or **interrogative sentence**) is followed by a question mark. However, do not use a question mark after a declarative sentence containing an indirect question.

Are you familiar with the paintings of Hokusai? [question]

He asked me whether or not I had been to Utah. [declarative sentence]

A polite request is often put in question form even when it isn't actually a question. In that case, the sentence may be followed by either a period or a question mark.

Would you please sign here.   *or*   Would you please sign here?

An **imperative sentence** is followed by either a period or an exclamation point.

MILD COMMAND: Sit down.   STRONG COMMAND: Get out!

An **exclamation** is followed by an exclamation point. An interjection at the beginning of a sentence is usually followed by a comma but may be followed by an exclamation point.

Hey, watch out for snakes!   Hey! Watch out for that snake!

A question mark or an exclamation point should be placed inside closing quotation marks when the quotation itself is a question or an exclamation. Otherwise, these punctuation marks belong *outside* the quotation marks.

Then Margarita asked, "What do you want?" [The quotation is a question.]

Did you say, "Never mind"? [The sentence as a whole is a question.]

Exercise For each of the following sentences, provide an appropriate end mark. Add closing quotation marks if necessary.

EXAMPLE: 1. The audience cried, "Bravo*!*"

1. The child shouted anxiously, "Wait for me

2. Karin asked, "Do you know anyone who has hiked the Appalachian Trail

3. Why would you say, "I give up

4. Mother shouted to the toddler, "Don't touch the stove

5. Wasn't the article titled "Geological Wonders of the East

6. The bus driver commanded, "Everyone, take your seats

7. The host said suavely, "Would you follow me, please

8. You mean he actually said, "No homework tonight, class

9. Janet asked whether or not I was going to band practice

10. Terene won't be able to attend

Name _____ Date _____ Class _____

 **WORKSHEET 2** *Other Uses of the Period*

An abbreviation is usually followed by a period.

Ms. Irene B. Dobbs   Oak St.   8:00 A.M. (*or* a.m.)   Airco Corp.   510 B.C.

When an abbreviation that ends with a period is the last word in a statement, do not add another period as an end mark. *Do* add a question mark or an exclamation point if one is needed.

Gautama Buddha died around 463 B.C.   Did they arrive at 5 A.M.?

Some common abbreviations, such as two-letter state codes, are written without periods.

AZ   NJ   FBI   ft   psi   TV

Note that state codes are used only when the ZIP Code is included.

Austin, TX 78748   *but*   Santa Barbara, Calif.

Each letter or number in an outline or a list is followed by a period.

Camping gear   Care of Tropical Fish
1. Tent   I. Equipment
2. Sleeping bag   A. Aquarium
3. First-aid kit   B. Filter
4. Food   II. Feeding

Exercise   Each of the following sentences contains one or more errors in the use of periods. Delete or insert periods as needed.

EXAMPLE: 1. Mr. Lively's address is 12 Dimick St, Boston, M⌃A⌃ 02134.

1. They said they would be here by 6 P.M..

2. We'll need another 10 ft. of plywood for the floor in the attic

3. Please meet John A Venge at 7:30 PM in my office, at 125 Sunnyside Dr.

4. Where on Fifth Avenue is the New York office of Viramax, Inc?

5. Scholars believe that the most complete version of the *Epic of Gilgamesh* was written around 1300 BC.

6. Our new address will be Acme, Inc, at 512 East Hampton Dr., New York, N.Y. 10017.

7. Dr Butler will see you now, Ms Parkes.

8. You can avoid the problem with a transition if you change your outline to read "B The Iron Horse" and eliminate "B Some important inventions."

9. The air pressure gauge reads 25.5 p.s.i.

10. My new address is as follows: 7106 El Paso Blvd, Fort Stockton, Tex; please send my mail there.

Chapter 12: Punctuation

 **WORKSHEET 3** *Commas to Separate Items*

MECHANICS

Use commas to separate items in a series. When *and, or,* or *nor* joins the last two items in a series, you may omit the comma before the conjunction if the comma isn't needed to make the meaning clear.

CLEAR: The pizza was hot, spicy and delicious.

UNCLEAR: Pete, Abdul and Luisa are waiting. [Is Pete waiting, or is he being addressed?]

CLEAR: Pete, Abdul, and Luisa are waiting.

If all the items in a series are linked by *and, or,* or *nor,* do not use commas to separate them.

Denmark **and** France **and** England have all vetoed the proposal.

Do not place a comma before the first item in a series.

INCORRECT: She has written books about, Mozart, Bach, and Beethoven.

CORRECT: She has written books about Mozart, Bach, and Beethoven.

Short independent clauses may be separated by commas.

The flowers bloomed, the birds sang, and children came outside to play.

Use a comma to separate two or more adjectives preceding a noun. When the last adjective before the noun is thought of as part of the noun, as in the compound noun *red pine,* the comma before the adjective is omitted. If one word in a series modifies the word following it, do not separate them with a comma.

Roxanne's apartment building has **long, narrow halls.**

I'd like a house with a **big front yard.** [*Front* is part of a compound noun.]

Where did I put my **light blue scarf**? [*Light* modifies *blue.*]

Exercise: Proofreading For each of the following sentences, add or delete commas as necessary.

1. Marcelo threw a long wobbly pass to the halfback, who caught it.

2. The students live in dorms sorority houses fraternity houses or apartments.

3. Eula Vikki or Marlene could answer the door.

4. Houses along the coast were battered by, high winds heavy rains and hail.

5. My favorite natural science museum has a huge exciting exhibit on fossils.

6. I buy only environmentally safe products and healthful, organic foods.

7. Dad mows I rake and Henry bags the clippings.

8. The building was made of light, gray granite.

9. Go north two blocks turn right and you'll be able to see the building.

10. We watched, dump trucks, cement mixers, and a roller, pull into the vacant lot.

Name _____ Date _____ Class _____

 **WORKSHEET 4** *Commas to Join Clauses*

Use a comma before *and, but, or, nor, for, so,* and *yet* when they join independent clauses.

    The speaker was late, so the meeting didn't start until nine o'clock.

    Yesterday was hot and humid, but today the weather is milder.

Don't confuse a compound sentence with a simple sentence that has a compound verb. Compound verbs, compound subjects, and compound objects are not separated by commas.

    COMPOUND SENTENCE: We enjoyed the music, and we found the lyrics very clever.

    COMPOUND VERB: We enjoyed the music and found the lyrics very clever.

    COMPOUND SUBJECT: The words and the music blended perfectly.

    COMPOUND OBJECT: One musician wrote both the words and the music.

Exercise A: Proofreading   Add commas as needed to the following sentences. If a sentence is punctuated correctly, write *C* on the line provided.

_____ 1. We got up late but we still had time for a hearty breakfast.

_____ 2. Have you finished the test or do you need a few more minutes?

_____ 3. Wendel will look for Rafael and Susan will try to find Eric.

_____ 4. My sister got her bachelor's degree at Tulane and her master's at Purdue.

_____ 5. I had only an hour before my bus left so I just threw my clothes into a bag.

Exercise B: Revising   On the line provided, rewrite each pair of sentences as a compound sentence or as a simple sentence with a compound subject, verb, or object. Add conjunctions and commas as needed.

    EXAMPLE: 1. I washed the floor. I didn't wash the windows.
           I washed the floor, but I didn't wash the windows.

1. I wanted to rent the new Wynona Ryder movie. It wasn't available.

_____

2. The Salk vaccine prevents polio. It should be given to all children.

_____

3. I might go to the basketball game. I might stay home and finish my report.

_____

4. I'll meet you at the concert. Don't worry if I'm late.

_____

5. Jamont called Mia. Mia passed the news to Chow.

_____

Name _____ Date _____ Class _____

 **WORKSHEET 5**

Commas with Nonessential Elements

MECHANICS

Use commas to set off nonessential clauses and nonessential participial phrases. A **nonessential** (or **nonrestrictive**) clause or participial phrase is one containing information that isn't needed to understand the main idea of the sentence.

> NONESSENTIAL CLAUSE: This postcard is from Will, **who lives in Ohio.**
>
> NONESSENTIAL PHRASE: Melvin, **convinced of the answer,** raised his hand.

If a nonessential element is removed from a sentence, the main idea of the sentence remains clear.

> This postcard is from Will.   Melvin raised his hand.

In contrast, an **essential** (or **restrictive**) clause or phrase is one that can't be left out without changing the meaning of the sentence. Essential clauses and phrases are *not* set off by commas.

> ESSENTIAL CLAUSE: All poets **whose works are in this book** are women.
>
> ESSENTIAL PHRASE: Actors **trying out for the play** must be good singers.

The meaning of each of these sentences changes if the essential element is removed.

> All poets are women.   Actors must be good singers.

Exercise   On the line before each sentence, write *N* if the italicized clause or phrase is nonessential. Write *E* if it is essential. Then add commas as needed.

> EXAMPLE: ___N___ 1. Joe, *having forgotten the man's name,* stalled for time.

_____ 1. Only people *who like anchovies and garlic* will enjoy this pizza.

_____ 2. Any car *carrying more than two passengers* is allowed in the express lane.

_____ 3. Uncle Ramón *who is my mother's brother* just bought a bowling alley.

_____ 4. All people *taking this course* must be licensed veterinarians.

_____ 5. The poet *whom I admire the most* is Maya Angelou.

_____ 6. Natalie Curtis *always interested in the music of Native Americans* was an early recorder of their songs.

_____ 7. Margaret Mead *who was a disciple of Ruth Benedict* was a noted anthropologist.

_____ 8. The birds *soaring overhead* are hawks.

_____ 9. Pablo Casals *one of the world's great cellists* founded the annual musical festival in Puerto Rico.

_____10. Parvis *who is planning to play in the golf tournament* is reading the NCAA rules.

Name _____ Date _____ Class _____

WORSHEET 6

Commas with Introductory Elements

Use commas after one-word adverbs such as *first, yes,* and *no* or after any mild exclamation such as *well* or *why* at the beginning of a sentence.

> **No,** I don't know how to skate.   **Okay,** I'll teach you.   **Why,** thank you.

Use a comma after an introductory **participial phrase** or a series of introductory **prepositional phrases**. A single prepositional phrase does not usually require a comma.

> PARTICIPIAL PHRASE: **Putting on her skates,** she joined us on the ice.
>
> PREPOSITIONAL PHRASES: **In the corner of the far end of the rink,** she fell.
>
> SINGLE PREPOSITIONAL PHRASE: **After some practice** she felt more confident.

Use a comma after an **adverb clause** at the beginning of a sentence or before any independent clause in the sentence.

> **When Hank's cousin offered us a ride,** we were grateful.
>
> Dog kennels can be expensive; **if you want me to,** I'll take care of Peaches over the winter vacation.

Exercise A: Proofreading   Add commas where they are necessary in each of the following sentences. Some sentences may not require any insertions.

1. Entering the store we were greeted by huge crowds.

2. In the beginning of *Raiders of the Lost Ark* Indy outruns a rolling boulder.

3. Rushing to answer the phone Lana tripped over an electric cord.

4. On a clear day you can see the tip of Mt. Monadnock from this field.

5. Nearly blinded by the whirling snow the climbers sought shelter.

6. While we were attending the concert we ran into Maribeth and Tom.

7. Yes I want to compete in the tournament; when you schedule it give me a call.

8. In a church in the center of a small town in Mexico my parents were married.

9. Before we entered the exhibition we had to check our packages and cameras.

10. Before my next song I'd like to say a few words about the lyricist, Ira Gershwin.

Exercise B   On the line following each of these introductory elements, add words and punctuation marks to form complete sentences.

1. In April _____

2. Well _____

3. Waiting in line for tickets _____

4. Under the table in the library _____

5. When we asked him for directions _____

Name _____ Date _____ Class _____

Commas with Elements That Interrupt

Use commas to set off elements that interrupt a sentence. For instance, appositives and appositive phrases are usually set off by commas. An **appositive** is a noun or pronoun placed beside another noun or pronoun to identify or explain it. An **appositive phrase** consists of an appositive and its modifiers.

Paul Szep, **the political cartoonist,** has won several Pulitzer Prizes.

Sometimes an appositive is so closely related to the word or words near it that it should not be set off by commas. Such an appositive is called a **restrictive appositive**.

The actor **Joanne Woodward** is married to Paul Newman.

Words used in direct address are set off by commas.

Tanya, would you like more soup?   Thank you, **Jon.**

Compound comparisons are set off by commas.

My mother's spaghetti is as good as, **if not better than,** that fancy restaurant's.

Parenthetical expressions are set off by commas. **Parenthetical expressions** are remarks that add incidental information or that relate ideas to each other.

I need to buy, **among other things,** a rake and a bucket.

Therefore, I'm going to the hardware store today.

It's Jay's Hardware, **not Star Hardware,** that's having the big sale.

Exercise: Proofreading   Add commas as necessary to the following sentences. Some sentences may not need any insertions.

1. Maine the largest of the New England states has a beautiful coastline.

2. Benjamin Franklin by the way also invented bifocal lenses.

3. Waneta would you like to play tennis or squash?

4. Kim has decided to major in nursing not business.

5. Lake Tanganyika is I believe the world's longest freshwater lake.

6. Eva Jessye was choral director for *Porgy and Bess* a popular American folk opera.

7. One of my cousins Frank has signed up for a summer program at Ohio State.

8. Did you know Larry that lawrencium is the name of a chemical element?

9. A traditional storyteller can be as gripping as if not more gripping than a TV show.

10. The play was mediocre; we did however enjoy the music and choreography.

Chapter 12: Punctuation

 **WORKSHEET 8** *Commas Used for Clarity*

Use a comma between words or phrases that might otherwise confuse a reader. For instance, use a comma after an introductory adverb that might be confused with a preposition.

> Below, the salmon strained against the cold currents of the river. [comma needed to prevent reading *below the salmon*]

Use a comma between a verbal and a noun that follows it if there is any possibility of misreading.

> On waking, Peter smelled pancakes cooking. [comma needed to prevent reading *on waking Peter*]

Use a comma in an **elliptical construction** that replaces an independent clause. (Reminder: An elliptical construction is a word group from which one or more words have been left out.)

> Its design was impeccable; its performance, flawless. [The construction *its performance, flawless* takes the place of the independent clause *its performance was flawless*. The comma takes the place of *was*.]

Use a comma to separate most words that are repeated. However, do not use a comma between repeated words that are part of a verb phrase.

> COMMA: The only clothes we had, had been soaked.
>
> NO COMMA: By late afternoon, we had had dozens of new customers.

Exercise Each of the following sentences needs a comma for clarity. Add commas where they are needed.

> EXAMPLE: 1. Before visiting‸Hugo had been in class.

1. Everything that is is composed of matter and energy.

2. After painting Shelley is going to sell the house.

3. Now, the meetings are attended by more than a hundred people; before they had had only a few participants.

4. Before meeting Julie and the president had talked on the telephone.

5. My hair is red; my eyes brown.

6. Whoever they are are they friendly?

7. Summer having ended Emil's thoughts turned to school.

8. Beyond the mountains reached to the sky.

9. Jerry's pitching is good; his batting outstanding.

10. Outside the neighborhood was quiet.

Name _____ Date _____ Class _____

Conventional Uses of Commas

MECHANICS

Use commas to separate items in dates and addresses.

    On Saturday, March 28, 1992, Blake returned to West Chester.

    Send the check to Valerie at 26 Simpson Road, Spring, TX 77034.

In dates, if the day is given before the month or only the month and year are given, no comma is used.

    Mom was born on 24 December 1947. She came to America in June 1952.

Use a comma after the salutation of a friendly letter and after the closing of any letter.

    Dear Nikki,   Yours truly,

Use a comma after a personal name followed by an abbreviation such as *Jr., Sr., R.N.,* or *M.D.* or after a business name followed by an abbreviation such as *Ltd.* or *Inc.* Used within a sentence, such abbreviations are followed by a comma as well.

    Mr. William P. Mann, Jr., strode up to the platform and began to speak.

Use a comma in numbers of more than three digits. Place the comma between groups of three digits, counting from the left of the decimal. However, do not use commas in ZIP Codes (10022), telephone numbers, house numbers, and four-digit years (1850).

    $63,079.32   8,956 yards   23,000,000 light years

Exercise A   Add commas as necessary to the following sentences. Some sentences may not require any insertions.

1. On October 3, 1990, East Germany united with West Germany.

2. Teresa Catawba M.D. will be our guest speaker on Tuesday July 12 1998.

3. My friend Guillermo Savilla Rodrigues Jr. was born on 1 June 1976.

4. Please forward my mail to 3001 Clermont Street Haymarket VA 22069.

5. Wordsmith Inc. has an office on Oak Street in Downingtown.

Exercise B: Proofreading   In the following personal letter, four commas are missing, and one of the existing commas should be removed. Correct each error.

Dear Lorraine

    As you know, on Saturday June 18 I will be moving to Lancaster,

Pennsylvania. My new address will be 1,407 Tulane Avenue, Lancaster PA

17061. Please keep in touch.

                Sincerely,

                Geraldine Washington

Chapter 12: Punctuation

WORKSHEET 10 *Semicolons*

Use a **semicolon** between independent clauses that are closely related in thought and are not joined by *and, but, for, nor, or, so,* or *yet.*

I was happy about the trip; California has always appealed to me.

Do not join independent clauses unless there is a close relationship between the main ideas.

NONSTANDARD: The weather is mild today; let's go camping this summer.

STANDARD: The weather is mild today. Let's go camping this summer.

Use a semicolon between independent clauses joined by a transitional expression or a conjunctive adverb. Use a comma after the transitional expression or conjunctive adverb.

TRANSITIONAL EXPRESSION: Al's a great runner; **in fact,** he's unbeatable.

CONJUNCTIVE ADVERB: I was tired; **therefore,** I stopped to rest.

A semicolon (rather than a comma) may be needed to separate independent clauses joined by a coordinating conjunction when there are commas within the clauses.

I've visited Texas, Mexico, New Mexico, and Arizona; and I hope to see Utah.

Use a semicolon between items in a series if the items contain commas.

My favorite poems include "Fire and Ice," by Robert Frost; "Mother to Son," by Langston Hughes; and "Lament," by Edna St. Vincent Millay.

Exercise A Replace commas below with semicolons where necessary.

1. One side, ours, was willing to negotiate, however, the other side refused.

2. Lenise was born in Ames, Iowa, Jack in Waco, Texas, and Stella in Cancún, Mexico.

3. Please, Patrice, adjust the dial carefully, the mechanism is sensitive.

4. Ed, Jim, and Li sang, and we all listened intently.

Exercise B Some of the following sentence pairs contain closely related ideas that could be combined into one sentence punctuated with a semicolon. On the line provided, combine the related sentences. If the sentence pair is not related, write C on the line.

1. Ms. Kyung is a fantastic teacher. In fact, she's the best.

_____

2. Guadalupe ran toward home plate. Her run tied the game.

_____

3. I was born in Pittsburgh. However, I moved to Erie at age two.

_____

4. We flew to Dallas. Have you ever been to Des Moines?

_____

Name _____ Date _____ Class _____

Colons

WORKSHEET 11

Use a **colon** to mean "note what follows." For example, use a colon before a list of items, especially after expressions such as *as follows* and *the following*.

Items you will need are as follows: hiking boots, heavy socks, and rain gear.

Do not use a colon before a list that directly follows a verb or a preposition.

VERB: Perennial flowers **include** asters, peonies, and irises.

PREPOSITION: Vitamin A is **in** carrots, yams, and squash.

Use a colon before a quotation that lacks a speaker tag such as *he said,* or *she remarked.* Additionally, use a colon before a long, formal statement or quotation.

The sergeant barked the command: "Attention."

Use a colon between independent clauses when the second clause explains or restates the first clause. Capitalize the first word of the independent clause following the colon.

His report was clear: The committee knew exactly what he meant.

Use a colon between the hour and minute *(4:30),* between chapter and verse in referring to passages from the Bible *(Genesis 3:2),* between a title and subtitle *(John Muir: Man of the Mountains),* and after the salutation of a business letter *(Dear Senator Specter:).*

Exercise A   Insert colons where necessary in the following sentences.

1. The exam will cover unit materials as follows Chapters 8, 9, and 10.

2. Her book was titled *Charles Drew Pioneer in Health and Medicine.*

3. The guide's instructions were explicit Stay with the group and walk slowly.

4. With relief, we heard the judge's decision "Case dismissed."

5. Take the following trains the 4 22 from Penn Station and the 5 07 from Newark.

Exercise B: Proofreading   The following business letter contains five errors in punctuation. Correct each error.

Dear Ms. Rodrigues

I have now had a chance to review: the manuscript of your article. I'd like to

meet with you to discuss suggested changes. Would Monday morning, around

9 45, be convenient? Please bring: one copy of the manuscript, your research

notes, and your signed contract.

Yours truly:

Howard Peel

Chapter 12: Punctuation

 **WORKSHEET 12** *Review*

Exercise A Add commas, periods for abbreviations, and end marks to the following sentences. Some sentences will require the addition of closing quotation marks as well as end marks.

EXAMPLE: 1. He asked me whether he really needed to get up at 6:30 A.M.

1. The first thing she said to me was "Where did you get that haircut

2. The tour leader started waving his arms and yelling, "Stop the bus at once

3. Please sit next to me Juan.

4. I'll be happy to go over Chapter 8 with you tomorrow

5. John Amsterdam is the president of the student council

6. Did Dante really say, "If Stella wants my ticket, she can have it

7. Have you ever read *The Women of Brewster Place* by Gloria Naylor

8. Hilary watch out for the falling boulder

9. Come and join me for a sandwich at the diner

10. Then Alice turned around and said, "Where in the world have you been

11. Is Maria R Sanchez M.D. the staff doctor for Talmadge & Co

12. She grew her flowers from seeds young seedlings and cuttings from my garden

13. Have you heard any more from Bill or Luis or Alf

14. I'm not sure that a big shaggy cocker spaniel would be my first choice as a pet

15. He wanted to do well on the test so he carefully studied all the chapter reviews

16. Are those trucks carrying dangerous cargoes banned from this bridge

17. Jeremy who is my next-door neighbor wants to go to Connecticut College

18. When you finish reading that book may I borrow it

19. No I've never seen a mockingbird; if you spot one please point it out to me

20. Irene hoping to get a job as a lifeguard took the Red Cross senior lifesaving course

21. Alan Richman originally a writer for the *Boston Globe* now writes for *Esquire*

22. Isn't he the writer whose columns you've kept in a scrapbook Rafael

23. On Saturday 19 April 1992 my older sister was married in Miami Florida

24. On June 17 1982, the offices of Nordair moved to 143 Cook Ave Akron OH 45590

25. Can people who want to volunteer still reach you at your Los Angeles office

Exercise B The following sentences are punctuated incorrectly. For each sentence, cross out the incorrect mark of punctuation and, if needed, fill in the correct mark above it. Add punctuation where necessary.

> EXAMPLE: 1. Please bring the following: your lunch, hiking boots, and a large, full water bottle.

1. Wow, Little Bear. Who taught you to draw like that.

2. First performed in March, 1959, on Broadway in New York City, Lorraine Hansberry's play *A Raisin in the Sun* which was later made into a movie was awarded the New York Drama Critics Circle Award.

3. Although the house was a mess. Mom said that if we all helped put away toys and books; picked up all the clothes lying around; dusted the furniture; and vacuumed the rug; it would look presentable by the time Grandma arrived.

4. After all you could look at the map to see if there is an exit off Interstate 70 to a state road that will take us south to Greenville Illinois; instead of just complaining that I don't know the way.

5. It is the pressure of getting work in on time not the work itself that gets on my nerves.

6. City buses can be a pleasant way to travel but why do they run so infrequently; and when they do arrive why are they in bunches of three or four or more.

7. Gen Benjamin O Davis Sr the first African American, promoted to the rank of lieutenant general in the U.S. Army, was the grandson of a slave.

8. If you are going to paint window frames; cover the panes of glass with masking tape: which will protect the glass from being spattered.

9. On a beautiful fall day in New England it is wise to go for a walk play a game outdoors or go for a drive; for it won't be long before the weather turns cold, and windy, and cloudy.

10. Students will receive paper pencils and rulers at the beginning of the test.

Exercise C: Proofreading In most of the following ten sentences, a comma or no mark of punctuation at all has been used where the writer should have used a semicolon (;) or a colon (:). On the line provided, write the word that comes just before the error and add a semicolon or colon, whichever is needed. If a sentence is already correct, write *C* on the line.

> EXAMPLE: 1. I don't have time to watch Tony tonight, besides, Geoffrey would love to baby-sit him. *tonight;*

1. Nevada borders the following states, California, Oregon, Idaho, Utah, and Arizona.   _____

2. We all hoped the weather would be good, however, the meteorologist had forecast rain and sleet.   _____

3. As you read each poem, keep in mind the judge's criteria, sharp imagery and originality.   _____

MECHANICS

Chapter 12, Worksheet 12, *continued*

4. In general, the longest-lasting mechanical devices in a house or an apartment are furnaces, stoves, and refrigerators. _____

5. The play was very well attended, few empty seats, if any, were left by curtain time. _____

6. My cousins were supposed to meet me at the station at noon, they were fifteen minutes late, however. _____

7. Rainy days at camp were discouraging there was nowhere to go and almost nothing to do. _____

8. The three parts of a composition are the introduction, the body, and the conclusion. _____

9. To hang the picture properly, you will need the following equipment, a small hammer, a picture hook, and a two-foot length of wire. _____

10. The reasons for her leaving are clear, she is overworked, underpaid, and bored. _____

Chapter 13: Punctuation

 **WORKSHEET 1** *Italics*

Italics are printed characters that slant to the right. To indicate italics in handwritten or typewritten work, use underlining. If you use a personal computer, you may be able to code words to print out in italics.

> PRINTED: I enjoyed the book *A Tale of Two Cities.*
>
> HANDWRITTEN: *I enjoyed the book* A Tale of Two Cities.

Use italics (underlining) for the following kinds of titles.

books	plays	long poems
periodicals	newspapers	works of art
films	television series	long musical compositions
recordings	comic strips	computer software

> I read a review of the movie *Fried Green Tomatoes* in *Newsweek.*

Also use italics for the names of court cases, trains, ships, aircraft, and spacecraft.

> The case of *Boosler County v. Smythe* involves the speedboat *Maribella.*

Use italics (underlining) for words, letters, and symbols referred to as such and for foreign words. However, many borrowed words are now part of English vocabulary and are not italicized.

> The symbol for the Greek word *pi* is π.
>
> The word *Arabian* always begins with a capital *A.*
>
> My favorite soup is *sopa gallego.*   *but*   Are you going to the **rodeo**?

Exercise   Underline all items that should appear in italics in the following sentences.

1. Our neighbor, Kim Wong, was a contestant on Jeopardy.

2. Do you ever get the words to, too, and two confused?

3. Composer Andrew Lloyd Webber wrote both The Phantom of the Opera and Cats.

4. The adjective jumbo comes from the name of a famous elephant.

5. ¡Hola! is a popular Spanish magazine.

6. Schubert's greatest musical composition is The Unfinished Symphony.

7. Spirit of St. Louis is the plane in which Charles Lindbergh made the first nonstop flight from New York to Paris.

8. The Spanish word alcalde means "mayor" or "governor."

9. In Italian, the vowel i is pronounced like the English letters ee in the word see.

10. USA Today reported that the space-shuttle launch had been postponed.

Chapter 13: Punctuation

 **WORKSHEET 2** *Quotation Marks A*

Use quotation marks to enclose a **direct quotation**—a person's exact words. Do not use quotation marks to enclose an indirect quotation. Notice that a direct quotation begins with a capital letter. However, if the quotation is only a word or a phrase, do not set it off with commas or capitalize the first word.

> DIRECT QUOTATION: Nigel and Nora said, **"We** were very sorry to hear the news.**"**
> INDIRECT QUOTATION: Nigel and Nora said they were very sorry to hear the news.
> DIRECT QUOTATION: Nigel and Nora said they were **"very sorry"** to hear the news.

When the expression identifying the speaker divides a quoted sentence, the second part begins with a lowercase letter. However, when the second part of a divided quotation is a sentence, it begins with a capital letter.

> "I know you will find," Angela said, "that this course is challenging."
> "Yes, it is," agreed Pat. "We've been looking forward to it."

When a direct quotation of two or more sentences is *not* divided, only one set of quotation marks is used.

> "Please take a seat. We are discussing Shaka's place in African history,"
> Ms. Han said.

A direct quotation is set off from the rest of the sentence by a comma, a question mark, or an exclamation point, but not by a period.

> "Let's go to the film festival**,**" said Lola.
> "What's playing**?**" I asked.
> "The best movie ever made**!**" she answered: "It's *Citizen Kane*!"

Exercise For each of the following sentences, insert or delete quotation marks and other marks of punctuation as needed. Correct each capitalization error by striking through the incorrect letter and writing the correct letter above it. Some sentences will also require the insertion of end marks.

1. I was wondering about something, Paul said when was the first baseball game played?

2. We don't know for sure Coach Clark responded, but we do know that the game developed from an old English sport called rounders

3. I thought, Dawn interjected, That Abner Doubleday invented the game.

4. The coach replied "that's an interesting point." "Historians now say that the story of Doubleday's inventing the game is merely folklore."

5. Coach Clark said "That American colonists in the 1700s played a ball game that they sometimes called baseball"

Name _____ Date _____ Class _____

Quotation Marks B

When used with quotation marks, the other marks of punctuation are placed according to the following rules: Commas and periods are always placed inside the closing quotation marks.

"Be quiet**,**" Terry whispered. "The curtain is going up**.**"

Semicolons and colons are always placed outside the closing quotation marks.

He told me that he was "too tired"**;** he told Shelley that he felt "just fine"**:** He's lying to one of us.

Question marks and exclamation points are placed inside the closing quotation marks if the quotation itself is a question or an exclamation. Otherwise, they are placed outside.

INSIDE: Zach asked, "Why are you so upset**?**"

OUTSIDE: Why do you say, "I don't want to talk about it"**?**

Use single quotation marks to enclose a quotation within a quotation.

Mr. Finn urged, "Tell me what he meant by writing, **'**All the world's a stage**.'**" [Notice that the period is placed inside the single quotation mark.]

"What did Mike mean when he said, **'**Hold the line**'?**"Olga asked. [The question mark is placed inside the double quotation marks, not the single quotation mark, because Olga's words, not Mike's, form a question.]

When writing **dialogue** (a conversation), begin a new paragraph every time the speaker changes, and enclose the speaker's words in quotation marks.

"It's a beautiful day. Let's get our bathing suits, pack some lunches, and ride out to the lake**,**" suggested Theresa.

"Sure**,**" Otis agreed, **"**let's go!**"**

"Wait a minute**,**" interrupted Jan. **"**Didn't I hear Dad say, 'Mow the lawn before you run off'?**"**

Exercise For each of the following sentences, insert quotation marks and other marks of punctuation as needed. Insert ¶ before a word that should begin a new paragraph.

EXAMPLE: 1. As Muhammad Ali always said,**"**I am the greatest!**"**

1. I asked, "When you said Catch as catch can, what did you mean?

2. He clearly said, I'll be here at six; now, where is he?

3. When Karl Marx was near death, his housekeeper came to him. Do you have any final messages for the world? she asked. Get out! Marx responded. Last words are for fools who haven't said enough.

4. Acclaimed composer Ludwig van Beethoven attended an opera written by another composer. After the performance, the composer asked, How did you like it? I liked your opera, Beethoven answered. I think I will set it to music.

Chapter 13: Punctuation

Quotation Marks C

Use quotation marks to enclose titles of short works, such as short stories, poems, essays, articles, songs, episodes of television series, and chapter titles and the titles of other parts of books.

> My favorite poem by Sylvia Plath is "The Colossus."
>
> Chapter 6 of *A Portrait of a Town* is entitled "Over There."

Neither italics nor quotation marks are used for the titles of major religious texts (the Bible, the Koran) or of legal or historical documents (Declaration of Independence).

Use quotation marks to enclose the title of a short work that appears in an italicized title. Use single quotation marks for the title of a short work that appears in a title enclosed in quotation marks.

> *"The Wasteland" and Other Poems*   "Imagery in 'The Open Boat'"

Use italics for the title of a longer work contained in a title (such as the title of an essay) enclosed in quotation marks.

> "Alice Walker and *The Color Purple*"

Use quotation marks to enclose slang words, invented words, technical terms, and dictionary definitions of words.

> I felt relieved to have "kicked" the habit of biting my nails.
>
> The French expression *raison d'être* means "reason for being."

Exercise   Add single and double quotation marks to these sentences as needed. Some sentences may also require the addition of end marks.

1. Form and Meaning in *The Joy Luck Club* is the title of the article Professor Williams is writing.

2. Chapter 5, titled In the Woods, was pretty frightening.

3. We'll be reading excerpts from the Bible as well as an article called, I think, The History of the Bible.

4. Wasn't an essay called Good and Evil in Hawthorne's story The Minister's Black Veil on our reading list?

5. Isn't *burrah sahib* a Hindi term meaning a bad person.

6. My grandfather said that my new outfit was the cat's pajamas, which means cool to you and me.

7. Yes, I have a title for my research paper; it's The Symbol of the Sword in *Hamlet*.

8. Please copy the article Robert Frost's Poem Fire and Ice for me.

9. As we drove home, the twins must have sung a hundred verses of This Old Man

10. My nephew calls the refrigerator a fooderator.

Chapter 13: Punctuation

WORKSHEET 5   *Ellipsis Points*

Use **ellipsis points** (. . .) to mark omissions from quoted material and pauses in a written passage. If the quoted material that comes before the ellipsis points is not a complete sentence, use three points with a space before the first point.

"A dark horse **. . .** rushed past the grandstand in sweeping triumph."

Benjamin Disraeli

If the quoted material that comes before or after the ellipsis is a complete sentence, use an end mark before the ellipsis points.

"The play unfolds in my mind**. . . .**"

To show that a full line or more of poetry has been omitted, use an entire line of spaced periods.

To indicate a speaker's pause or hesitation in a written passage, use three ellipsis points with a space before the first point.

"Well **. . .** I guess I'm not sure," admitted the defendant in a low voice.

Exercise   Omit the italicized parts of the following passages. Use ellipsis points to punctuate each omission correctly.

1. Hilde said, "I really enjoy ice skating, *but I can't stand the cold!"*

   _____

2. Send your finest thoughts out into the world. Let them beam *like the rays of the sun* into the lives of others.

   _____

   _____

3. The years of a tree are measured in rings.
   And so it is with all of nature.
   The years of the human heart are measured in courage.

   _____

   _____

   _____

4. "Mr. Clayton called. *He's going out.* Call him back at 4:30," said Mrs. Kwan.

   _____

5. Love, *even that which springs naturally from the heart,* is often hard work.

   _____

   _____

Chapter 13: Punctuation

| WORSHEET 6 | *Apostrophes A* |

The **possessive case** of a noun or pronoun shows ownership or relationship. To form the possessive of a singular noun or an indefinite pronoun, add an apostrophe and an *s*.

a **cat's** bed   a **summer's** day   **Nick's** car   **anybody's** guess

To form the possessive of a singular noun ending in an *s* sound, add only an apostrophe if the noun has two or more syllables and if the addition of *'s* will make the noun awkward to pronounce. Otherwise, add *'s*.

for **appearance'** sake   **Moses'** rage   the **princess's** carriage

To form the possessive of a plural noun ending in *s*, add only the apostrophe.

the **Burnses'** party   his **dogs'** kennels   my **brothers'** room

Plural nouns that do not end in an *s* form the possessive by adding an apostrophe and an *s*.

the **women's** team   the **mice's** nest   **children's** literature

Form the possessive of only the last word in a compound word, in the name of an organization or business firm, or in a word group showing joint possession. However, form the possessive of each noun in a word group showing individual possession of similar items.

my **mother-in-law's** trailer   Becker and **Becker's** report   **Joe's**, **Thelma's**, and **her** tickets

When used in the possessive form, words indicating time, such as *minute, hour, day, week, month,* and *year,* and words indicating amounts in cents or dollars require apostrophes.

a **day's** work   six **months'** pay   my two **cents'** worth

Possessive personal pronouns include *my, mine, your, yours, his, her, hers, its, our, ours, their,* and *theirs.* Do not use an apostrophe with these pronouns or with the possessive *whose.*

Exercise   Most of the following items contain incorrect possessive forms. On the line provided, give the correct form of each word. If an item is correct, write *C.*

EXAMPLE: 1. Chris' tapes *Chris's tapes*

1. It is her's. _____

2. womens' department _____

3. that boys' radio _____

4. Dolly's and Kenny's song _____

5. scissors' blades _____

6. no ones' fault _____

7. San Jose's industries _____

8. a weeks's vacation _____

9. leaves' color _____

10. a horses' hooves _____

Chapter 13: Punctuation

 **WORKSHEET 7** *Apostrophes B*

A **contraction** is a shortened form of a word, word group, or figure in which an apostrophe takes the place of all the letters, words, or numbers that are omitted.

   isn't [is not]   o'clock [of the clock]   they're [they are]   '63 [1963]

Do not confuse contractions with possessive pronouns.

   It's late. [contraction]   The dog ate **its** bone. [possessive]

Use an apostrophe and an *s* to form the plural of all lowercase letters, some uppercase letters, and some words referred to as words. You may add only an *s* to form the plurals of such items—except lowercase letters—if the plural forms will not cause misreading.

   Cross your *t*'s and dot your *i*'s.   Say your *please*'s and *thank you*'s.
   *T*s mean "Tuesdays" in this schedule.   These **VCRs** are too expensive.

NOTE: To form the plural of an abbreviation that ends with a period, always add '*s*.
   M.B.A.'s   M.D.'s   M.A.'s

Use apostrophes consistently.

   These two *I*'s on my report card stand for "incomplete"; the *S*'s stand for "satisfactory."
   [Without the apostrophe, the plural of the letter *I* would spell *Is*. The apostrophe in
   the plural of the letter *S* is unnecessary but is included for consistency.]

Exercise: Proofreading   On the lines provided, rewrite words that are punctuated incorrectly, adding or deleting apostrophes as needed. [Note: You may need to change the spellings of some words.]

   EXAMPLE: 1. Lets try to find a modern puzzle maze that wont be too
                difficult for us to explore. *Let's; won't*

 1. Your lucky if youve ever been through an old-fashioned hedge
    maze.   _____

 2. Public TVs program about the ABCs of mazes got me interested
    in mazes' history.   _____

 3. From above, some of the bushes looked like *h*s, *t*s, and other
    letters.   _____

 4. I b'lieve Id need a lot of help to find my way out by dusk or even
    ten o clock.   _____

 5. Ive read that mazes became popular in Europe during the 1500s
    and 1600s; however, my uncle said that hes read about mazes
    that were built two thousand years ago.   _____

Chapter 13: Punctuation

 **WORKSHEET 8** *Hyphens*

Use a **hyphen** to divide a word at the end of a line. Divide a word only between syllables.

Lillian Hellman is my favorite **playwright**.

Do not divide a one-syllable word.

INCORRECT: Hellman's characters seem very realistic.

CORRECT: Hellman's characters
seem very realistic.

Divide a word that is already hyphenated only at the hyphen.

INCORRECT: Her plays contain well-writ-
ten dialogue.

CORRECT: Her plays contain **well-
written** dialogue.

Use a hyphen with the prefixes *ex–*, *self–*, and *all–*, with the suffix *–elect*, and with all prefixes before proper nouns or proper adjectives.

ex-president   **self-**esteem   **all-**knowing   senator**-elect**   **post-**Victorian

Use hyphens with compound numbers from *twenty-one* to *ninety-nine* and with fractions used as modifiers.

two hundred **thirty-six**   **two-thirds** majority   **one-half** cup

In general, hyphenate a compound adjective only when it precedes the noun it modifies. However, do not use a hyphen if one of the modifiers is an adverb ending in *–ly*.

a well**-**defined rule   a clearly defined rule   a rule that is well defined

Exercise A   On the lines provided, write the following words with hyphens, showing how they could be divided at the end of a line. If a word should not be divided, write *no hyphen*.

EXAMPLE: 1. frankly *frank-ly*

1. fifty-four   _____
2. mid-September   _____
3. baseball   _____

4. merciful   _____
5. plunge   _____

Exercise B   In each phrase below, place a caret (^) to indicate where a hyphen should be inserted. Some phrases may not require the insertion of hyphens.

EXAMPLE: 1. a well groomed dog
                      ^

1. a tender hearted man
2. one fourth cup of water
3. a storm in the mid Atlantic

4. the new president elect
5. a finely tuned instrument

Name _____ Date _____ Class _____

Dashes

Use a dash to indicate an abrupt break in thought. If the sentence continues, use a second dash after the interruption.

My coach—there he is now—wants to meet with me after school.

Use a dash to mean *namely, in other words, that is,* and similar expressions that come before an explanation.

Ten people—the entire junior varsity team—were absent.

Use dashes to set off an appositive or a parenthetical expression that contains commas.

The contents of their luggage—a paper bag, a cardboard box tied with string, and an old typewriter case—had been unpacked and neatly laid out.

Use a dash to set off an introductory list or group of examples.

A hamster, three mice, and a parakeet named Mr. Biscuit—each coolly watched the progress of our wallpapering project.

Exercise For each of the following sentences, insert dashes where they are needed.

Example: 1. The Crosby triplets͜Barry, Harry, and Larry͜were at the picnic.

1. Your puppy I can't believe how much he's grown is really cute.

2. Two men are walking down a street stop me if you've heard this joke before and meet a man with an elephant.

3. A suitcase and ten dollars these were all my grandfather had when he came to this country.

4. No matter what anyone else says, you have to do only one thing your best.

5. Household cleaning fluids bleach, ammonia, alcohol should be stored well out of the reach of children.

6. Punctuation marks parentheses, dashes, and even brackets can suggest the complexity of thought as words sometimes cannot.

7. On a shelf over her bed were her favorite books Greek myths, Nathaniel

   Hawthorne's stories and old cameras of all kinds.

8. Could you tell me where oh, never mind, I see it now.

9. Separate the egg oops more carefully than I just did.

10. Is the boy over there that one in the red shirt your brother?

Chapter 13: Punctuation

 **WORKSHEET 10** *Parentheses*

Use parentheses to enclose informative or explanatory material of minor importance. Be sure that the material enclosed in parentheses can be omitted without losing important information or changing the basic meaning and construction of the sentence.

> Joan (she is Becky's stepmother) works for a publishing company.
>
> Hadrian's Wall (built A.D. 122–128) protected the people of Britain from attack.

A parenthetical sentence that falls within another sentence should not begin with a capital letter unless it begins with a word that should always be capitalized. A parenthetical sentence that falls within another sentence should not end with a period but may end with a question mark or an exclamation point.

> A mastiff (see figure on page 34) makes a fine guard dog.
>
> That summer (what a delight it was!) we swam almost every day.

A parenthetical sentence that stands by itself following a sentence should begin with a capital letter and should end with a period, a question mark, or an exclamation point before the closing parenthesis.

> These parklands will be at the mouth of the river. (See map on page 478.)

When parenthetical material falls within a sentence, punctuation should never come before the opening parenthesis but may follow the closing parenthesis.

> At the inauguration of Bill Clinton (1993), Maya Angelou read a poem.

In a formal research paper, use parentheses to identify the source of quoted or paraphrased material.

> A person sings the blues to get into a particular mood (Jahn, *Muntu*, 224).

Exercise   Parentheses are missing in each of the following items. Insert parentheses, capital letters, and end marks where appropriate.

1. For years people thought that Abner Doubleday 1819–1893 invented baseball.

2. The passageways leading to the tombs see figure 3 are of complex design and were sometimes armed with devices to trap thieves.

3. Then, the detective frowns thoughtfully and opens a hidden door that's my favorite part where she finds the key to the mystery.

4. During the war years, peoples from many different cultures came to the cities and had to find ways to live together Baker, 382.

5. The Amazon River area is populated by fierce yet friendly people. Years ago, my father mapped the area and met many of them.

Chapter 13: Punctuation

 **WORKSHEET 11** *Brackets and Slashes*

Use brackets to enclose an explanation within quoted or parenthetical material.

The book states, "That architect [Louis Sullivan] lived in Chicago."

Louis Sullivan (an architect [1856–1924]) taught Frank Lloyd Wright.

Use brackets and the Latin word *sic* to indicate that an error existed in the original of a quoted passage.

"Louis Sulivan's [*sic*] most famous student was Frank Lloyd Wright," the article continued.

Use a slash between words to indicate that both terms apply. There is no space before or after the slash.

Uncle Tim has invented a lawn mower/edger.

In the event that he/she fails to fulfill this contract, legal action will be taken. [Avoid using the terms *he/she* and *and/or* as much as possible because they can make your writing choppy.]

Within a paragraph, use a slash to mark the end of a line quoted from poetry or from a verse play. In verse excerpts quoted within paragraphs, the slash has a space on either side of it.

Wordsworth shows his knowledge of the darker aspects of life with these words: "Suffering is permanent, obscure and dark, / And shares the nature of infinity."

NOTE: The slash is also commonly used in writing fractions and ratios.

FRACTIONS: 1/2 qt   3 7/8 ft

RATIOS: 35 mi/hr   32 lb/sq in.

Exercise: Proofreading   Proofread the following sentences and correct any errors in the use of punctuation. If a sentence is correct, write C.   [   ]

EXAMPLE: 1. Adu said his main problem was "finding one (a car) that I can afford."

_____ 1. George Herman Ruth (commonly called "Babe" (1895–1948)) was a great player.

_____ 2. The manual instructed us to "use the cable to connect the tellevision—*sic*—with the VCR."

_____ 3. The model boasts some impressive figures (more than 90 mi gal) as well as an affordable sticker price.

_____ 4. In class, we analyzed the poem "The Cross of Snow" (Henry Wadsworth Longfellow 1807–1882).

_____ 5. Explain the image in the following lines from Longfellow's "The Tide Rises, the Tide Falls": "Darkness settles on roofs and walls, / But the sea, the sea in the darkness calls . . ."

Chapter 13: Punctuation

WORSHEET 12 *Review*

Exercise A   Correct the following sentences by adding italics (underlining), quotation marks, other marks of punctuation, and capitalization.

> EXAMPLE: 1.   In one of his books, Mark Twain wrote It is easier to stay out than get out
>
> *In one of his books, Mark Twain wrote, "It is easier to stay out than get out."*

1. The first section in People Weekly has some interesting facts about celebrities.

_____

2. Are you going to the Greek Festival asked Mr. Doney or didn't you know that it's scheduled for this weekend _____

_____

3. Our teacher quoted John F. Kennedy's words: And so, my fellow Americans, ask not what your country can do for you; ask what you can do for your country.

_____

4. How do I find out who wrote the poem Dream Deferred Jill asked her English teacher.

_____

5. The phrase frosting on the cake has nothing to do with dessert; it refers to something additional that is a pleasant surprise. _____

_____

6. I'm still hungry complained Donna after finishing a plate of stew that baked apple looks tempting _____

_____

7. When faced with a frightening situation, I often recite Psalm 23:4, which starts Yea, though I walk through the valley of the shadow of death, I will fear no evil. _____

_____

8. Perhaps the finest memorial to Abraham Lincoln is the poem When Lilacs Last in the Dooryard Bloom'd in Walt Whitman's book Sequel to Drum-Taps. _____

_____

9. Are you saying I don't know the answer or I don't understand the question.

_____

10. Margaret Walker's first book, For My People, included a tribute to grandmothers in a poem called Lineage. _____

_____

Exercise B   The following expressions involve the use of dashes, parentheses, hyphens, and apostrophes. Each item consists of three expressions. Two of the expressions are correct; one is wrong. Find the wrong expression and then write the expression correctly on the line provided.

1. [a] the womens' hats [b] a well-known actor's signature [c] each girl's score

_____

2. [a] looking for its owner [b] Bill and Joe's party [c] either our car or your's

_____

3. [a] Mayor-elect Smith's speech [b] Peg's twenty-fourth birthday [c] does'nt cross her *t*'s

_____

4. [a] Very few students—only two—failed the test. [b] See the definitions in the first column (Column A). [c] Gina is well-liked by everyone.

_____

5. [a] She left the manuscript—a year's work—in the taxi. [b] By the third day of the trip (Friday,) I was exhausted. [c] The last chapter (pages 67–91) is the best.

_____

Exercise C   On the lines provided, rewrite the following items, omitting the parts that appear in italics. Use ellipsis points to indicate where the material has been omitted.

1. I don't enjoy reading *exaggerated* tall tales.

_____

2. Kind words can *heal many wounds and* cure human errors.

_____

3. Rafael is at the library. *He has to write a report.* He'll be back soon.

_____

4. Although Esperanza dislikes most vegetables, *and peas in particular,* she never turns down a serving of carrots.

_____

_____

Exercise D Revise the following groups of words by inserting apostrophes and hyphens where needed.

1. the ex presidents home
2. transAlaskan
3. Achilles heel
4. Youre from Peru, arent you?
5. three quarters full
6. Isnt soda bread Irish?
7. His speech is filled with *uhs*.
8. three quarter length sleeves
9. There are three *as* in *alphabetical*.
10. Its theirs, not ours.
11. our mayor elect
12. post World War II Europe
13. dotted all of your *is*
14. Didnt Anthony make your piñata?
15. self appointed critic
16. Its after five oclock.
17. part time job
18. Why didn't someone answer the phone?
19. Thats all there is to know.
20. Wheres the Shaker box you bought?

Exercise E On the lines, write these words with hyphens showing how they should be broken at the ends of lines. If a word should not be divided, write *no hyphen*.

1. rebate   _____

2. brunch   _____

3. cozy   _____

4. three-fourths   _____

5. bluebird   _____

Exercise F: Proofreading Proofread and correct each item by deleting incorrect punctuation and inserting slashes or brackets as needed. If an item is correct, write C.

1. He, she must be present to win. _____

2. We need 8 and 7 8 feet of fencing. _____

3. "Everybodies' *sic* invited!" _____

4. Annie is a teacher/writer. _____

5. (ten dollars [$10.00] _____

Name _____ Date _____ Class _____

 **WORKSHEET 1** *Improving Your Spelling*

Using the following techniques will improve your spelling.

Pronounce words carefully. Most people spell "by ear"—that is, by how a word sounds. When you are not sure about the correct pronunciation of a word, look it up in a current dictionary.

　　bach • e • lor [*not* bach • lor]　　tem • per • a • ture [*not* tem • per • ture]

Spell by syllables. A syllable is a word part that can be pronounced by itself.

　　awk • ward [two syllables]　　hand • ker • chief [three syllables]

Use a dictionary. By using a dictionary, you will become familiar with the correct pronunciations and divisions of words. When you check the spelling of a word, make sure that its use isn't limited by a label such as *British* or *chiefly British*. Also check for labels such as *obsolete* or *archaic*.

Proofread for careless spelling errors. Always reread what you have written so that you can eliminate careless spelling errors. For example, avoid errors such as transpositions (*beleive* for *believe*), missing letters (*seprate* for *separate*), and the misuse of similar-sounding words (*then* for *than*).

Keep a spelling notebook. Divide each page into four columns.

　　Column 1: Write correctly any word you find troublesome.

　　Column 2: Write the word again, dividing it into syllables and marking the stressed syllable(s).

　　Column 3: Write the word again, circling any part that causes you trouble.

　　Column 4: Jot down any comments that will help you remember the correct spelling.

Exercise　On the lines provided, write the syllables of each of the following words, using hyphens between the syllables. Do not look up the words in a dictionary. Be sure that the division of each word includes all of the letters of the word.

　　　　　EXAMPLE:　1. accommodate *ac-com-mo-date*

1. adversary　_____　6. deficit　_____

2. alias　_____　7. genuine　_____

3. barbarous　_____　8. incidentally　_____

4. chimney　_____　9. legislature　_____

5. costume　_____　10. procrastinate　_____

MECHANICS

Chapter 14: Spelling and Vocabulary

WORKSHEET 2   *Roots and Prefixes*

The **root** of a word is the part that carries the word's core meaning. Many roots come from ancient Latin and Greek words. For example, the root –*micr*– comes from the Greek word *mikros*, meaning "small." The English words with this root—*microscope, microbe,* and *microns,* for example—all have something to do with smallness. Here are some Greek and Latin roots that appear in many English words.

Latin Root	Meaning	Greek Root	Meaning
–aud–, –audit–	hear	–anthro–	human
–bene–	well, good	–bibli–	book
–cogn–	know	–bio–	life
–magn–	large	–chro–	time
–omni–	all	–dem–	people
–par–	equal	–graph–	write, writing, study
–prim–	first, early	–log–, –logue–	study, word
–uni–	one	–phil–	like, love
–vid–, –vis–	see	–tele–	far, distant

A **prefix** is one or more than one letter or syllable added to the beginning of a word to create a new word with a different meaning. Here are some Greek, Latin and Latin-French, and Old English prefixes that appear in English words. Their meanings are shown in parentheses.

Old English	Latin and Latin-French	Greek
be– (around, about)	de– (away, from, off)	anti– (against)
for– (away, off, from)	dis– (away, not)	dia– (through, across)
mis– (badly, not, wrongly)	in–, im– (not)	hyper– (excessive, over)
over– (above, excessive)	pre– (before)	para– (beside, beyond)
un– (not, reverse of)	semi– (half)	sym–, syn– (together, with)

When adding a prefix, do not change the spelling of the original word.

Exercise   The following words contain prefixes and roots from the charts above. In the space provided, write the prefixes and roots. Then write a definition of each word based on the meanings of the prefixes and roots. Check your definition in a dictionary.

1. disunity _____

2. bibliography _____

3. dialogue _____

4. synchronize _____

5. inaudible _____

Name _____ Date _____ Class _____

WORKSHEET 3 | *Suffixes*

MECHANICS

A **suffix** is one or more than one letter or syllable added to the end of a word to create a new word with a different meaning.

Source	Suffix	Meaning	Example
Old English	–ness	state, quality	happiness

NOUN SUFFIXES

Greek,	–cy	state, condition	leniency
Latin, and	–ism	act, manner	cynicism
French	–tude	quality, state	multitude
	–ty, –y	quality, state	certainty

ADJECTIVE SUFFIXES

Greek,	–able, –ible	able, likely	manageable
Latin, and	–ic	person or thing showing	classic
French	–ous	marked by	famous
Old English	–ful	full of	hopeful
	–some	apt to, like	bothersome

VERB SUFFIXES

Greek,	–ate	become, cause	animate
Latin, and	–fy	make, cause	beautify
French	–ize	make, cause	finalize

Exercise Underline the suffix or suffixes in each word. Then guess the meaning of each word. Check your guess in a dictionary.

1. audible _____

2. unify _____

3. kindness _____

4. primacy _____

5. meddlesome _____

6. magnitude _____

7. porous _____

8. consumerism _____

9. bountiful _____

10. mythic _____

Chapter 14: Spelling and Vocabulary

WORSHEET 4 | *Choosing Between ie and ei and Using the Suffix –sede*

Write *ie* when the sound is long *e*, except after *c*.

EXAMPLES: **thief**   **fierce**   **receive**   **chief**

EXCEPTIONS: **neither**   **seize**   **weird**   **protein**

Write *ei* when the sound is not long *e*.

EXAMPLES: **eighteen**   **neighbor**   **vein**   **weigh**

EXCEPTIONS: **patient**   **quiet**   **interview**   **friend**

NOTE: These rules apply only when the *i* and the *e* are in the same syllable.

The only English word ending in *–sede* is *supersede*. The only English words ending in *–ceed* are *exceed, proceed,* and *succeed*. All other English words with this sound end in *–cede*.

EXAMPLES: **accede**   **concede**   **intercede**   **precede**   **recede**

Exercise A   On the line provided, spell each of the following words correctly by supplying *ie* or *ei*.

1. gr. . .f   _____   11. p. . .rce   _____

2. th. . .r   _____   12. s. . .ge   _____

3. v. . .l   _____   13. rel. . .ve   _____

4. h. . .r   _____   14. sl. . .gh   _____

5. bel. . .f   _____   15. bes. . .ge   _____

6. counterf. . .t   _____   16. shr. . .k   _____

7. dec. . .ve   _____   17. f. . .rce   _____

8. ch. . .ftain   _____   18. . . .ght   _____

9. perc. . .ve   _____   19. cash. . .r   _____

10. rec. . .pt   _____   20. y. . .ld   _____

Exercise B: Proofreading   Correct any errors in spelling in the following sentences.

EXAMPLE: 1. ~~Cheif~~ *Chief* among our concerns are the ~~greivances~~ *grievances* expressed by the lunchroom staff.

1. After a lengthy discussion, they agreed to accede to our wishes.

2. Some people believe that environmental concerns must supercede all other considerations.

3. Students will procede in an orderly manner to the nearest stairway.

4. The results have exceded all our wildest hopes.

5. What was the first state to sesede from the Union?

Chapter 14: Spelling and Vocabulary

WORSHEET 5 *Spelling Rules A*

When adding a prefix, do not change the spelling of the original word.

> inter + active = **inter**active   re + write = **re**write   mis + place = **mis**place

When adding the suffix *–ness* or *–ly*, do not change the spelling of the original word. One-syllable adjectives ending in *y* also generally follow this rule.

> soft + ness = soft**ness**   quick + ly = quick**ly**   wry + ly = wry**ly**

However, for most words ending in *y*, change the *y* to *i* before adding *–ness* or *–ly*.

> happy + ly = happ**ily**   spicy + ness = spic**iness**

Drop the final silent *e* before a suffix beginning with a vowel.

> move + able = mov**able**   give + ing = giv**ing**   pure + ist = pur**ist**

Keep the final silent *e* in words ending in *ce* or *ge* before a suffix beginning with *a* or *o*.

> trace + able = trace**able**   outrage + ous = outrag**eous**

Additionally, keep the silent *e* when adding *–ing* to the words *dye* and *singe (dyeing, singeing)* or when adding *–age* to the word *mile (mileage)*.

When adding *–ing* to words that end in *ie*, drop the *e* and change the *i* to *y*.

> EXAMPLES: lie + ing = **lying**   tie + ing = **tying**

Keep the final silent *e* before a suffix beginning with a consonant.

> EXAMPLES: brave + ly = brav**ely**   peace + ful = peace**ful**
>
> EXCEPTIONS: judge + ment = judg**ment**   wise + dom = wis**dom**
>
> whole + ly = whol**ly**   nine + th = nin**th**

For words ending in *y* preceded by a consonant, change the *y* to *i* before any suffix that does not begin with *i*.

> EXAMPLES: heavy + est = heav**iest**   hurry + ing = hurry**ing**

For words ending in *y* preceded by a vowel, keep the *y* when adding a suffix.

> EXAMPLES: play + ful = play**ful**   employ + ment = employ**ment**
>
> EXCEPTIONS: day + ly = da**ily**   pay + ed = pa**id** [the *-ed* drops its *e*]

Exercise   On the lines provided, spell each of the following words with the given suffix.

1. joy + ful _____

2. base + ment _____

3. prepare + ed _____

4. untie + ing _____

5. notice + able _____

6. icy + ness _____

7. shy + ly _____

8. noisy + ly _____

9. gray + ness _____

10. marry + age _____

Name _____ Date _____ Class _____

 **WORKSHEET 6** *Spelling Rules B*

Double the final consonant before a suffix that begins with a vowel if the word *both* (1) has only one syllable or has the accent on the last syllable *and* (2) ends in a single consonant preceded by a single vowel.

> EXAMPLES: commit + ing = commit**ting**   control + ed = control**led**

For words ending in *w* or *x*, do not double the final consonant.

> EXAMPLES: plow + ed = plow**ed**   wax + ing = wax**ing**

For words ending in *c,* add *k* before the suffix instead of doubling the *c.*

> EXAMPLES: frolic + ing = frolic**king**   mimic + ed = mimic**ked**

Do not double the final consonant unless the word satisfies the conditions (1 and 2) above.

> EXAMPLES: feed + ing = feed**ing** [has one syllable but does not end in a single consonant preceded by a single vowel]
>
> cancel + ed = cancel**ed** [ends in a single consonant preceded by a single vowel but does not have accent on the last syllable]

When a word satisfies both conditions but the addition of the suffix causes the accent to shift, do not double the final consonant.

> EXAMPLES: refer + ence = refer**ence** [*but:* referred]
>
> prefer + able = prefer**able** [*but:* preferred]
>
> EXCEPTIONS: excel—excel**lent**, excel**lence**, excel**lency**

NOTE: The final consonant of some words may or may not be doubled. Either spelling is acceptable.

> EXAMPLE: travel + er = traveler or traveller

Exercise   On the lines provided, spell each of the following words with the given suffix.

1. shop + er   _____
2. picnic + ing   _____
3. relax + ation   _____
4. propel + er   _____
5. confer + ence   _____

6. tax + ing   _____
7. volunteer + ism   _____
8. outlaw + ed   _____
9. plan + ers   _____
10. forget + ing   _____

Name _____ Date _____ Class _____

Plurals A

Remembering the following rules will help you spell the plural forms of nouns. For most nouns, including proper nouns, add *s*.

    secret → secret**s**   donkey → donkey**s**   Daly → Daly**s**

For nouns ending in *s, x, z, ch,* or *sh*, add *es*.

    glass → glass**es**   dish → dish**es**   tax → tax**es**

For nouns ending in *y* preceded by a vowel, add *s*.

    decoy → decoy**s**   stray → stray**s**   toy → toy**s**

For nouns ending in *y* preceded by a consonant, change the *y* to *i* and add *es*. For proper nouns ending in *y*, add *s*.

    puppy → pupp**ies**   county → count**ies**   fly → fl**ies**   Kennedy → Kennedy**s**

For some nouns ending in *f* or *fe*, add *s*. For others, change the *f* or *fe* to *v* and add *es*. For proper nouns, add *s*.

    roof → roof**s**   loaf → loa**ves**   knife → kni**ves**   fife → fif**es**   Wolfe → Wolf**es**

For nouns ending in *o* preceded by a vowel, add *s*.

    radio → radio**s**   patio → patio**s**   stereo → stereo**s**

For nouns ending in *o* preceded by a consonant, add *es*.

    echo → ech**oes**   potato → potat**oes**   hero → her**oes**

For some common nouns ending in *o* preceded by a consonant, especially those referring to music, and for proper nouns, add only an *s*.

    solo → solo**s**   piano → piano**s**   Ibo → Ibo**s**

NOTE: For some nouns ending in *o* preceded by a consonant, you may add either *s* or *es* (mosquito—mosquito**es** *or* mosquito**s**; volcano—volcano**es** *or* volcano**s**). When in doubt about how to form a plural, consult a current dictionary.

Exercise On the lines provided, spell the plural form of each of the following nouns.

    1. gulf   _____   6. soprano   _____

    2. penny   _____   7. tomato   _____

    3. portfolio   _____   8. Murphy   _____

    4. waltz   _____   9. valley   _____

    5. house   _____   10. elf   _____

Name _____ Date _____ Class _____

 **WORKSHEET 8** *Plurals B*

Remembering the following rules will help you spell the plural forms of nouns.

The plurals of a few nouns are formed in irregular ways.

 man → men   goose → geese   child → children

For a few nouns, the singular and plural forms are the same.

 sheep   Chinese   scissors   fish

For most compound nouns, form the plural of only the last word of the compound.

 football → footballs   ten-year-old → ten-year-olds   baby sitter → baby sitters

For compound nouns in which one of the words is modified by the other word or words, form the plural of the noun modified.

 justice of the peace → justices of the peace   editor in chief → editors in chief

For some nouns borrowed from other languages, the plurals are formed as in the original languages.

 analysis → analyses   alumna → alumnae   radius → radii

To form the plurals of figures, most uppercase letters, signs, and words used as words, add an *s* or both an apostrophe and an *s*.

SINGULAR:	9	1600	R	&	*him*
PLURAL:	9s	1600s	Rs	&s	*hims*
	or	*or*	*or*	*or*	*or*
	9's	1600's	R's	&'s	*him's*

To prevent confusion, add both an apostrophe and an *s* to form the plural of all lowercase letters, certain uppercase letters, and some words used as words.

 These *I*'s on my report card stand for "incomplete." [Without an apostrophe, the plural of *I* could be confused with *Is.*]

Exercise   On the lines provided, spell the plural form of each of the following nouns. (NOTE: Italics indicate words used as words or letters used as letters.)

1. father-in-law _____

2. *o* _____

3. politics _____

4. trout _____

5. 1700 _____

6. tooth _____

7. *and* _____

8. turntable _____

9. datum _____

10. *A* _____

Name _____ Date _____ Class _____

Using Context Clues A

WORSHEET 9

Often you can figure out the meanings of unfamiliar words by using **context clues**. The **context** of a word is made up of the phrases and sentences that surround it. Here are three types of context clues:

Definitions or restatements: Look for words that define or restate the meaning of a word.

> She was totally **enervated,** or weakened, by the difficult task. [*Enervated* is defined, or restated, as "weakened."]

Examples: A word may be accompanied by examples that illustrate its meaning.

> We wanted to plant a row of **conifers**—pine trees, fir trees, or blue spruces— behind the community center. [Examples suggest that *conifers* are evergreen trees.]

Synonyms: Look for clues that indicate that an unfamiliar word is similar in meaning to a familiar word.

> At first, I enjoyed the newness of the video game. However, the **novelty** quickly wore off, and I became bored. [Clues indicate that *novelty* means "newness."]

Exercise For the italicized word in each of the following sentences, write a short definition based on the clues you find in the context. Check your definitions in a dictionary.

1. Most *citrus* trees, including lime trees, orange trees, and lemon trees, thrive in semitropical

   climates. _____

   _____

2. The amount of *arable* land—that is, land that can be cultivated—is very small.

   _____

3. When I am sick with a cold for more than a few days, I always become *querulous*, or

   complaining. _____

   _____

4. Mr. Weatherall was frequently so nervous and confused that he irritated co-workers with

   his *distraught* behavior. _____

   _____

5. Radio advertisements use *concise* language because they must convey a great deal of

   information in very little time. _____

   _____

MECHANICS

Name _____ Date _____ Class _____

 **Using Context Clues B**

Often you can figure out the meanings of unfamiliar words by using **context clues**. The **context** of a word is made up of the phrases and sentences that surround it. Here are three types of context clues:

Comparisons: Sometimes an unknown word may be compared with a more familiar word.

> A ship's **hawser** is often the strongest of all its ropes. [Clues indicate that *hawser* means "one of the ropes used on a ship."]

Contrast: An unfamiliar word may sometimes be contrasted with a more familiar word.

> Unlike women's clothing shops, **haberdasheries** often employ full-time tailors. [Clues suggest that *haberdashery* means "men's clothing store."]

Cause and effect: Look for clues that indicate that an unfamiliar word is related to the cause of, or is the result of, an action, feeling, or idea.

> The temperature rose so high that we were soon **sweltering** even in the shade. [Clues indicate that *sweltering* means "very hot."]

When context clues are subtle, you must use your general knowledge. You can also draw connections between the unfamiliar word and other information in the material.

> Everyone rose as the priest said a **benediction**. [The general context suggests that *benediction* means "prayer."]

Exercise   Use context clues in the following sentences to determine which definition from the list below matches each italicized word. On the line before each sentence, write the letter of the correct definition.

_____ 1. The icy roads made driving *perilous*.

_____ 2. Crystal seems very mature, but her brother is incredibly *puerile*.

_____ 3. Perhaps my mother is so *frugal* because my grandmother was thrifty, too.

_____ 4. Unlike many types of pasta, *manicotti* is hollow in the middle.

_____ 5. Because Uncle Bert had heart problems, he saw a *cardiologist* often.

_____ 6. The village contained both large mansions and tiny, humble *casitas*.

_____ 7. Common types of wool come from sheep, but *cashmere* comes from goats.

_____ 8. Do you have *cognizance* of his whereabouts, or is it still a mystery?

_____ 9. Her story was completely believable, but his story seemed *dubious*.

_____ 10. Although several primates have thick, furry coats, others are quite *glabrous*.

a. knowledge   b. dangerous   c. heart specialist   d. thrifty   e. type of pasta
f. childish   g. small houses   h. hairless   i. doubtful   j. goat's wool

Chapter 14: Spelling and Vocabulary

 **WORSHEET 11** *Forming New Words*

New English words are formed in the following ways:

(1) by **combining** two base words (words that can stand alone and that are complete in themselves) to make a compound or by combining a word with an **affix** (a prefix or a suffix) or with a word root

    BASE WORDS COMBINED: foot + ball = football   self + aware = self-aware

    AFFIX ADDED: re– ("again") + build = rebuild

(2) by **omitting** part of an original word to shorten it or to use it as another part of speech

    telephone → phone   elevated train → el   omnibus → bus

(3) **shortening** and **combining** two words

    breakfast + lunch = brunch   smoke + fog = smog

(4) by **expanding** the use of a word by using it as different parts of speech

    videotape (n.) → videotape (v.)

Exercise A   Each of the following words has come into the English language by one of the methods described above. Study the construction of the word. Then, on the line provided, write the letter of the correct definition of the word.

_____ 1. sub   a. to squeeze or crush (blend of *squirt* and *swish*)

_____ 2. bench   b. (verb) to remove from a game

_____ 3. blurt   c. a short worm

_____ 4. squish   d. to speak out abruptly (blend of *blow* and *spurt*)

_____ 5. inchworm   e. an underwater ship

Exercise B   Each of the following sentences contains an italicized word that has come into the English language by one of the methods described above. On the line provided, write the original word(s) or word parts from which you would guess the new word was formed.

1. The announcer spoke into a *mike* so that everyone could hear her. _____

2. Our math teacher was absent, so we had a *sub* today. _____

3. The movie star was driven to the theater in a sleek, white *limo*. _____

4. The rocket will be launched into space at the end of the *countdown*. _____

5. As the boat rolled in the rough water, Soledad suffered from *seasickness*. _____

Name _____ Date _____ Class _____

Choosing the Appropriate Word

Synonyms are words that have the same or nearly the same meaning. However, synonyms often have subtle shades of differences in meaning. Use a dictionary or a thesaurus to make sure you understand the exact differences in meaning between synonyms.

Many words have two kinds of meaning. The **denotative** meaning of a word is the meaning given by a dictionary. The **connotative** meaning of a word is the feeling or tone associated with it.

> At the top of the hill stood a vine-covered **cottage**. [The word *cottage* denotes a small building. *Cottage* connotes a cozy, romantic, rustic place.]

> At the top of the hill stood a vine-covered **shack**. [Although *shack* also denotes a small building, the word carries the connotations of disrepair and poverty.]

Exercise For each pair of words in parentheses, underline the word with the more appropriate connotation.

> EXAMPLE: 1. The way the poet uses words is very (sly, <u>clever</u>).

1. I gave my mother a meaningful but (cheap, inexpensive) gift on her birthday.

2. Wanting to look conservative yet elegant, Martha wore a (tailored, plain) suit to the job interview.

3. Your footsteps in the room (shocked, startled) me slightly since I was concentrating on my reading.

4. With great contempt he (snickered, laughed) at their opinions.

5. Mark has never told a lie; he is always (unaffected, honest) in what he says.

6. Upon winning a gold medal, the courageous young gymnast became instantly (famous, notorious).

7. "I'm still hungry," the boy (whined, said) after refusing to eat his lima beans.

8. Some days I feel (older, more ancient) than my fourteen years.

9. Ms. Cole (designs, plans) clothes suitable for any occasion.

10. To grab people's attention, the opening scene of the movie should be absolutely (riveting, interesting).

Chapter 14: Spelling and Vocabulary

 **Review**

Exercise A   Underline the root and, where appropriate, the prefix or suffix in each of the following words. Then use the meanings of the word parts and your own knowledge to match each word with its correct definition. Write the letter of the correct definition on the line.

_____ 1. benevolent   a. life forms on the earth

_____ 2. biosphere   b. one who dislikes human beings

_____ 3. graphology   c. in disguise

_____ 4. incognito   d. kindly

_____ 5. misanthrope   e. study of handwriting

Exercise B   On the lines provided, spell each of the following words, adding the prefix or suffix given.

1. modify + cation _____

2. il + legal _____

3. un + certain _____

4. share + ing _____

5. dis + appear _____

6. sad + ness _____

7. jog + er _____

8. politic + ing _____

9. mis + inform _____

10. steady + ly _____

Exercise C: Proofreading   Proofread the following sentences and circle any misspelled words. On the lines provided, write any misspelled words correctly. If a sentence does not contain any spelling errors, write *C*.

1. Isaac Bashevis Singer was borne in Poland in 1904. _____

2. The son of a rabbi, Singer went to a religous school, hoping at first to become a rabbi also. _____

3. But after leaving the Rabbinical Seminary in Warsaw, he decided instead to become a journelist. _____

4. In 1935, Singer moved to the United States; there, he wrote articles and book reviews for New York's *Forward*. _____

5. This newspaper, like the paper for which Singer wrote in Poland, was printed in the Yiddish langage. _____

6. Singer wanted to write in Yiddish because he hoped to make the custums and idioms of traditional Jewish culture more familiar to modern readers. _____

7. For almost fifty years, Singer wrote novels, short stories, and childern's books. _____

MECHANICS

8. He wrote stories in Yiddish and than translated them into
English.   _____

9. Singer won many awards, including the National Book Award
and the Nobel Prize for litrature, the most distinguished award a
writer can receive.   _____

10. One of his most popular stories, "Yentl," was made into a movie. _____

Exercise D Write the correct plural form of each of the following words.

1. journey   _____   6. son-in-law   _____

2. witch   _____   7. flurry   _____

3. belief   _____   8. thief   _____

4. curio   _____   9. torpedo   _____

5. cupful   _____   10. lens   _____

Exercise E On the line provided, write the letter of the definition that best fits the
meaning of the italicized word in each sentence. Use context clues for guidance.

a. continuous   b. too small or little   c. painfully
d. go up   e. mistaken idea

_____ 1. *Ascend* to the fifth floor for the meeting, and then come down here for lunch.

_____ 2. We have a large supply of food, but our water supply is *scant*.

_____ 3. For the entire night I was troubled by a *persistent* cough.

_____ 4. It's true that cats are strong, but it's a *fallacy* that they have nine lives.

_____ 5. I don't have the patience to listen to such an *excruciatingly* silly argument.

Exercise F For each pair of words in parentheses, underline the word with the
appropriate connotation.

1. I hate it when (obnoxious, unpleasant) people sit near me at the movies and make
too much noise.

2. During the (cold, freezing) weather, animals only brave the elements when they are
very hungry.

3. I (cherish, like) having peas mixed in with my corn.

4. The teacher explained the subject with such (clarity, clearness) that every student
understood.

5. Today in biology class, we studied the (interior, internal) organs of the human body.

Name _____ Date _____ Class _____

Chapter 15: The Writing Process

WORKSHEET 1

Freewriting and Brainstorming

When you're **freewriting,** you jot down whatever pops into your head.

1. Write for three to five minutes. Keep writing until your time is up.

2. Start with any topic or word, such as *photography* or *sports cars* or *honesty.*

3. Don't worry about using complete sentences or proper punctuation. Your thoughts may be disorganized. You may repeat yourself. That's perfectly OK.

4. From time to time, choose one key word or phrase from your freewriting and use it as a starting point for more writing. This **focused freewriting,** or **looping,** allows you to "loop" from what you've already written to something new.

Another way to generate ideas is through **brainstorming,** or using free association. You can brainstorm alone or with others by using the following steps:

1. Write a word, phrase, or topic on your paper or on the board.

2. Without any careful thought, begin listing every related word or idea that enters your mind. One person can write for a group.

3. Don't stop to evaluate the ideas. Anything goes, even jokes and ideas that seem to be off the topic.

Exercise A   You can freewrite anywhere: if you have started a journal, you can freewrite there. Start with this question: What's your favorite song? Write a few lines of the lyrics. Then give yourself three minutes to write anything about the song.

_____

_____

_____

_____

_____

Exercise B   Choose one of the following subjects. Brainstorm about this subject either by yourself, with another student, or with a small group. Keep going until you've exhausted every possible idea. On the lines below, list the writing topics from your brainstorming session.

Subjects:

movies	advertising	vacations
the U.S. president	professional wrestling	automobiles

Subject chosen for brainstorming: _____

Possible topics gathered from brainstorming: _____

_____

_____

COMPOSITION

Name _____ Date _____ Class _____

Clustering and Asking Questions

Clustering is another free-association technique. It is used to break up a large subject into its smaller parts or to gather information, but unlike brainstorming, it also shows connections. Clustering is sometimes called *webbing* or *making connections*.

1. Write a subject in the center of a sheet of paper. Draw a circle around the subject.
2. In the space around the circle, write all the words or ideas that come to mind. Circle each addition, and then connect it to the original circled subject with a line.
3. Create offshoots by adding and connecting related ideas. Then circle each related idea and connect it to the appropriate circle.

One good way to gather information is to use the reporter's **5W-How? questions:** *Who? What? Where? When? Why?* and *How?* Although not every question applies to every situation, the *5W-How?* questions are a good basic approach. You can also ask the same *5W-How?* question more than once about various aspects of your topic.

Exercise A   Choose one of the following subjects or use one of your own. Then create a cluster diagram on a separate piece of paper by thinking of ideas related to the subject.

Subjects:

school spirit	a family tradition	robotics
Fridays	situation comedies	a current news event

Exercise B   You are a television news reporter and have been assigned to interview a scientist who has discovered a low-cost, highly efficient new source of energy. Prepare a list of *5W-How?* questions you intend to ask during the interview.

_____

_____

_____

_____

_____

_____

_____

_____

_____

_____

_____

Name _____ Date _____ Class _____

WORKSHEET 3

Reading and Listening with a Focus

When you read to gather information, you have to be clearly focused. Once you've found a possible source of information, use these hints for finding and collecting information on a specific topic.

1. Give the source of information a "once-over." Look for key words in the index, the table of contents, and chapter headings and subheadings.

2. Skim passages until you find something about your topic; then slow down and take notes in your own words. Be sure to record publishing information for later use.

To listen with a focus, use these hints:

1. Think ahead. Prepare questions you need to ask.

2. In an interview, concentrate on the question the person is answering.

3. Take notes even if you are recording. Don't try to write every word—use abbreviations and listen for main ideas and important details.

Exercise A   Your task is to find material for a report on a famous African American in our nation's history. Some possibilities are Benjamin Banneker, Sojourner Truth, Rosa Parks, Frederick Douglass, Jackie Robinson, and Martin Luther King, Jr. Choose one of these or another African American you would like to research. Next, find a source—perhaps your American history textbook or a biographical dictionary. Make notes that answer the following questions.

1. When and where did the person live? _____

_____

2. For what is he or she famous? _____

_____

3. What was one major event in the person's life? _____

_____

Exercise B   Tune in to a local evening news broadcast on television. Listen for answers to these questions.

1. What is the lead news story—the event covered first? How much time does the station devote to the lead story?

_____

2. What is the first feature story presented—that is, a story that wouldn't be considered an up-to-the-minute news report?

_____

3. How much time is given to each kind of news: local, state, and national?

_____

COMPOSITION

Name _____ Date _____ Class _____

WORKSHEET 4 | # *Observing and Imagining*

One way to gather material for your writing is to look closely at the world around you. Remember, observation is purposeful and deliberate. It's important to use all five of your senses—sight, sound, smell, taste, and touch. It's also important to use your imagination. Try activating your imagination by asking *"What if?"* Here are some sample "What if?" questions:

- What if I could change my circumstances? (What if I were an only child or what if I were *not* an only child? What if I had lived during the Middle Ages?)

- What if a familiar thing in our world no longer existed? (What if we had no music? What if we had no public schools?)

- What if major social changes were made overnight? (What if racial prejudice no longer existed? What if everyone earned the same amount of money?)

Exercise   A good story can be about almost anything. Think about the four places listed below. Then choose one and observe it carefully. Write down some descriptive details about each event or place as you might experience it through your five senses. Finally, go one step further by writing a few "What if?" questions that might lead to good story plots.

   a bus or subway train   a shopping mall   a city park   a river

EXAMPLES: Inside an airplane: sensory perceptions

1. *blue sky; deep roar of the engines on takeoff; swaying sensation as the plane hits turbulence; inviting smell of the in-flight meal*

Inside an airplane: "What if?"

1. *What if you were seated next to a celebrity? What if the plane had to make a forced landing in a cornfield?*

Sensory perceptions:

   1. _____

   2. _____

   3. _____

   4. _____

"What if?"

   1. _____

   2. _____

   3. _____

   4. _____

Name _____ Date _____ Class _____

Purpose, Audience, and Tone

Your **purpose** is your reason for writing. You can write to express yourself; to create literary works; to explain, explore, or inform; or to persuade.

Your **audience** is the people who will read or listen to your writing. The audience you choose will affect what you say and how you say it. When writing for a particular audience, you need to consider what the audience already knows about your subject, what will interest that audience, and what level of language will be appropriate.

Your **tone** is your attitude toward the subject and toward your readers. The tone of a piece of writing can often be described in a single word: *lively, sarcastic, amused,* or *serious,* for example. To create a particular tone, you must be careful in your choice of words, details, sentence lengths, and sentence structures.

Exercise   Read each of the following paragraphs. Then record its purpose, suggest a possible audience, and describe its tone.

1. Before we even started the fourth quarter, I knew it was all over. Angie, our leading scorer, wasn't performing. The Cougars still looked fresh and fierce, while we looked like a bunch of amateurs. I felt so frustrated I could have cried.

    Purpose: _____

    Audience: _____

    Tone: _____

2. Feel the luxury. Harness the power. Own the best. The legendary Auriga is simply the finest car you'll ever buy.

    Purpose: _____

    Audience: _____

    Tone: _____

3. Want to burn down 10,000 acres of forest in a jiffy? Well, it's easy to do. Just leave a campfire burning. Just be a little careless the next time you're in the woods on a hot, dry summer day. Anyone can do it. It's a snap.

    Purpose: _____

    Audience: _____

    Tone: _____

COMPOSITION

Name _____ Date _____ Class _____

Arranging Ideas

Arranging your ideas is an important part of planning. The following chart shows four common ways of arranging ideas.

TYPE OF ORDER	DEFINITION	EXAMPLES
Chronological	Narration: presents events as they happen in time	Story; narrative poem; explanation of a process; history; biography; drama
Spatial	Description: describes objects according to location	Descriptions (near to far; left to right; top to bottom; and so on)
Importance	Evaluation: gives details from least to most important or the reverse	Persuasive writing; descriptions; explanations (main idea and supporting details); evaluative writing
Logical	Classification: relates items and groups	Definitions; classifications; comparisons and contrasts

Exercise   Read the topics below and decide which of the four types of order discussed above would be most suitable for developing each topic. On the lines provided, write *C* for chronological order, *S* for spatial order, *I* for order of importance, or *L* for logical order. Be prepared to explain your response.

EXAMPLE: ___*I*___ 1. Pets are beneficial to the elderly.

_____ 1. The house, built in 1920, has an unusual layout.

_____ 2. The provinces of China share remarkable similarities in their governments, but differ in their populations and standards of living.

_____ 3. Fumiyo has always had trouble keeping track of her belongings.

_____ 4. When I get married, my spouse and I will follow certain rules of good communication.

_____ 5. The reading room of the Cooperville Library is often a cluttered, disorganized mess.

_____ 6. Between January and March there are five birthdays in our family.

_____ 7. Three major systems in the body are the circulatory system, the respiratory system, and the digestive system.

_____ 8. Recent changes in the government of Vietnam have made it possible for people to enjoy a better standard of living.

_____ 9. The ancient history of Korea deserves to be better known.

_____ 10. Regular exercise results in four major benefits to your health and looks.

Name _____ Date _____ Class _____

WORKSHEET 7 *Using Charts*

Charts are a practical, graphic way to arrange your prewriting notes. Charts group related bits of information and allow you to see the overall arrangement clearly.

When you make a chart, you use the skill of classifying: grouping related information. When classifying information, ask yourself these questions:

- Which items are similar in some way? What heading will show what they have in common?
- Do some items include other items? Which ones?
- Do you have any items left over? Should you create another heading? Should you eliminate the leftovers?

Exercise Look at the following ideas for a paper on college football, and complete the assignment that follows.

a. Teaches teamwork

b. Encourages school spirit

c. Many football players on scholarship not completing their degrees

d. Scholarship program intended to offer a college education to economically disadvantaged students

e. Competition encouraging colleges to violate recruiting rules

f. Can give a college national recognition

g. Colleges often emphasizing sports over academics

h. Alumni fans donating money to alma maters with good football teams

i. Prepares players for professional football careers

j. Star football players often given passing grades for poor academic work; some players actually illiterate

k. Alumni pressure and money possibly corrupting to college football; alumni known to reward star players with money and cars

1. One natural way to classify the information is in two groups: favorable ideas about college football and unfavorable ones. Below, list all the positive details under *Pro* (by letter) and all the negative details under *Con*.

   Pro: _____

   Con: _____

2. Another classification is items about players and items about schools. On a separate sheet of paper, make a chart that groups these pros and cons under headings of "students" or "schools." Does every item in the list fit in the chart?

COMPOSITION

Chapter 15: The Writing Process

Writing a First Draft

There's no magic formula, no *one* right way, to write a first draft. Your prewriting notes may be rough, or you may create a detailed outline. You may like to write fast, or you may write slowly, carefully shaping each sentence. Do whatever feels right for your style of writing a draft. Consider these suggestions:

- Use your prewriting notes or outline as a guide.
- Write freely. Concentrate on expressing your ideas.
- Include any new ideas that come to you as you write.
- Don't worry about making errors in grammar, usage, and mechanics. You can fix them later.

Exercise   Have you ever daydreamed about being a famous performer like Hammer or Gloria Estefan? Here are some prewriting notes about the imagined life of a performer. Arrange or group the notes, and add to them if you like. Then use the details to write the first draft of a paragraph.

make millions of dollars

can't safely go out alone in
    public

own big house and expensive
    clothes

difficult to have personal
    relationships

people love you who don't even
    know you

travel a lot

sleep in strange hotels all over
    the country

followed by groupies
    everywhere you go

have to have bodyguards for
    personal protection

great satisfaction performing
    before crowds of people

_____

_____

_____

_____

_____

_____

_____

_____

_____

_____

Name _____ Date _____ Class _____

WORSHEET 9 | *Peer Evaluation*

Every writer needs an editor—a person who can read critically and with a different viewpoint. You can get your own editor through peer evaluation. Members of a peer-evaluation group read and comment on each other's papers. Take the following steps when you evaluate the work of a classmate.

1. Be sure to tell the writer what's right as well as what's wrong.

2. Make suggestions for improvement. If you see a weakness, give the writer some suggestions to correct it.

3. Concentrate on content and organization. Don't worry about mechanical errors such as spelling or punctuation.

4. Be sensitive to the writer's feelings. Make sure that your comments are constructive—offer solutions, not criticism.

Exercise Read the following paragraph. Then use the questions that follow to write an evaluation of the paragraph.

     Maxine Hong Kingston is the daughter of Chinese immigrant parents. Maxine Hong Kingston was raised in Stocktons Chinatown in California. And attended the university of California at Berkeley. Maxine Hong Kingston taught mathematics and english. She became a writer. She wrote *The Woman Warrior: Memoirs of A Girlhood Among Ghosts.* Later, she wrote *China Men.*

1. What purpose does the paragraph serve? Does it fully accomplish its purpose?

2. What might the writer do to increase the sentence variety and to avoid repetition in sentence structure?

3. What other problems might the writer address during revision and proofreading?

_____

_____

_____

_____

_____

_____

_____

_____

_____

_____

_____

COMPOSITION

Chapter 15: The Writing Process

WORKSHEET 10

Revising by Adding and Cutting

Two revising techniques are adding and cutting.

You can **add** new information and details in new words, phrases, sentences, and paragraphs.

You can **cut** information, details, examples, or words. For example, you might cut repetition, wordiness, and details unrelated to the main idea.

Exercise Study the revisions made to the following paragraph. Then answer the questions that follow.

> *most fascinating creatures* *Egyptian* *magnificent gold and purple*
> One of the ~~neatest things~~ in ancient mythology is the phoenix. This bird lived alone in
>
> the desert. ~~I wonder if they named the city of Phoenix, Arizona, after this bird?~~ After living
> *the bird suddenly burst into flames.* *from its own ashes*
> 500 to 600 years, ~~it died.~~ But then it rose to live another lifetime. That's why the phoenix is
>
> a symbol of immortality.

1. What details did the writer add to make the paragraph more vivid and concrete?

   _____

   _____

   _____

   _____

2. Why did the writer cross out the sentence, "I wonder if they named the city of Phoenix, Arizona, after this bird"?

   _____

   _____

Name _____ Date _____ Class _____

Revising by Replacing and Reordering

Two ways to revise are replacing and reordering.

You can **replace** weak words, clichés, awkward-sounding sentences, and unnecessary information or details.

You can **reorder** words, phrases, sentences, or paragraphs to add variety or to improve clarity.

Exercise   Study the revisions made to the following paragraph. Then answer the questions below.

Of these,
⌐Swahili is the most widely spoken and understood ~~active language in Africa.~~ (There are
                                                                                        prefix
more than eight hundred native languages spoken on the continent of Africa.) (Ki is a ~~word~~
                    refer to   *to*
that makes the word ~~tell about~~ a language instead of ~~about~~ a people.) The actual name of
                        For example, a person who   *s*   *would*
the language is *Kiswahili.* ~~That means if you~~ speak Swahili, ~~you~~ refer to the language

spoken by the Ganda people as "Kiganda" and the language spoken by the Luo people

as "Kiluo."

1. Why did the writer reorder the second sentence?

   _____

   _____

2. Why did the writer reorder the third sentence?

   _____

   _____

3. Why did the writer replace "word" with "prefix"?

   _____

   _____

4. Why did the writer replace "you" with "a person"?

   _____

   _____

COMPOSITION

Chapter 15: The Writing Process

WORKSHEET 12 | *Proofreading*

When you proofread, you catch and correct any remaining errors in grammar, usage, and mechanics (spelling, capitalization, punctuation). If you put aside your paper for a while, you'll spot these mistakes more easily. The following guidelines are designed to help you locate and correct a few of the most common errors.

1. Is each sentence a complete sentence?
2. Does every sentence end with the appropriate punctuation mark?
3. Does every sentence begin with a capital letter? Are all proper nouns and proper adjectives capitalized?
4. Does every verb agree in number with its subject?
5. Are verb forms and tenses used correctly?
6. Are subject and object forms of personal pronouns used correctly?
7. Does every pronoun agree with its antecedent in number and gender? Are pronoun references clear?
8. Are frequently confused words (such as *except* and *accept, imply* and *infer*) used correctly?
9. Are all words spelled correctly? Are the plural forms of nouns correct?
10. Is the paper neat and in correct manuscript form?

Exercise: Proofreading   The paragraph below has ten errors in grammar, usage, and mechanics. If necessary, use a college dictionary and your handbook to identify and correct each mistake.

Most people have strong feelings about there pets. Especially when it comes to dogs and cats. Both Mara and Fran said she preferred dogs because dogs are more friendlier than cats. Chad disagreed, pointing out that he had never been chased or bited by a cat. Jennifer asked Chad if he had ever heard of a cat, that had tried to save someone's life. After listening to what Jennifer had to say, Chad said that she had a good arguement. I'm glad that each kind of pet are admired by somebody. The important thing is to love and take care of your pet, weather it's a dog, a cat, or some other kind of animal.

Name _____ Date _____ Class _____

 **WORSHEET 1** *Topic Sentences*

A **paragraph** is usually defined as a group of sentences that develop a main idea. A **composition**, in turn, can be described as a group of paragraphs that develop a main idea.

A **topic sentence** is a specific, limiting statement about the subject of the paragraph. You can find a topic sentence anywhere in a paragraph. Not all paragraphs have or need topic sentences. However, they provide a focus for the reader, and they help the writer avoid straying from the topic.

Exercise   On the lines provided, write the main idea and topic sentence of each paragraph. If the paragraph does not have a topic sentence, write *No Topic Sentence*.

1. For the Sioux, who were forced to resettle in the late 1800s, reservation life was miserable. Christian missionaries attacked and undermined their beliefs. Religious ceremonies such as the sun dance were banned by government officials. The Sioux were no longer able to roam and to hunt. Their very food and clothing changed.

   Main idea: _____

   Topic sentence: _____

2. One story maintains that a Sioux brave approached one of the agents from the Bureau of Indian Affairs who ran the Pine Ridge reservation. The brave picked up some earth, rolled it into a ball, and gave it to the agent. "We have given up nearly all our land," said the brave, "and you had better take the balance. Now here, . . . I hand it to you."

   Main idea: _____

   Topic sentence: _____

3. Defeated Native Americans were given areas of land called reservations. Yet they did not even have control over their reservations. The reservations were run instead by agents from the Bureau of Indian Affairs. For example, the Native Americans did not divide up the land themselves. Instead, the Dawes Act of 1887 divided the land into plots for each family so that the Native Americans, many of whom had no interest in farming, would farm in the same way that the white settlers farmed.

   Main idea: _____

   Topic sentence: _____

4. The deprivation of life on the reservation continues today for many Native Americans. For example, the Pine Ridge Reservation in South Dakota includes the poorest county in the United States. About half of the approximately two million American Indians in the United States live on reservations. Many of them live in severe poverty, and their economic and educational opportunities are limited.

   Main idea: _____

   Topic sentence: _____

COMPOSITION

Chapter 16: Paragraph and Composition Structure

WORKSHEET 2 *Using Details*

Supporting sentences give details to support or develop a paragraph's main idea. Supporting sentences often consist of sensory details, facts, or statistics. A paragraph may be developed with one type of detail or with a combination of types.

Sensory details are images of sight, sound, taste, smell, and texture that bring the subject to life for readers.

A **fact** is something that can be proven true by concrete information.

John F. Kennedy became the first Irish Catholic president of the United States.

A **statistic** is a fact based on numbers. To verify the accuracy of facts or statistics, you can check a reliable reference.

More than 40 million Americans claim Irish descent.

Exercise A   Choose one of the following topics or one of your own. On the lines provided, write the topic and five sensory details related to the topic. If possible, write one detail for each of the five senses.

Possible Topics: my dream vacation; my grandparents' cellar, attic, house, or farm; the mall; the ideal birthday; a favorite holiday

Topic: _____

1. _____
2. _____
3. _____
4. _____
5. _____

Exercise B   Choose one of the following topics or one of your own. On the lines provided, write your topic and three facts or statistics that you could use to support your topic.

Possible Topics: the best sporting goods store; the best CD store; an outstanding athlete, film star, inventor; why your state, city, or county is a great place to live

Topic: _____

1. _____
   _____

2. _____
   _____

3. _____
   _____

Name _____ Date _____ Class _____

WORSHEET 3

Using Examples and Anecdotes

To make the main idea of a paragraph clear, you may have to develop that idea in detail. Two ways to elaborate on a main idea are to use examples and anecdotes.

Examples are specific instances or illustrations of a main idea.

> MAIN IDEA: Thai food offers many interesting flavors.
>
> EXAMPLE: Lemon grass, an unusual herb used in Thai food, has a tangy, aromatic flavor.

An **anecdote,** a little story that is usually biographical or autobiographical, can also be used to support, or prove, a main idea.

> MAIN IDEA: Mark Twain's sense of humor was always at work.
>
> ANECDOTE: When Twain lived in Hartford, Connecticut, his mansion was among the largest and most ornate in the country and included an indoor greenhouse. Twain was not, however, always able to keep up with the expenses of his lavish lifestyle. So it was that he enjoyed his billiards room, which had a small veranda. When bill collectors would call, Twain would step out onto the veranda and instruct a servant to tell the bill collector, "Mr. Twain has just stepped out."

Exercise A   Choose one of the following topics or one of your own. Write the main idea and two sentences that present examples related to the topic.

Possible topics: Bicycling is the best individual sport; aerobic dancing is the best for exercise; chess is the most challenging board game; a good way to learn a second language is to watch movies and television in that language.

Main idea: _____

1. _____

2. _____

Exercise B   Choose one of the following main ideas or one of your own. Underline your main idea. Then write an anecdote to support it.

Possible main ideas: I was a creative child; taking a chance paid off for me, my sister, or my grandfather; good people often do finish first.

Anecdote: _____

_____

_____

_____

_____

_____

COMPOSITION

Name _____ Date _____ Class _____

The Clincher Sentence

A **clincher sentence** is a final sentence that emphasizes or summarizes the main idea or draws a conclusion.

> EXAMPLE: In recent years doctors have been urging people to eat low-fat, low-cholesterol diets. One result has been the creation of new cereals for adults, including "natural" and high-fiber cereals. These cereals often contain honey instead of sugar and whole grains instead of refined grains. Bran flakes and other forms of bran are also increasingly popular as breakfast foods. **The days of bacon and eggs may be gone for good.**

Exercise For each of the following paragraphs, write an appropriate clincher sentence.

1. Twice each year the clothing industry tries to convince people that their clothes are out of fashion and that they need to buy the latest designs. In March an army of fashion writers and photographers attends showings of fall and winter clothes in Milan. They travel on to London and Paris later that month and to New York in April. Spring and summer clothes are shown in October in Milan, Paris, London, and New York. Designers, manufacturers, and retail-store owners wait nervously to see what fashion writers choose to adore or to scorn.

   Clincher sentence: _____

   _____

2. From the minute we wake up to the minute we fall asleep, we are bombarded with information about our world. Some of this information is presented in news broadcasts on radio and television. Some comes from books, newspapers, and magazines. And as if all that were not enough, we now have computers that can bring whole libraries of information into our homes.

   Clincher sentence: _____

   _____

Name _____ Date _____ Class _____

Achieving Unity

Unity simply means that the paragraph "hangs together." In other words, all the supporting sentences work together to develop the main idea. Unity can exist whether the main idea is clearly stated in a topic sentence or is implied (suggested). In paragraphs that relate a series of actions or events, the main idea is often implied rather than stated.

In a paragraph with unity, all sentences relate to the stated main idea, to an implied main idea, or to a sequence of events.

Exercise   Each of the following paragraphs contains one sentence that destroys its unity. Find that unrelated sentence in each paragraph and draw a line through it.

1. Extracurricular activities help develop well-rounded personalities. In many clubs or on teams, members learn cooperation and leadership. Dues are low, and there are few if any entrance requirements. Working on school newspapers, yearbooks, and dramatic productions teaches responsibility toward others and the ability to meet a schedule or deadline. Such activities help students develop talents that might otherwise remain undiscovered or undeveloped.

2. Polio, once a killer and crippler of adults and children, fell to the Salk and Sabin vaccines. Measles, once an inevitable experience during childhood, can now be totally avoided with proper immunization. Many diseases did not exist in North America until the Europeans brought them here. Smallpox, once a dreaded killer worldwide, is now virtually unheard of. Thanks to vaccines, these and many other diseases are now, for the most part, historical curiosities.

3. Scientists who work in the field of artificial intelligence, or AI, are concentrating their energies on replicating some seemingly simple but actually quite complicated human abilities. Some AI researchers are trying to teach machines how to recognize patterns. Others are attempting to write programs that imitate natural human language. Still others are working on manual skills and locomotion. In recent years computers have gotten much, much smaller than they were in the 1950s and 1960s.

Name _____ Date _____ Class _____

Achieving Coherence A

In a **coherent** paragraph, the relationship between ideas is clear—the paragraph flows smoothly. You can make paragraphs coherent by paying attention to the order in which you arrange your ideas. The chart below lists four basic ways of arranging ideas.

CHRONOLOGICAL ORDER: Arrange events in the order they happen.

SPATIAL ORDER: Arrange details in the order that the eye sees them.

ORDER OF IMPORTANCE: Arrange ideas or details according to how important they are.

LOGICAL ORDER: Arrange ideas or details into related groups.

Exercise A The ideas in the paragraph are not in an order that makes sense. On the line provided, list each sentence by number in order of importance—from the least important supporting sentence to the most important.

(1) Much evidence may be cited to show George Washington's enormous popularity immediately following his leadership and victories during the American Revolution. (2) People generally thought of Washington as a genuine hero and a model citizen. (3) The most important testament of Washington's esteem came from Congress. (4) Members of Congress approved a bronze equestrian statue of Washington for the future capital in which the general was to be dressed in Roman clothes and was to wear a laurel wreath on his head. (5) In addition, many cities, including Boston and Richmond, celebrated Washington's birthday, February 22.

Order of importance (least to most): _____

Exercise B The sentences in the paragraph are not arranged in an order that makes sense. On the line provided, list each sentence by number in spatial order, from the farthest point to the nearest.

(1) The mountain towered above the landscape. (2) Halfway down the mountain, the timberline began, the trees almost buried in deep snowdrifts. (3) At the foot of the mountain, the boy made his camp. (4) Near the camp, an icy stream rushed by, swollen with the slowly melting snow. (5) The boy knew that deer foraged in those drifts and that some had already starved during the long, cold winter. (6) Wreaths of heavy, smoky clouds hid the heavy rocks high up the mountain that would make the climb so dangerous. (7) At night, curious animals came close on all sides of the camp—the boy often saw the fresh tracks in the snow the next morning.

Spatial order (far to near): _____

Name _____ Date _____ Class _____

WORKSHEET 7 | *Achieving Coherence B*

Direct references and *transitional words and expressions* can help you achieve coherence. These words and phrases act as connectors between ideas so that the paragraph is clear to readers.

Referring to a word or an idea that you've used earlier in the paragraph is a **direct reference**. You can make direct references by (1) using a noun or pronoun that refers to a word or an idea used earlier, (2) repeating a word used earlier, or (3) using a word or phrase that means the same thing as one used earlier.

Words and phrases that make a transition from one idea to another are called **transitional words and expressions**. These words and phrases include prepositions that indicate chronological or spatial order, as well as conjunctions, which connect and show relationships.

In the following paragraph the direct references are shown in boldface. The transitional words and phrases are italicized.

> In 1936, a Mexican American named Joseph Montoya was elected to the House of Representatives of his home state, New Mexico. *At that time* **Montoya,** a Democrat, was only twenty-one years of age. That election made **him** the youngest man *ever* to be seated on the **state legislature.** *Two years later* **he** was reelected. *During the same year,* **he** was named the majority floor leader. *Later,* **Montoya** was elected to the state senate; *subsequently,* **he** became the lieutenant governor of **his state.**

Exercise   In the paragraph below, underline the direct references and circle the transitional words and phrases.

> The earth is full of volcanoes, which are named after Vulcan, the Roman god of fire. Some volcanoes are extinct and, therefore, pose no threat. Many of them, however, are only dormant, and they could explode. The dormant volcano Mount St. Helens did erupt in Washington in 1980. Of course, you know that volcanoes are found mostly on land. But did you know that they are also on the ocean floor? Because most of the land volcanoes circle the Pacific Ocean, they are known as the Ring of Fire. An ancient Roman probably would have called the circle Vulcan's Ring.

COMPOSITION

Chapter 16: Paragraph and Composition Structure

WORSHEET 8 — Description and Narration

In a **description** you use sensory details (details of sight, sound, taste, touch, and smell) for support. You'll often use *spatial order* to organize a description, but, depending on your subject or purpose, you might also use *order of importance* or *chronological order.*

The strategy of **narration** examines changes over time. You may use narration to *tell a story, to explain a process,* or *to explain causes and effects.* You usually use *chronological order* to present ideas and information in paragraphs of narration.

Exercise A   Choose one of the following subjects. Then, on the lines provided, list five sensory details (details of sight, sound, taste, smell, and touch) that you could use to describe the specific features of the subject.

1. the school gymnasium
2. the kitchen—when you have to clean it up
3. a character from *Star Trek* or a science fiction book or movie
4. an old, abandoned house
5. a disturbing insect

_____

_____

_____

_____

_____

Exercise B   You have probably used the strategy of narration many times, perhaps without even knowing that you were doing so. Now practice the strategy by following the instructions given below.

1. Imagine you are telling someone how to make your favorite food. Remember to include all the important steps and ingredients.

_____

_____

_____

2. Give at least three causes for the popularity of credit cards, and then identify three potentially harmful effects of credit cards.

Causes: **Effects:**

_____   _____

_____   _____

_____   _____

Name _____ Date _____ Class _____

Classification and Evaluation

The strategy of **classification** examines a subject and its relationship to other subjects. You can classify a subject by dividing it into its parts, defining it, or comparing and contrasting it with something else. In paragraphs that classify, writers usually use **logical order:** grouping related ideas together. Classifying by **dividing** means looking at the parts of a subject in order to understand the subject as a whole.

Evaluation means judging the value of something. You often evaluate a subject in order to inform readers or to persuade them to think or act differently. An evaluation should be supported with reasons showing *why* you made the judgment about the subject. A good way to arrange these reasons is **order of importance:** You emphasize a point by listing it first or last in the paragraph.

Exercise A   Select one of the following topics or one of your own. Write three or more parts into which the topic could be divided.

> a child's education   the senior year
>
> the baseball season   adulthood

Topic: _____

Parts: _____   _____

_____   _____

Exercise B   Select one of the following topics or one of your own. Write the name of the larger group or class to which your topic belongs. Then list three details that distinguish the topic from other members of that group or class.

> chess   haunted houses at amusement parks
>
> pizza   jazz

Topic: _____

Larger group or class: _____

Details: _____

_____

_____

Exercise C   Select one subject from the following list. Then, on a separate sheet of paper, state your overall opinion (good, bad, somewhere in between), and list three reasons why you hold this opinion.

1. a movie you've seen (at the theater or on videotape)
2. a place you have visited
3. a book or story you've read
4. a recording (tape or CD) you have listened to

COMPOSITION

Name _____ Date _____ Class _____

 WORKSHEET 10 **The Thesis Statement**

The **thesis statement** of a composition is like the topic sentence of a paragraph; it expresses the main idea, or thesis, of your paper. Your thesis is not your topic (such as youth football) but what you want to say about it (youth football causes serious, unnecessary injuries).

Exercise A   In the list below, find the four effective thesis statements: They should each have a specific topic and a clear main idea. The remaining thesis statement is weak. It is missing a specific topic or a clear main idea. On the line provided, rewrite it as needed to make it more effective.

1. New technology has made it possible for millions of Americans to work at home.

2. Alaska's reputation as a rugged land is reflected in the resourcefulness and independent spirit of its people.

3. Japanese Americans have made many important contributions to art and music in the United States.

4. Shopping malls are important to Americans.

5. The citizens of Massachusetts are taking positive actions to preserve their state's natural resources.

_____

Exercise B   The limited topic of the following list of details is the famous 369th Infantry Regiment. What is a specific main idea you can form from the details? Write a thesis statement for the following topic and list of details. Express both the topic and the main idea clearly and specifically in the statement.

Limited Topic: the 369th Infantry Regiment

Details

• famous African American regiment in World War I
  went to France in 1918
  attended training school in France

• bravery
  received eleven citations for bravery
  entire regiment received the French *Croix de Guerre*
  not one soldier from regiment was ever captured

• service
  served in France more than a year
  "Battle of Henry Johnson" named for member of regiment who showed
      great bravery in battle
  first troop to march through Washington Square Arch in New York City
      after returning home

Thesis Statement: _____

_____

Name _____ Date _____ Class _____

Early Plans

The **early plan**—sometimes called a rough, or informal, outline—gives you a general idea of the kinds of information you want to include in your composition.

- Sort related ideas and details into separate groups.
- Make a separate list of details that don't fit into any group. You may use them at some later stage.
- Give each group of details a separate label.

Once your grouping is complete, you must choose a strategy for organizing and developing your composition. The four strategies of paragraph development—narration, description, classification, evaluation—and the four basic orders—chronological (time), spatial (space), logical, order of importance—are also used for the larger structure of a composition.

Exercise A   On the lines provided, organize the following details about a dog into two groups. Above each group of details, write a heading that identifies what the details have in common.

sits, heels	big, brown eyes	long, floppy ears
a long, thin body	fetches the newspaper	rolls over
short, bobbed tail		

_____   _____

_____   _____

_____   _____

_____   _____

_____   _____

Exercise B   Identify the details from the list above that relate to the dog's appearance. On the first line below, explain one way of putting these details in spatial order (for example, from head to tail). Then list the details in that order.

Order: _____

1. _____

2. _____

3. _____

4. _____

COMPOSITION

Chapter 16: Paragraph and Composition Structure

WORKSHEET 12 **Formal Outlines**

Structured outlines sometimes grow out of early plans. A **formal outline** has numerals and letters to identify headings and subheadings. Indentations show levels of subordination. You may choose a **topic outline,** which uses single words and phrases, or a **sentence outline,** which uses only complete sentences. Formal outlines may be used for planning, but they are more often written after the composition is complete, providing an overview, or summary, for the reader.

Exercise A   Complete the topic outline below by filling in information from the following list.

Pay television   New office technologies

New entertainment technologies   Computer games

Fax modems

  I. _____

     A. _____

     B. Cable television

     C. Virtual reality arcade games

     D. Laser discs

     E. _____

     F. Digital movies

 II. _____

     A. Facsimile machines

     B. Modems

     C. _____

     D. Personal computers

     E. Laptop computers

     F. Computer networks

Exercise B   Write a thesis statement based on the outline given above.

_____

_____

_____

_____

Name _____ Date _____ Class _____

 **WORKSHEET 13** # *The Introduction*

The **introduction** of an article or composition should

- catch the audience's attention (otherwise they may not read on)
- set the tone, or show the writer's attitude toward the topic (humorous, serious, critical)
- present the thesis (sometimes at the beginning, but often at the end, of the introduction)

Techniques for writing introductions include beginning with

an interesting or dramatic quote   an anecdote

an extended example   an unusual or enlightening fact

a question or a challenge   a stand on some issue

an outrageous or comical statement   a simple statement of your thesis

Many introductions use a combination of these techniques.

Exercise   For each of the following introductions, identify the thesis statement, the tone, and the technique used for writing the introduction.

1.   According to E.O. Wilson of Harvard University, the ants and other insects on our planet outweigh us by about ten to one. So, for every 150-pound person on earth, there are as much as 1,500 pounds of beetles, flies, ants, wasps, gnats, cockroaches, and other creatures that you don't want to invite in for dinner.
     Think about that 1,500-pound figure for a minute. A single insect weighs less than the shadow of a doubt. So how many insects does it take to equal 1,500 pounds? Kids have a word for it—*gazillions*. That's how many insects showed up in my tent the last time I went camping. It's a sport that I recommend highly—to people I don't like very much.

Thesis statement: _____

Tone: _____

Technique: _____

2.   Did you know that an amazing journey is taking place in your body? This journey begins with your heart, a powerful pump that sends five liters or more of blood through your body every minute. The journey includes stopovers in your lungs, your arteries and veins, your capillaries, and every cell in your body. What is the pathway for this journey? It is your circulatory system. The circulatory system is one of the most important transportation networks in your body.

Thesis statement: _____

Tone: _____

Technique: _____

COMPOSITION

Chapter 16: Paragraph and Composition Structure

WORKSHEET 14 | *The Body*

The **body** of a composition is the part where you develop the main idea of your thesis statement. One or more paragraphs express a major point of your thesis and support, or prove, it with details. These paragraphs should connect with one another and should relate directly to your thesis statement. You can achieve these goals if the body has *unity, coherence,* and *emphasis.*

Coherence is an ordered flow of ideas within and between sentences and paragraphs. You can achieve coherence by using three techniques—*transitional expressions, direct references,* and *a short transitional paragraph.*

Exercise   The following paragraphs form part of the body of a composition. Add transitional words and phrases and direct references on the lines provided. Circle any sentence that is out of order and draw an arrow to show where it belongs. Cross out any sentence that does not directly relate to the topic of its paragraph.

In 1889, _____ Rudyard Kipling was 24 years old, he decided to visit the

United States. _____ he would win the Nobel Prize for literature in 1907, in

1889, _____ was a virtually unknown newspaper reporter. One of his aims in

visiting the United States was to interview Mark Twain, _____ had achieved

international fame.

Kipling had a hard time finding Mark Twain. In Buffalo, New York, someone told

_____ to try Hartford; someone else said he should try Europe. A third

person suggested Elmira. _____ , Kipling boarded a train for Elmira, reached

_____ at midnight, and was told that _____ was probably not

in town.

That was wrong, _____ . After a little sleuthing, Kipling learned where

Twain lived. Kipling is probably best known for his famous *Jungle Book.* Arriving finally at

Twain's house, Quarry Farm, Kipling was told, "Mr. Clemens has just gone downtown." Of

Kipling, Twain later said: "Between us, we cover all knowledge. He knows all that can be

known, and _____ know the rest."

Back to town the journalist went. When Kipling _____ found the writer,

Kipling was exhausted. Twain, _____ , invited him to chat.

And that is just what _____ did. Twain told stories about his life and

talked about his writing. _____ the end of the interview, Kipling had plenty

of material for a superb article.

Chapter 16: Paragraph and Composition Structure

 **WORSHEET 15** *The Conclusion*

Compositions need **conclusions** that allow readers to feel that the ideas are tied together and are complete. The following techniques are some options writers have for creating effective conclusions.

1. Refer to the introduction.
2. Offer a solution or make a recommendation.
3. Restate your thesis.
4. Summarize your major points.
5. Point out consequences or areas for future research.
6. End with an appropriate quotation.

Exercise On the lines provided, identify the techniques used by the writers of the following conclusions.

1. Technological advances in preparation, storage, and distribution processes help ensure that the food we grow will be used efficiently. Such advances balance the natural cycles of bounty and shortage and make modern society possible.

   Technique: _____

2. We began by asking the question, "Why were the Easter Island statues built?" We are now forced to admit that, while we have some tantalizing clues, we still have no definitive answer.

   Technique: _____

3. Although the damage to the ozone is severe and cannot be easily reversed, this is not the time for the "I-can't-make-a-difference" attitude. Indeed, you can and must attempt to make a difference. Begin by writing to your congressional representatives today.

   Technique: _____

4. In the 1970s and 1980s, dramatic progress was made in increasing children's awareness of the dangers of cigarette smoking. Yet teenage smoking among some socioeconomic groups is actually on the rise. The solution to this problem may lie in renewed emphasis on and commitment to early-childhood education about smoking.

   Technique: _____

Name _____ Date _____ Class _____

WORKSHEET 16

Transitional Words and Phrases

Whether your piece of writing is made up of a single paragraph or many paragraphs, you will always be connecting ideas. The following chart is a handy guide to words that make the right connections.

TRANSITIONAL WORDS AND PHRASES			
Comparing Ideas/ Classification and Definition	also and	another moreover	similarly too
Contrasting Ideas/ Classification and Definition	although but however	in spite of nevertheless	on the other hand still yet
Showing Cause and Effect/ Narration	as a result because	consequently since	so that therefore
Showing Time/Narration	after at last at once before	eventually finally first meanwhile	next then thereafter
Showing Place/Description	above across around before beyond	down here in inside into	next over there to under
Showing Importance/ Evaluation	first last	mainly more important	then to begin with

Chapter 17: The Research Paper

 **WORKSHEET 1** *Choosing a Suitable Topic*

In exploring subjects for a research paper, begin with your own interests: You will be thinking and reading about your final topic and working hard on it for some time. Also remember that the library is only one place to start your exploration.

FAMILY AND FRIENDS: Does someone you know have an interesting job or hobby?

HEROES: Whom do you admire and wish you knew more about?

PLACES NEAR AND FAR: What places have you visited or wanted to visit?

CURRENT EVENTS: Which events and subjects grab your attention?

LIBRARY AND MEDIA: What subjects arouse your curiosity?

Once you have found a subject, you need to narrow your focus to a specific aspect that intrigues you and that can be covered in a composition. To limit a topic, you can analyze it on your own or you can look for subtopics in the card catalog, in the *Readers' Guide to Periodical Literature*, and in encyclopedias and specialized dictionaries. Then, make sure your limited topic is suitable for a research paper. Use the following criteria.

AVAILABILITY OF SOURCES: Be sure you can find five or six good sources.

OBJECTIVITY AND FACTS: Can you maintain objectivity and stick to the facts?

AUDIENCE INTEREST: If your topic isn't appealing or is widely known, what approach could intrigue your readers?

Exercise Which of the following topics are suitable for a seven-to-ten-page research report? Some may be too broad, too narrow, or too personal. For each topic that seems unsuitable, first tell why you think it's unsuitable and then suggest a more workable topic.

1. how the War of Jenkins' Ear got its name
2. a television program worth watching
3. daily life of women in the Iroquois Nation
4. John Bardeen's contributions to developing the transistor
5. the American space-exploration program

1. _____

_____

2. _____

_____

3. _____

_____

4. _____

_____

5. _____

_____

COMPOSITION

Name _____ Date _____ Class _____

Evaluating Sources

You can use general reference works like encyclopedias to get an overview of your topic. If you already have a solid background in your topic, go directly to more focused sources, such as the card catalog or on-line catalog, or the *Readers' Guide to Periodical Literature*. Before using a source, you need to evaluate its usefulness to you. One good way to evaluate a source is to use the "4R" test.

RELEVANT: Does the source relate directly to your limited topic? For a book, check the table of contents and index. Skim magazine articles.

RELIABLE: Can you trust it? A respected scholar or a respected magazine such as *Scientific American* can usually be relied on for accuracy.

RECENT: Be sure you aren't using outdated information, especially for rapidly changing topics.

REPRESENTATIVE: If you are working on a controversial topic, you must show different points of view. Your task as a researcher is to study, balance, and interpret the views on all sides.

Exercise   The items below are from the *Readers' Guide to Periodical Literature.*

CATHER, Willa Sibert

Ⓐ Wee Winkie's wanderings: story. Vogue 161: 113 Je '73*

   about

Ⓑ American woman: Willa Cather centennial. il por Vogue 161:113 + Je '73*

Ⓒ Two women: a centennial. J. W. Donohue. America 128:276–80 Mr 31 '73*

Ⓓ Willa Cather; understanding God's ways. Chr Today 18:31 D 7 '73*

Ⓔ Willa Cather's Song of the lark. L. Olson. New Repub 169:28–31 Jl 7 '73*

Ⓕ Menuhins: remembering Cather. T. Price. pors Hi Fi 24: MA28 Ap '74

Ⓖ Willa Cather: the light behind her books. M. H. Freydberg. Am Scholar 43:282–7 Spr '74*

From *Readers' Guide to Periodical Literature, 1974.* Copyright ©1974 by The H. W. Wilson Company. Reprinted by permission of The H. W. Wilson Company.

You are researching the life of Willa Cather. Answer the following questions by writing *yes, no,* or the appropriate key letter or letters for the entries in the spaces provided to the right of the questions below.

1. Which entry refers to a work by Cather?   _____

2. Which article is about a specific Cather novel?   _____

3. Which articles probably contain biographical information?   _____

4. Are any of the articles likely to contain the most current research on Cather?   _____

Chapter 17: The Research Paper

Taking Notes

When you find possible sources, it's important to keep accurate and complete information on them. Your Works Cited list—the list of sources at the end of your report—must contain specific information because some of your readers may want to consult your sources.

The best system for collecting accurate information is to put each source on a 3" × 5" card. On each card, record full publishing information, note the call number or location of the source, and assign each source a number.

Read or listen to the source (or a complete section of it) before you begin taking notes. Then go back over the information using 4" × 6" cards to record your notes. Later, when you're organizing your report, cards make it easy to arrange and rearrange information.

Exercise   The following excerpt is from a recent article you are reading about playwrights. Assume that you're researching a paper about the problems of modern city life in drama. You've given this article the source number 9. Develop a list of questions using the *5W-How?* questions. Then, in the space provided, take notes to answer the questions you have written.

> Alfonso Sastre, who is one of Spain's leading playwrights, has been influenced by the works of Luigi Pirandello and Arthur Miller. Sastre, along with these playwrights, usually sets his plays in urban locations. A major theme throughout his plays is the difficulties of city life. The characters in almost every play face the problem of maintaining a sense of self within overcrowded and often demeaning situations. Despair over social injustices pervades Sastre's works. However, he, as well as Miller, infuses a sense of hope into the despair. Perhaps the play that stands as the finest example of the themes of despair and hope is *Anna Kleiber*.

Questions: _____

_____

_____

_____

Answers: _____

_____

_____

_____

_____

_____

_____

COMPOSITION

Chapter 17: The Research Paper

| WORKSHEET 4 | *Writing a Thesis Statement* |

The thesis statement is a sentence or two stating both your topic and what you will say about it. Your thesis statement may change or be reworded as your writing progresses.

Exercise A   For each topic, write a thesis statement.

> EXAMPLE: 1. **Topic:** The salaries of professional athletes
>
> **Thesis Statement:** *The salaries of professional athletes have skyrocketed in the past decade.*

1. **Topic:** Household chemicals that are poisonous

   Thesis Statement: _____

   _____

2. **Topic:** Changes in divorce laws

   Thesis Statement: _____

   _____

3. **Topic:** Americans' dependence on the automobile

   Thesis Statement: _____

   _____

4. **Topic:** the efforts of ecology-minded groups

   Thesis Statement: _____

   _____

5. **Topic:** Violence on television and in films

   Thesis Statement: _____

   _____

Exercise B   Choose one of the thesis statements you have written in Exercise A (or another of your choice), and write an introductory paragraph for a research report. In the introduction include your thesis statement, as well as interesting details, ideas, a question, examples, or definitions. Write your introduction on the lines provided, and underline your thesis statement.

_____

_____

_____

_____

_____

_____

Chapter 17: The Research Paper

WORKSHEET 5   *Developing an Outline*

To create your writing plan, start by sorting your note cards into stacks according to their labels. These stacks may immediately suggest the main sections of your report and the ideas you will want to emphasize. Then you can decide how best to order the ideas and which supporting details to use in which sequence.

Your working outline can be rough in form, as long as it is sufficiently detailed to give shape and direction to your drafting. But for your completed paper, your teacher may request a final **formal outline** like the one below. Such an outline serves as a table of contents and is prepared *after* you've finished the report.

    I. What we learn from mythology
        A. Clues to how people lived in the past
            1. Their values
            2. Their culture
        B. Implications of how to live in the present
            1. What myths reveal about human nature
                a. Myth of King Midas
                b. Myth of Phaëthon
            2. Need to tolerate different points of view and attitudes toward life

Exercise   In the left-hand column is an incomplete outline for a paper titled "Twentieth-Century Heroes." Using the information in the right-hand column, fill in the blank spaces in the outline. Note that some of the outline is already given. You will not use all of the information in the column at the right.

I. Definition of a hero	Heroes from music
II. Heroes from sports	Babe Ruth
A. _____	Movie heroes
B. _____	Jesse Owens
C. _____	Elvis Presley
D. _____	Women heroes in literature
III. _____	The Beatles
A. _____	Billie Jean King
B. _____	Paula Abdul
C. _____	Heroes of tomorrow
IV. _____	Importance of heroes
A. Role models (people to look up to)	Chris Evert
B. _____	Identification with heroes

COMPOSITION

Name _____ Date _____ Class _____

 **WORKSHEET 6** | *Documenting Sources*

Deciding which information you must **document,** or give credit for, in a research paper sometimes requires thought. That thought process can start with noticing what is or is not documented when you read reports of research. The following guidelines will also help you avoid pitfalls when documenting your information.

1. In general, don't document information that appears in several sources or facts that appear in standard reference books. For example, a statement like *"Their Eyes Were Watching God* is generally considered Hurston's finest novel" needs no documentation because it clearly relies on several sources. The main facts of her life that are available in encyclopedias and other standard references also do not need to be credited.

2. Document the source of each direct quotation (unless it's very widely known, such as Patrick Henry's "Give me liberty or give me death!").

3. Document any original theory or opinion other than your own. Since ideas belong to their authors, you must not present the ideas of other people as your own.

4. Document the sources of data or other information from surveys, scientific experiments, and research studies.

5. Document unusual, little-known, or questionable facts and statistics.

NOTE: Remember that you must give credit when you use another writer's *words or ideas.* Not to do so is **plagiarism,** an extremely serious offense. Even a summary or a paraphrase of someone else's original idea must be credited. When in doubt about plagiarism, give credit.

Exercise If each of the following items were to appear in a research paper on the baseball player Christy Mathewson, which ones would you need to document? On the line provided, write *D* for an item requiring documentation and *ND* for an item that does not require documentation.

_____ 1. Christy Mathewson, a right-handed pitcher, played for the New York Giants from 1900 to 1916.

_____ 2. Using his famous screwball, Mathewson won thirty games three years in succession (1903–1905).

_____ 3. About Mathewson's pitching style, Connie Mack once said, "With Mathewson, it was knowledge, judgment, perfect control, and form."

_____ 4. The grave of Christy Mathewson is in Lewisburg, Pennsylvania, near Bucknell University.

_____ 5. Matty's control is demonstrated by his number of strikeouts as opposed to his number of walks—2,505 to 837.

Name _____ Date _____ Class _____

 **WORKSHEET 7** *Parenthetical Citations*

A **parenthetical citation** gives source information in parentheses in the body of a research paper. The citation should provide just enough information to lead the reader to the full source listing on the Works Cited page. Since the Works Cited list is alphabetized by authors' last names, an author's last name and the page numbers are usually enough for a parenthetical citation.

WORKS BY ONE AUTHOR:	(Kingston 32)
SEPARATE PASSAGES IN A SINGLE WORK:	(Kingston 24, 53–59)
MORE THAN ONE WORK BY THE SAME AUTHOR:	(Kingston, *Woman Warrior* 87)
WORKS BY MORE THAN ONE AUTHOR:	(Brooks and Warren 102)
MULTIVOLUME WORKS:	(Sandburg 3: 124–125)
WORKS WITH A TITLE ONLY:	(*World Almanac* 523)
CLASSIC LITERARY WORKS PUBLISHED IN MANY EDITIONS:	*Prose:* (Twain, *The Adventures of Huckleberry Finn*, ch. 1, 3) *Poems and verse plays:* (Shakespeare, *Macbeth* 5. 5.17) [Note use of Arabic numbers.]
INDIRECT SOURCES:	(qtd. in Lawson 349)
MORE THAN ONE WORK IN THE SAME CITATION:	(Smith 46; Williams 98)

Place the citation as close as possible to the material it documents, if possible at the end of a sentence or at another point of punctuation. Additionally, place the citation *before* the punctuation mark of the sentence, clause, or phrase you are documenting. For a quotation that ends a sentence, put the citation after the quotation mark but before the end punctuation mark. For an indented quotation, put the citation *two spaces after* the final punctuation mark.

NOTE: A nonprint source such as an interview or audiotape will not have a page number; a print source fewer than two pages will not require a page number. If you name the author in your sentence, you need give only the page number. If the author has more than one work in the Works Cited list, you will also have to give a short form of the title.

Exercise On the line provided, write a parenthetical citation for each of the following items. Treat the items as if they were all citations in the same research paper. Watch for more than one work by the same author.

1. Page 76 of *Animal Law* by Godfrey Sandys-Winsch, published in 1978 by Shaw & Sons, a company in Wheaton, Illinois _____

2. Page 58 from an article entitled "Fighting to Free Animals" by H. Quinn. The article appeared in the December 3, 1984, issue of *Macleans* magazine. _____

COMPOSITION

3. "USDA Animal Research Under Fire" by Jeffrey L. Fox, *Bio Science* magazine, volume 35, number 1, pages 6–7, January 1985 _____

4. Page 1414 of *Science* magazine, published June 1984, "Animal Rights Bill Defeated in California," written by Jeffrey L. Fox _____

5. Henry Foster and James Fox, editors of *The Mouse in Biomedical Research*, volume 3, pages 302–03, published in 1983 by Academic Press, San Diego, California _____

6. S. Begley's article entitled "Liberation in the Labs" in *Newsweek* magazine, August 27, 1984, pages 66–67 _____

7. "Animal Research: The Case for Experimentation" by Frederick A. King, *Psychology Today*, pages 56–58, volume 18, September 1984 _____

8. Heather McGiffin and Nancie Brownley, editors of *Animals in Education*, published in 1980 by the Institute for the Study of Animal Problems, which is in Washington, D.C., pages 247–53 _____

9. *Vertebrates*, which is in volume 2 in the two-volume set *Animals in Schools*, by L. Comber and M. Hogg, page 68, published in 1980 by Heinemann Educational Books in Portsmouth, NH _____

10. Pages 11–16 in *Animals and Science for Man: A Study Guide* by Rodney F. Plimpton, Jr., and Fred J. Stephens, Burgess Publishers in Minneapolis, MN, 1979 _____

Name _____ Date _____ Class _____

List of Works Cited

The Works Cited list contains all the sources, print and nonprint, that you credit in your report. (The term *Works Cited* is a broader title than *Bibliography*, which refers to print sources only.)

BOOKS: Joyce, Carey. <u>Art and Reality: Ways of the Creative Process</u>. Garden City: Doubleday, 1958

JOURNAL ARTICLES: Watkins, Floyd C., and Thomas Daniel Young. "Revisions of Style in Faulkner's *The Hamlet*." <u>Modern Fiction Studies</u> 5 (1959–60): 327–36. [article by two authors in a scholarly journal]

MAGAZINE ARTICLES: "Rabies." <u>Sciquest</u> Mar. 1980: 28. [unsigned article in a monthly magazine]

NEWSPAPER ARTICLES: "Panama Suspends Deportation." <u>Tallahassee Democrat</u> 16 Apr. 1987, late ed.: A3. [unsigned article]

Use the following guidelines for preparing the list of Works Cited.

- Center the words *Works Cited* on a new sheet of paper.
- Begin each entry on a separate line. Position the first line of the entry evenly with the left margin and indent the second and all other lines five spaces. Double-space all entries.
- Alphabetize the sources by the author's last name. If there is no author, alphabetize by title, ignoring *A, An*, and *The* and using the first letter of the next word.
- If you use two or more sources by the same author, include the author's name only in the first entry. For all other entries, use three hyphens followed by a period (---.) in place of the author's name. Order the entries alphabetically by title.

Exercise   Use the following items to prepare entries for a Works Cited list. Use correct punctuation and styling and refer to the examples above. In the space before each item, number the items from 1 to 5 to indicate the correct alphabetical order.

1. _____ A book by A. S. Byatt entitled Degrees of Freedom: The Novels of Iris Murdoch, published in London by Chatto and Windus in 1965.

_____

_____

_____

2. _____ An article by Bernard McCabe entitled The Guises of Love, published in Commonweal, pages 270–73, on December 3, 1965.

_____

_____

_____

COMPOSITION

3. _____ An anonymous article entitled A Murdoch Checklist, published in
volume 10 of Books and Bookmen, pages 10–11, in 1966.

_____

_____

_____

4. _____ An article by Sharon Kaehele and Howard German entitled The Discovery
of Reality in Iris Murdoch's *The Bell*, published in volume 72 of the journal
PMLA, pages 554–63, in 1967.

_____

_____

_____

5. _____ An article by Iris Murdoch entitled The Novelist as Metaphysician,
published in The Listener, pages 473 and 476, on May 16, 1950.

_____

_____

_____

Name _____ Date _____ Class _____

 **WORKSHEET 9** *Proofreading and Publishing*

Checking the mechanics of your documentation (parenthetical citations and list of Works Cited) is a very important part of proofreading a research paper. Remember that your documentation is there for readers to use: accuracy is necessary because they may want to find one of your sources.

A research report is a substantial piece of work, a paper to be proud of and to *use*. Try one of the following suggestions for publishing your paper.

- If you discover persons or groups especially interested in your subject, consider sending them a copy of your report.
- Save a copy of your report as an example of your writing and research skills for a college or job application.
- You might make your report the basis of a videotape documentary or you could make an audiotape of the report, adding sound effects or music.

Exercise: Proofreading   The following paragraphs are part of a research report. Proofread for errors in grammar, spelling, punctuation, and capitalization, and put the Works Cited list in the correct form.

An even temprement and a good mental attitude is essential in any sport, but this seems especially true for tennis. When two people having roughly the same abilitys play each other, it's the loser who usually beats himself or herself.

Getting angry on the court can have disasterous effects on one's game, even when that anger is directed at oneself. Psychologists agree: "Losing players become openly hostile toward themselves, criticizing their shots in a manner destined to lead straight to disintegration. Its only in rare cases that such self-criticism leads to better play." (Cath, Kahn, and Cobb, 45) A far better approach is to forget a bad point just played and consentrate on the next point.

Of course, the best mental attitude in the world won't help an unskilled player. No matter how well you control your emotions, that won't help a bit "if your stroking pattern doesn't honor the basic laws of physics." (Braden, 21) The more correctly an individual practices, the less frustrated the individual is in a game. And the less frustrated he or she is, the better he or she performs.

Works Cited

Braden, Vic. "Five Myths That May Be Holding you Back." <u>Tennis</u> Mar. 1981: 21.

<u>Love and Hate on the Tennis Court.</u> Stanley H. Cath, Alvin Kahn, and Nathan Cobb.
    Charles Scribner's Sons: New York, 1977.

COMPOSITION

Name _____ Date _____ Class _____

Using Notes in a Research Paper

Exercise   You are writing a research paper about communication among animals. The purpose of your paper is to answer the question "Does any nonhuman animal have language?" Below are two notes for your report. Each note deals with communication among honeybees. Use the notes to write a paragraph for your paper on a separate sheet of paper. Quote from one note directly; paraphrase or summarize material from the other. Be sure to include a list of Works Cited.

Note 1:

"Sure, bees communicate, but so does every other animal. Birds have alarm calls. Dogs bark at strangers. Cats cry when they want to be fed. But none of that is language. Those are all just signals—one-liners that mean 'help' or 'go away' or 'I'm hungry.' Real language is much more subtle and complex. A real language is infinite in its possibilities of expression. And a real language is creative. Think about this sentence: 'My nephew Humphrey said that the pygmy hippos at the Sydney Zoo all have Hungarian names.' Now, the chances are pretty good that no one has ever uttered that sentence before. It's no great shakes, that sentence, but it's completely original. Speakers of languages are constantly coming up with original statements. Animals, on the other hand, have a limited repertoire of signals. They say the same dumb, dull things over and over."

> —Interview with Roberta Whorf, Associate Professor of Linguistics, Saussure Community College, June 1993.

Note 2:

"Some creatures communicate by means of calls—songs, grunts, or words. Honeybees communicate by means of dance. Karl von Frisch and his colleagues discovered that when a bee finds a good food supply—a bunch of clover, for example—it flies back to the hive and does a dance that communicates highly specific and accurate information. The movements in the dance tell the other bees which direction to fly to find the food, how far to fly, and how rich the food source is. This language of the bees is one of many examples of language in the animal kingdom."

> —Angela Suarez, *Empires in the Grass: Life and Death in Your Own Backyard*. Rockport, MA: Wordworks Publishing Services, 1993.

Your paragraph will be judged on the basis of these criteria:

1. The paragraph is developed from both sources.
2. A thesis statement explains what the paragraph is about.
3. The tone of the paragraph is appropriate for a research paper.
4. Facts and ideas are stated mostly in the writer's own words.
5. Both sources are credited.
6. The paragraph is relatively free of errors in spelling, grammar, usage, mechanics, and manuscript form.

Name _____ Date _____ Class _____

 **WORKSHEET 1** *Finding Books in the Library*

In most libraries, books are assigned **call numbers** to identify each book and to indicate where it's shelved. Call numbers are assigned according to one of two classification systems: the *Dewey decimal system* or the *Library of Congress system*. In the **Dewey decimal system,** nonfiction books and some works of literature are grouped by subject into ten general subject areas, each assigned a range of numbers. Books of fiction are grouped together in alphabetical order according to the authors' last names. The **Library of Congress system** uses code letters to identify subject categories. The first letter of a book's call number tells the general category. The librarian can provide you with a complete list of letter codes for Library of Congress categories.

The **card catalog** is a cabinet of drawers filled with alphabetically arranged cards: *title cards, author cards,* and *subject cards*. Catalog cards may give publication facts, list the number of pages, and tell whether the book contains illustrations or diagrams. The **on-line catalog** is a computerized version of the card catalog. The on-line catalog can locate information quickly and may tell you if a book you are looking for is checked out or if it is available at another library.

Exercise A On a separate sheet of paper, draw a diagram of your school library, and label the areas where the following resources are found. List below your diagram any items that you could not find.

1. the card catalog (or on-line catalog)   4. current magazines

2. the fiction section   5. the librarian's desk

3. the reference section   6. computers

Exercise B Use the card catalog to find the following books. For each book, give its title, author or editor, and call number.

1. a biography of Benjamin Franklin _____

_____

2. a collection of plays by Amiri Baraka, Tennessee Williams, or Lillian Hellman

_____

_____

3. a guide to colleges and universities _____

_____

4. a collection of essays about American history _____

_____

5. a recent book on movie making _____

_____

Name _____ Date _____ Class _____

 **Using Reference Materials**

Your library may contain many or all of the following sources of information.

- *Readers' Guide to Periodical Literature* The *Readers' Guide* indexes articles, poems, and stories from more than one hundred magazines.
- **Vertical File** A vertical file is a cabinet with up-to-date materials organized by subject; it often contains government, business, and educational publications.
- **Microfilm and Microfiche** Many libraries photographically reduce periodicals and newspapers and store them on microfilm or microfiche.
- **Audiovisual Materials** Libraries often keep audiocassettes of famous speeches or poetry readings as well as videotapes of documentaries.
- **Reference Section** Most libraries have a separate reference section. Ask your librarian about its location and what works are available.

Exercise A In your school or your local library, find answers to the following questions about the *Readers' Guide.*

1. Where are the volumes of the *Readers' Guide* kept in this library? _____

   _____

2. In the *Readers' Guide,* find a heading for an article on the subject of recycling. Write the title of the article, the name of the author, the name of the magazine, the date the article was published, and the page numbers listed for this article. In addition, list any *see* or *see also* references you find for this heading.

   _____

   _____

3. Check in the *Readers' Guide* under a subject heading of a career that interests you. Write down the title, author, magazine, date, and page numbers for three articles listed.

   _____

   _____

4. List the title, author, name of the magazine, date, and page numbers of an entry for a review of a recent television program or movie that interests you.

   _____

Exercise B Name a reference book you could use to find each of the following items of information.

1. the source of the expression "All the world's a stage" _____

2. a description of the climate of the Falkland Islands _____

3. a critique of a prominent author's works _____

4. entrance requirements for Yale and the University of Texas at Austin _____

Name _____ Date _____ Class _____

WORKSHEET 3

Types of Dictionaries

An **unabridged dictionary** is the most comprehensive source for finding information about a word. Unabridged dictionaries offer more word entries and usually give more detailed information, such as fuller word histories or longer lists of synonyms or antonyms, than an abridged dictionary does.

The *Oxford English Dictionary* (*OED*) is the largest unabridged dictionary. The *OED* gives the approximate date of a word's first appearance in English and shows, in a quotation, how the word was used at that time. The *OED* also traces any changes in the spelling or meaning of a word.

An **abridged** or **college dictionary** is one of the most commonly used reference books in the United States. Abridged dictionaries do not contain as many entries or as much information about entry words as unabridged dictionaries do. However, abridged dictionaries are revised frequently, so they give the most up-to-date information on meanings and uses of words. Besides word entries, most abridged dictionaries contain other useful information, such as tables of commonly used abbreviations, selected biographical entries, and tables of signs and symbols.

A **specialized dictionary** contains entries that relate to a specific subject or field. For example, there are specialized dictionaries for terms used in art, music, sports, gardening, mythology, and many other subjects.

Exercise   Using an abridged or college dictionary, look up the answers to the following questions.

1. What was Galileo's full name? _____

2. What is the scientific notation for pyridoxine? _____

3. What is the meaning of the Latin phrase *mare liberum*? _____

4. When was the Great Wall of China constructed? _____

5. From what language is *pest* derived? _____

6. Copy the correct pronunciation of *foliicolous*, including diacritical marks. Be sure that you are able to pronounce the word correctly. _____

7. How many different meanings are given in your dictionary for the word *gauge*?

   _____

8. What is the height of Mount Everest? _____

9. Where does the word *Wednesday* come from? _____

10. From what language is the word *pajamas* derived? _____

Name _____ Date _____ Class _____

The Dictionary Entry

A **dictionary entry** contains a lot of information about a word. The boldfaced **entry word** shows how the word is spelled and how it is divided into syllables. The entry word may also show capitalization and provide alternative spellings. The **pronunciation** is shown by the use of accent marks and either diacritical marks or phonetic respelling.

Part-of-speech labels (usually in abbreviated form) indicate how the entry word should be used. Some words may be used as more than one part of speech. For these words, a part-of-speech label is given before each numbered (or lettered) series of definitions.

The **etymology** is the origin and history of a word. Etymology tells how the word (or its parts) came into English. The etymology for the word *opossum* looks something like this:

[<Algonquian (*apässum*), lit., white beast]

The example shows that *opossum* comes from an Algonquian word that literally means "white beast." Sometimes etymologies contain symbols such as < or *. These symbols are usually explained in the front of the dictionary or at the bottom of each page.

Special usage labels (such as [archaic] or [slang]) may show that a definition is limited to certain forms of speech. Other labels, such as *Law, Med.* (medicine), or *Chem.* (chemistry), may indicate that a definition is used only in a certain field. Here are two usage labels for the word *law:*

[Math] a general principle   [Brit] a handicap in a race

Dictionaries may also contain the following information.

   examples: phrases or sentences that may demonstrate how the defined word is to be used

   other forms: full or partial spellings of plural forms of nouns, different tenses of verbs, or the comparison forms of adjectives and adverbs

   related word forms: usually created by adding suffixes or prefixes

   synonyms and antonyms: words with the same or opposite meanings

Exercise   Use a dictionary to answer the questions below. Write your answers on the lines provided.

   1. What is a noun form of the word *ornate?* _____

   2. How else can the word *stockroom* be written? _____

   3. Is the noun *thews* singular or plural? _____

   4. Which syllable is accented in the word *mischievous?* _____

   5. What language does the word *persimmon* come from? _____

Name _____ Date _____ Class _____

WORKSHEET 5 *Business Letters: Form*

A business letter contains six parts.

- The **heading** usually consists of three lines: your street address (or post office box number); your city, state, and ZIP Code; and the date of the letter.

- The **inside address** shows the name and the address of the person or organization you are writing to. If you're writing to a specific person, use a courtesy title (such as *Mr., Ms.,* or *Mrs.*) or a professional title (such as *Dr.*) in front of the person's name. After the person's name, include the person's business or job title (such as *Owner* or *Sales Manager*), followed by the name of the company or organization and the address.

- The **salutation** is your greeting. If you are writing to a specific person, begin with *Dear,* followed by a courtesy title or a professional title and the person's last name. End the salutation with a colon. If you don't have the name of a specific person, you can use a general salutation, such as *Dear Sir or Madam* or *Ladies and Gentlemen*. You can also use a department or a position title, with or without the word *Dear*.

- The **body** of your letter contains your message. If the body of your letter contains more than one paragraph, leave a space between paragraphs.

- **Closings** often used in business letters include *Sincerely, Yours truly, Respectfully yours,* and *Regards*. Capitalize only the first word of the closing.

- Write your **signature** in ink, directly below the closing. Sign your full name. If you type your letter, type your name neatly below your signature.

There are two styles used frequently for business letters. With the **block form,** every part of the letter begins at the left-hand margin, and paragraphs are not indented. In the **modified block form,** the heading, the closing, and the signature are aligned along an imaginary line just to the right of the center of the page. The other parts of the letter begin at the left-hand margin. All paragraphs are indented.

Exercise On the back of this sheet, write a business letter. Use block form. Invent all of the information. Your purpose can be to request information about a product or a service or to offer appreciation for a product or service.

Resources, Worksheet 5, continued

_____

_____

_____

_____

_____

_____

_____

_____

_____

_____

_____

_____

_____

_____

_____

_____

_____

_____

_____

_____

_____

_____

_____

_____

_____

_____

_____

_____

_____

_____

_____

_____

_____

_____

_____

_____

Name _____ Date _____ Class _____

Business Letters: Content

The purpose of a **request letter** is to ask for something. It may be a catalog, a brochure, or information about a product or service. An **order letter** is a special kind of request letter that is written to order merchandise by mail. Remember the following guidelines when you write a request or order letter.

1. State your request clearly.
2. If you're asking for information, enclose a self-addressed, stamped envelope.
3. Make sure that your request is reasonable and that you have allowed enough time for the person to respond.
4. Include all important details, such as size, color, style, catalog number, and price. Compute correctly any costs involved, including any necessary sales tax or shipping charges.

The purpose of a **complaint** or **adjustment letter** is to report a problem and to request a satisfactory resolution to the difficulty. Remember the following guidelines when writing a complaint or adjustment letter.

1. Register your complaint as soon as possible.
2. Explain exactly what is wrong, and provide all necessary information.
3. Keep the tone of the letter courteous.

An **appreciation** or **commendation letter** is written to compliment or to express appreciation to a person, a group, or an organization.

Remember that all business letters usually follow a few simple guidelines. *Use a courteous, positive, and professional tone.* Rude or insulting letters are counterproductive. *Use formal standard English.* Avoid slang, dialect, contractions, and abbreviations. *State your purpose clearly and quickly.* Assume that the person reading your letter is busy. *Include all necessary information.*

Exercise You would like to express dissatisfaction about the service that you recently received at a local restaurant. On the back of this sheet, write a letter of complaint to the restaurant manager. Keep the body of your letter short, but include the important facts.

Name _____ Date _____ Class _____

_____

_____

_____

_____

_____

_____

_____

_____

_____

_____

_____

_____

_____

_____

_____

_____

_____

_____

_____

_____

_____

_____

_____

_____

_____

_____

_____

_____

_____

_____

_____

_____

_____

_____

_____

_____

Resources

WORKSHEET 7

Letters of Application and Résumés

You write a **letter of application** to provide a selection committee or a possible employer enough information to determine whether you are a good candidate for a position. When you are writing a letter of application, remember the following points.

1. Identify the job or position you're applying for. Tell how you heard about it.
2. Depending on the position you are applying for, you might include
   - your age, grade in school, or grade-point average
   - your experience or your activities, awards, and honors
   - personal qualities or characteristics that make you a good choice
   - the date or times you are available
3. Offer to provide references. Your references should include two or three responsible adults (usually not relatives) who have agreed to recommend you. Be prepared to supply their addresses and telephone numbers.

A **résumé** is a summary of your background and experience. For many job positions, a résumé should be submitted along with a letter of application. There are many different styles of arranging the information on a résumé. Whatever style you select, be sure your résumé looks neat and businesslike.

Exercise A   You have seen an ad for an after-school job that suits your qualifications and needs. Write the body of a letter of application to the person in charge of hiring. Keep the body of your letter brief, but include enough information to show that you are a good candidate for the position.

_____

_____

_____

_____

_____

_____

_____

_____

_____

_____

_____

_____

_____

RESOURCES

Resources, Worksheet 7, continued

Exercise B Choose a job that interests you. On the lines below, write a personal résumé that shows you are qualified for such a position. Then, write a short letter explaining how you heard about the job and requesting a personal interview. You may invent some or all of the information.

_____

_____

_____

_____

_____

_____

_____

_____

_____

_____

_____

_____

_____

_____

_____

_____

_____

_____

_____

_____

_____

_____

_____

_____

_____

_____

_____

_____

Name _____ Date _____ Class _____

Printed Forms and Applications

As you enter the work force or begin applying to colleges, you'll be asked to fill out a variety of forms and applications. The person or organization who receives your form or application will be able to help you best if you fill the form out neatly and completely. When you fill out forms, keep the following guidelines in mind.

1. Always read the entire form to make sure you understand exactly what items of information you are being asked to supply.

2. Type neatly or print legibly, using a pen or pencil as directed.

3. Include all information requested. If a question does not apply to you, write *not applicable* or *N.A.* instead of leaving the space blank.

4. Keep the form neat and clean. Avoid smudges or cross-outs.

5. When you have completed the form, proofread it carefully in order to correct any spelling, usage, punctuation, or factual errors.

6. Submit the form to the correct person, or mail it to the correct address.

Exercise   Complete the form below. Make up any or all of the information. Print neatly.

Name _____ Tel. No. _____

Street _____ City _____ State _____ ZIP Code _____

(Do not complete the following section if your last name begins with M–Z.)

Describe any experience that you've had working with tools or business machines.

_____

_____

_____

_____

(Do not complete the following section if your last name begins with A–L.)

Circle the items that apply to you:

- over 6 feet tall
- brown or black hair
- red or blond hair
- athlete
- freshman/sophomore
- junior/senior

Describe any relevant experience that you have had caring for animals.

_____

_____

_____

_____

Resources

WORKSHEET 9 *Writing Social Letters*

When you want to thank someone formally, congratulate someone, send an invitation, or respond to an invitation extended to you, you should write a social letter.

Social letters are much less formal in style than business letters. For example, social letters don't include an inside address and most use the modified block form.

Thank-you letters. The purpose of a thank-you letter is to express appreciation for a gift or a favor you have received. Try to say more than just "thank you": Give details about how the person's gift or efforts were appreciated or helpful.

Invitations. An invitation should contain specific information about a planned event, such as the occasion, the time and place, and any other details guests might need to know.

Letters of regret. If you have been invited to a party or another social function and will be unable to attend, it is polite to send a letter of regret. A written reply is especially appropriate if you were sent a written invitation that included the letters *R.S.V.P.* (In French, these letters are an abbreviation for "please reply.")

Exercise On the lines provided, write a social letter for one of the following situations.

1. Write a thank-you letter expressing appreciation for a gift or favor.
2. Write an invitation letter for an upcoming event you are planning.
3. Write a letter of regret explaining that you will not be able to attend an event to which you have been invited.

_____

_____

_____

_____

_____

_____

_____

_____

_____

_____

_____

_____

_____

_____

Name _____ Date _____ Class _____

Manuscript Style A

Abbreviate given names only if the person is most commonly known that way. Leave a space between two such initials, but not between three or more.

N. Scott Momaday   **A. S.** Byatt   **W.E.B.** Du Bois

Abbreviate social titles whether used with the full name or with the last name alone. The social title of *Miss* is not considered an abbreviation, and so it is not followed by a period.

Mr.   **Mrs.**   **Ms.**   **Sr.** [*Señor*]   **Sra.** [*Señora*]   **Dr.**   **Miss**

Civil and military titles may be abbreviated when used before full names or before initials and last names. Spell them out before last names alone.

Brig. Gen. Clara Adams-Ender   **Brigadier General** Adams-Ender

Abbreviate titles and academic degrees after proper names. Use such abbreviations only after a person's full name, not after the last name alone. Except for numerals such as *III* or *IV*, abbreviations of titles and degrees used after a name are set off by commas. Do not include the title *Mr., Mrs., Ms.,* or *Dr.* when you use a title or degree after a name.

John Webb **II, RN,** assisted **Dr.** Gina Harrell during the operation.

Spell out most company names in text. They may be abbreviated in tables, notes, and bibliographies. The abbreviations *Inc.* and *Ltd.* are set off by commas; however, they may be omitted in text. *After* spelling out the first use of the names of agencies, organizations, and other groups commonly known by their initials, use abbreviations.

Exercise   Most of the following sentences contain errors in the use of abbreviations. On the line provided, correct each error. If a sentence is correct, write C.

1. Maj. Rogers suggests that we contact Mrs Van Wolverton at Wells and Co. soon.

   _____

2. Ms. Karen Ulmerton, Ph D will make the first speech at the seminar immediately after the Rev. Logan finishes his opening address.

   _____

3. Dr H.R. Post III, M.D. will demonstrate the procedure on Monday.

   _____

4. Children's World Learning Centers, Inc., has just purchased the lot; CWLC plans to have completed building by the fall.

   _____

5. Public Broadcasting Service (PBS) is well known for its quality programming. One of Public Broadcasting Service's most popular series is *Mystery!*

   _____

Name _____ Date _____ Class _____

WORKSHEET 11   *Manuscript Style B*

In a written passage (text), spell out the names of states, countries, and other political units whenever they stand alone or follow any other geographical term. Abbreviate them in tables, notes, and bibliographies.

    TEXT: Nevada   Germany   TABLES, ETC.: Nev.   Ger.

In text, *United States* may be abbreviated to *U.S.* only when it is used as an adjective. However, spelling it out is never incorrect.

    Many **U.S.** tourists flock to the Virgin Islands.
                                           or
    Many **United States** tourists flock to the Virgin Islands.

In text, spell out every word in an address. In letter and envelope addresses, the two-letter state code may be used when followed by a ZIP Code. Addresses may be abbreviated in tables, notes, and bibliographies.

    Before she moved here, she resided at 851 Englewood Boulevard.

In text, spell out references to the points of the compass.

    She told us to travel **southeast** [*not* SE] from Baton Rouge.

Exercise   On the line provided, correct the manuscript style in each of the following sentences. If a sentence is correct, write *C*.

1. Under the laws of the U.S., a United States citizen cannot have dual citizenship with Gr. Brit. or any other country.

_____

2. The chart heading read "Population Density of N.Y."

_____

3. We will be moving to Kalamazoo, Mich., in July.

_____

4. The compass is pointing E; we need to go N.

_____

5. On Thursday, the bird-watchers club will meet at 162 Alvarado St., just N of Main.

_____

Name _____ Date _____ Class _____

Manuscript Style C

Abbreviate the two most common era designations, *A.D.* and *B.C.* The abbreviation *A.D.* is used with dates in the Christian era. When used with a specific year number, *A.D.* precedes the number. When used with the name of a century, it follows the name. The abbreviation *B.C.* is used for dates before the Christian era. It follows either a specific year number or the name of a century.

> In A.D. 1492, Columbus sailed west, hoping to reach India.

> In India, the Indus Valley civilization thrived around 2500 B.C.

Spell out the names of months and days whether they appear alone or in dates. Both types of names may be abbreviated in tables, notes, and bibliographies.

> TEXT: Friday, January 5, 1994   TABLES, ETC.: Fri., Jan. 5, 1994

Abbreviate the designations for the two halves of the day measured by clock time *A.M.* (*ante meridiem*) and *P.M.* (*post meridiem*). Both abbreviations follow the numerals designating the specific time. Do not use *A.M.* or *P.M.* with numbers spelled out as words or as a substitute for the word *morning, afternoon,* or *evening.* Also, do not use the word *morning, afternoon,* or *evening* with numerals followed by *A.M.* or *P.M.*

> I will arrive at **8:00 A.M.**
>
>   *or*
>
> I will arrive at **eight o'clock in the morning.**

Spell out the English equivalents of common Latin expressions. For example, use *and so forth* rather than *etc.* In tables, notes, and bibliographies, use abbreviations for the Latin expressions. In text, spell out the words *volume, part, unit, chapter,* and *page* as well as the names of school subjects.

Exercise   On the line provided, correct the manuscript style in each of the following sentences.

1. As the author states on pg. 3, they saw quite a bit of wildlife; deer, raccoon, rabbits, etc., are common in this area.

   _____

2. By 5:00 P.M. in the evening, virtually everyone had heard the news.

   _____

3. Rome was destroyed by a fire in 64 A.D.

   _____

4. Applications will be accepted Mon. through Fri. during regular business hours.

   _____

5. The Sumerians built temples at Eridu, Ur, etc., around B.C. 3000.

   _____

Resources

WORKSHEET 13 · *Manuscript Style D*

In text, spell out the names of units of measurement whether they stand alone or follow a spelled-out number or a numeral. Such names may be abbreviated in tables and notes when the name follows a numeral.

Forty **feet** of rock lay between the prospectors and a rich vein of gold.

Spell out the words for the symbols % (percent), + (plus), – (minus), = (equals), and ¢ (cents). The dollar sign ($) may be used whenever it precedes numerals. Do not substitute the symbol for the word *money* or *dollars* after numerals.

When I was your age, I got fifty **cents** a week for an allowance.

Assets total in excess of $525,000.

Spell out a **cardinal number**—a number that states how many—if it can be expressed in one or two words. Otherwise, use numerals. Cardinal numbers in compounds, such as *thirty-three*, are hyphenated.

eleven miles   **one hundred** gallons   **735** bushels   **3,264** applicants

In a particular context, be consistent in your use of numerals. If any of the numbers require numerals, use numerals for all of them. However, to distinguish between numbers appearing beside each other, spell out one number and use numerals for the other.

We drove **40** miles on Saturday and **285** on Sunday.

How many biscuits will **three 5**-pound sacks of flour make?

Exercise   On the line provided, correct the manuscript style in each of the following sentences.

1. 19 tons of fill dirt will be needed to create the new playground.

   _____

2. In our class, seventy % of the students are bilingual.

   _____

3. In those days, forty two $ a week was a good rate of pay.

   _____

4. Over 80 percent of the budget is devoted to an additional 1,000 sq. ft. of parking space.

   _____

5. We watched two four-part miniseries last month.

   _____

Name _____ Date _____ Class _____

WORKSHEET 14

Manuscript Style E

Spell out a number that begins a sentence. Also, spell out an **ordinal number**—a number that expresses order.

Eight (*not* 8) beams lay ready to be nailed in place.

For the **fifth** (*not* 5th) time during dinner, the phone rang.

Use numerals to express numbers in conventional situations. Spell out a number used with *o'clock*.

January 19, 1951	ID# 135–03–778	16 ounces	9:15 A.M.
or	Interstate 35	the 1800's *or* the 1800s	*but*
19 January 1951	713 First Avenue	2 by 4 inches	three o'clock

Nonsexist language is language that applies to people in general, both male and female. When you are referring to a profession or people in general, use nonsexist expressions rather than gender-specific ones. For example, you might use the nonsexist terms *humanity*, *human beings*, and *people* instead of the gender-specific term *mankind*.

Exercise On the line provided, correct the manuscript style in each of the following sentences.

1. 25 of the people polled were positive about the third-party candidate.

   _____

2. We should have arrived by 4:00 in the afternoon; we definitely took a wrong turn off Interstate Sixty One.

   _____

3. For the 100th time, will you *please* put your roller skates in the closet!

   _____

4. One route from Houston, Texas, to San Antonio is Interstate Ten.

   _____

5. Realism was a literary and artistic movement of the nineteen hundreds.

   _____

RESOURCES

Resources

WORKSHEET 15 *Review*

Exercise A Go to a library to look for books with the following descriptions. Write the author, title, and call number of each book.

1. a nonfiction work by Isaac Asimov _____

_____

2. a book by Rachel Carson _____

_____

3. a book about civil rights _____

_____

4. a book about gardens or gardening _____

_____

Exercise B You are writing a paper about presidential election campaigns. Go to a recent volume of the *Readers' Guide*. Find four articles in the *Readers' Guide* under the subject heading "Presidential election." If there is no heading "Presidential election," find a related heading (Political campaign, President, Elections, and so on). For each article, write the name of the author, the description, the title of the article, the name of the periodical, and the date of publication. Also tell whether or not the article is illustrated.

1. _____

_____

2. _____

_____

3. _____

_____

4. _____

_____

Exercise C On the lines provided, write the titles of reference works that you might use to find the following information.

1. another word that means the same as *sad* _____

2. the number of immigrants from Russia to the United States in 1992 _____

3. general information about the invention of the telephone _____

4. the birth date of scientist Albert Einstein _____

5. the exact location of Chiclayo, in Peru _____

Name _____ Date _____ Class _____

Exercise D On the lines provided, write a letter to your state senator, requesting that he or she come to speak to your social studies class on Citizenship Day. Invent the necessary information.

_____

_____

_____

_____

_____

_____

_____

_____

_____

_____

_____

_____

_____

_____

_____

_____

_____

_____

_____

_____

_____

_____

_____

_____

_____

_____

_____

_____

_____

Exercise E   On the lines provided, revise each of the following sentences for errors in manuscript style.

1. Capt. A. Edward Newman will demonstrate the new system, and Mrs Eleanor Stone of New Electronics Inc. will be available to answer questions.

   _____

   _____

2. 3 tons of recyclable paper were collected by only one dedicated student over the course of twenty-four weeks.

   _____

   _____

3. For thirty-five $, you can have a working knowledge of French.

   _____

   _____

4. At 9:15 AM in the morning, Sen. Okimo will arrive at 320 E. Maine, Cleveland.

   _____

   _____

5. On Sat., Apr. 5, the 1st broadcast of a new series on classic rock will air on the radio.

   _____

   _____